California's Ancient Past: From the Pacific to the Range of Light

Jeanne E. Arnold and Michael R. Walsh

Contemporary Perspectives Series, Society for American Archaeology Press

SAA

SOCIETY FOR AMERICAN ARCHAEOLOGY

The SAA Press

The Society for American Archaeology, Washington, D.C. 20002

Printed in the United States of America

Printed on acid-free paper

Library of Congress Cataloging-in-Publication Data

Arnold, Jeanne E.
California's ancient past : from the Pacific to the range of light / Jeanne E. Arnold and Michael R. Walsh.
p. cm. -- (Contemporary perspectives series)
Includes bibliographical references and index.
ISBN 978-0-932839-40-4
1. Indians of North America--California--Antiquities. 2. California--Antiquities.
3. Archaeology--California. I. Walsh, Michael R. II. Title.
E78.C15A793 2010
979.4'01--dc22 2010012014

ISBN 978-0-932839-40-1

Contents

Acknowledgments

We are grateful to the SAA Press Editorial Board and to Paul Minnis (SAA Contemporary Perspectives series editor) for contacting the senior author about writing this book. John Niekirk and the SAA production staff (and Tobi Brimsek behind the scenes) were wonderfully accommodating, efficient, and supportive during the production process.

We thank our many colleagues and predecessors in California for their outstanding archaeological scholarship and for sharing information and newly published data. William Hildebrandt, Mark Sutton, Mark Allen, Jelmer Eerkens, William Clewlow, and Mark Basgall generously provided critical reviews of selected chapters at our request. Alan Garfinkel, Russell Kaldenberg, Michael J. Moratto, Martin Rosen, Shannon Tushingham, Claude Warren, Helen Wells, and David Whitley provided published and unpublished manuscripts or drew our attention to specific works. Renee Fraser assisted with editorial matters on selected chapters during the early stages of production. Kent Lightfoot and Torrey Rick reviewed the proposed manuscript for SAA Press, and both made insightful suggestions that resulted in important clarifications and expansions of the book's contents.

We contacted a number of institutions and individuals regarding images for the book, and we thank them for their generous assistance: Dan Rogers at the Smithsonian Institution; Michael J. Moratto; Jo Anne Van Tilburg and Gordon Hull at the UCLA Rock Art Archive; Susan Danforth and Kim Nusco at the John Carter Brown Library, Brown University; Janice Timbrook at the Santa Barbara Museum of Natural History; Shannon Tushingham at UC Davis; and Kim Hogeland at the University of California Press.

The substantial task of generating maps and several other illustrations for this book was placed in the capable hands of Clarus J. Backes, Jr. We are deeply appreciative of his careful attention to producing high-quality figures, occasionally on a tight schedule. We also thank UCLA's Lana Martin and Eric Gardner, who scanned and modified several images for the volume.

We hope this volume, and this series, will be embraced by professional scholars, students, the Native American community, and the many other people around the world who are deeply interested in science and in learning about and preserving America's archaeological heritage.

Jeanne E. Arnold and Michael R. Walsh, Los Angeles
2010

1

Introduction to California

California has a rich and well-studied archaeological record that reaches firmly back into the terminal Pleistocene and spans the entire Holocene. According to the traditional explanation, the first people came to the west coast by land after crossing the Bering Land Bridge and passing through the famed "ice-free corridor" in central Alaska, Canada, and the northern Great Plains. More recently it has been proposed that the first people to cross into North America may have paddled small boats along unglaciated shorelines from northeast Asia, along the low-lying Bering land mass, and southward from Alaska along the Pacific Coast, reaching the region by 13,200 years ago. Today we know that California has sites that are among the earliest in the Americas. Increasingly, archaeologists find it reasonable to consider that the peopling of the continent could have followed this coastal pathway (Erlandson 2002; Erlandson et al. 2007), although the hypothesis is not without controversy since it reverses decades of conventional thinking. But the Arlington Canyon skeleton from Santa Rosa Island, one of the northern Channel Islands (Figure 1.1), is more than 13,000 years old (Johnson et al. 2000), and evidence of human activities at the Daisy Cave site on nearby San Miguel Island belies persistent exploitation of the coastal environment at least 11,600 years ago (Rick et al. 2001). The Channel Islands have not been connected to the mainland in the last half-million years, so people reached these localities in boats and knew how to capture marine resources at a very early date.

At the end of the Pleistocene, California was of course much cooler and wetter than it is today, but its great physiographic variability contributed then as well as now to its many distinct ecological regions. Great pine forests extended far into southern California; huge lakes dotted what are now the interior deserts; and estuaries, rivers, littoral zones, and well-watered grass-

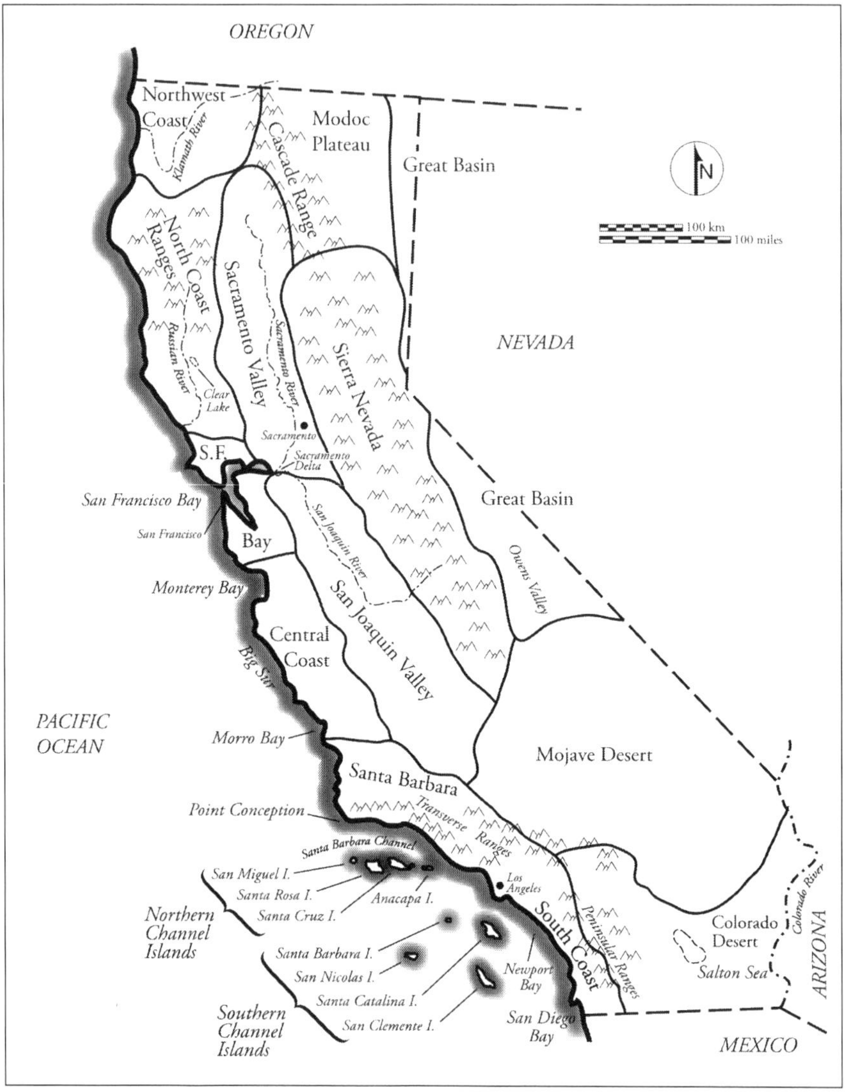

Figure 1.1. California's physiographic and cultural regions as defined in the text. Map by Clarus J. Backes, Jr.

lands supported initial settlers. Once in the region, people never left, although countless migrations and population shifts occurred through the ensuing Holocene.

A case can be made that California is among the premier places in the world for the archaeological study of hunter-gatherers and their varied adaptations over time and space. California is certainly singular in many respects. At the time that Europeans began their sustained colonial activities in western Mexico and Alta California during the 1760s, the total indigenous population in the state exceeded any region of comparable size in North America. This is a remarkable observation for a landscape inhabited entirely by hunter-gatherers. Credible population estimates range from about 310,000 to as many as 700,000 people (Anderson 2005:34), and portions of California's coast maintained population densities that exceed any found among hunter-gatherers the world over (Arnold and Graesch 2004:4; Kelly 1995:222–226).

Archaeological investigations are supported by an ethnographic record that is unusually vibrant. This record attests to a range of cultural-linguistic diversity unparalleled in the New World. At European contact no fewer than 60 broad linguistic groups speaking as many as 100 mutually unintelligible languages and dialects were found within the borders of the state (Anderson 2005:34–37; Golla 2007). Kroeber (1962) estimated that California was home to some 600 autonomous sociopolitical groups that he called "tribelets," each unified by dialect, residence, and common defense. The young and blossoming Anthropology department at the University of California, Berkeley and a few other institutions such as the Smithsonian sent many precocious faculty and students into remote areas of California to conduct ethnographic research. Dozens of these groups were documented starting around 1903 and lasting well into the 1940s. The ethnographic record that emerged from these efforts has greatly enriched our understanding of language, settlement, architecture, inheritance, political structure, and more, and we draw upon it with some frequency in this volume. The late colonization of the far west, where many tracts of land remained unclaimed by Euroamericans and still controlled by Native Californians in the late 1800s, also contributed significantly to the success of ethnographers in finding lifeways to observe and enhances our ability to discuss pre-contact cultures in ways that are barely possible in the U.S. northeast or southeast.

At the time of historic contact these social groups displayed a full range of sociopolitical complexity, from essentially band-level foragers through wealth-based chiefly polities. Moreover, there is ample evidence that this full scope of cultural complexity arose at various times in different places in the prehistoric past. It is possible to view these polities from incipience through fruition and, in some cases, decline. This richness and variability in political and economic organization means that our treatment of California's prehistory will tend toward the topical rather than the encyclopedic. Only in this chapter and the next are we able to cast our net wide enough to provide some sense of the immense variation that characterizes the state.

California as a modern state is a wholly arbitrary construct of nineteenth-century politics and does not itself reflect a single, unified archaeological province. Its boundaries encompass some 423,968 km^2 and, except for the unambiguous, 1,350 km-long Pacific Coast and a small portion of the Colorado River at the southeastern border, state boundaries were drawn without regard to geographic features, landmarks, environmental zones, or human populations. Some of the state's borderland areas therefore share as many features with neighboring states as with the remainder of California. To illustrate this in human terms, consider that the Smithsonian series *Handbook of North American Indians* discusses California groups in four distinct volumes: the Northwest Coast, California, the non-Puebloan Southwest, and the Great Basin. Anthropologists and archaeologists have expended considerable energy over the question of the "California culture area" (Heizer 1978:1–3), and to a large degree these efforts uniformly adjust the size of the culture area in accordance with the distribution of acorn-bearing oak trees. Without a doubt the acorn maintained a prominent place (arguably *the* prominent place) in the development and maintenance of most of California's social groups. However, as we shall see in the following chapters, California's indigenous economies flourished utilizing considerably more diverse flora and fauna than this one essential component would imply.

Systematic, data-driven archaeological investigations in California have been carried out since the days of Nels Nelson and Max Uhle, who were the first to investigate the massive shellmound sites near the San Francisco Bay, pioneering a series of foundational archaeological methods (Nelson 1909, 1910; Uhle 1907). Today, heritage preservation and CRM in California constitute growth industries, and no state in the union has more practicing professional archaeologists. Yet California's complex prehistory thwarts every effort to establish a single, coherent, state-wide chronological framework or culture-historical nomenclature. The prehistory is too varied and, indeed, the archaeological record is too rich to tell one simple story line.

As a result, California archaeologists and anthropologists have found it useful to partition the state into subregions (Arnold et al. 2004; Chartkoff and Chartkoff 1984; Jones and Klar, eds. 2007; Moratto 1984). Michael

Moratto's (1984) widely cited book provides a definitive history of archaeological research in California through the early 1980s—both the practitioners and the research—and should be consulted by any serious student of California prehistory who is interested in tracking the development of previous scholarship. Moratto also outlines the ecological and geographical underpinnings for notable regional distinctions in indigenous cultures and provides exceptional coverage of all major areas. Likewise, recent edited volumes such as Erlandson and Jones (2002) and Jones and Klar, eds. (2007) and syntheses such as Arnold, Walsh, and Holliman (2004) lay the foundation for an excellent understanding of the regional approach to California archaeology. In the end these are *cultural* regions based on commonalities in the prehistoric sequence and, particularly, in social, political, and economic life ways observed in the ethnographic present. As one might expect, strong concordance with geomorphic and biotic climes is inevitable and readily apparent, but these subregions are an archaeological convenience and may not necessarily please every physical geographer, biologist, or climatologist.

Our approach to the regional question in California is shown in Figure 1.1. Although there remains within each of these geographical provinces a high degree of cultural variability, these regions tend to share significant chronological hallmarks and, perhaps more significantly, archaeological nomenclatures. It must be emphasized that these subregions are convenient for archaeological purposes but are not in themselves strictly cultural borders or barriers of any sort. Native Californians routinely ventured over the regional borders that we have drawn.

What follows is a brief overview of the major cultural provinces of California and an introduction to the resident social groups largely as they were spatially situated at historic contact (Figure 1.2). We focus on the particular indigenous economies and the local ecological conditions that characterize the regions based on available geographical data, historical records, colonial-era archaeological data, and the memories of informants contacted by ethnographers during the early 1900s. We remain mindful, however, that environmental fluctuations during the Holocene (droughts, cold intervals, rising sea levels, and so on) occasionally altered the character of these regions. Still, the regions we present were distinct *from one another* throughout the prehistoric sequence, no matter the prevailing macroclimate. These fluctuations are further discussed for their relevance to observed variations in the archaeological record in Chapter 2.

Figure 1.2. Primary ethnolingistic territories of California. Map by Clarus J. Backes, Jr.

Northwest Coast

The northwestern corner of California is dominated by the Klamath Mountains (see Figure 1.1). These mountains are constituted by several smaller ranges, notably the Siskiyou Mountains at the Oregon border and the more southerly Trinity Alps. Elevations extend for the most part from 1500 to

Figure 1.3. Northwestern California: redwood forest along the Smith River. Photo by Shannon Tushingham.

2150 m (5000–7000') but rise to as many as 2724 m (8936') at Thompson Peak. This corner of the state is frequently fog-shrouded, seasonally snowy, and typically rainy for most of the year. Annual rainfall for the region as a whole averages between 180 and 250 cm, with 450 cm not uncommon in the northern Siskiyous. This heavy rain feeds three major river systems, the Klamath, Trinity, and Smith rivers (Figure 1.3). Of particular significance for our purposes, these rivers teem seasonally with anadromous fish, especially the Chinook (spring and fall runs) and Cojo (fall run) salmon. The ethnographic groups who plied the Klamath region in the historic era—the Tolowa, Hupa, Yurok, Karok, Chilula, and Wiyot (Figure 1.2)—are noteworthy for their substantial redwood or cedar plank housing, designed to withstand the weather, and the central importance of the seasonal mass captures of salmon. These factors led to distinctive economic and political adaptations, unusual for California but quite in keeping with wealth-based fishers of the greater Pacific Northwest.

Modoc Plateau

The Modoc Plateau is volcanic tableland bordered on the west by the Cascade Mountains, on the east and north by the Great Basin, and on the south by the Sierra Nevada (Figure 1.1). The Plateau is marked by a mixed terrain of volcanic cones, lava flows and benches, deeply cut river canyons, wide river valleys, and lakes. The Cascades form a minor rain shadow over the Plateau, which at 1820 m (6000') in elevation bleeds off residual precipitation long before it reaches the more arid Great Basin to the east. Owing to intensive volcanic activities in both the Cascades and the Modoc Plateau, obsidian sources are plentiful, and stone tool assemblages are dominated by volcanic glass during all periods in prehistory (McGuire 2007). Indeed, so plentiful are obsidian sources that there exists something of a "poverty of riches": finding all of the sources in order to devise source-specific hydration rates is a daunting task.

Indigenous economy, technology, and artifact styles appear to blend elements common to more westerly and southerly California groups, as well as to those of the Great Basin (McGuire 2007:176). Indeed, joined with ethnographic groups who claim ancestry to the Modoc Plateau—the Klamath/Modoc, the Achumawi, the Atsugawi, and elements of the Mountain Maidu—are the Northern Paiute, a group more generally associated with the Great Basin (Figure 1.2). Indigenous economies were based not on the acorn but on wild roots and bulbs such as camas and epos. People gathered these wild crops, which could be dried and stored for winter, from lakeside marshlands and marshy meadows. Fish and migratory water fowl they took from lakes and streams may have provided the bulk of meat resources, along with small mammals taken in drives. Hunters pursued large mammals (deer, elk, antelope, and mountain sheep) and excavated deadfalls to trap deer. Indeed, the primary watercourse on the Modoc Plateau—the Pit River—is named for these pit-traps, which in the nineteenth century also bagged their share of American settlers on horseback.

The Cascade-Modoc Plateau region of northeastern California is remote, largely undeveloped, and difficult of access today. It may have been so in prehistoric times as well, isolated from contact with the acorn-based "California" pattern to the west and south by the Cascade and Sierra Nevada cordillera. For this reason, the Modoc Plateau is often associated with, and considered an extension of, the economic adaptations witnessed in the Great Basin to the east (McGuire 2007:176).

North Coast Ranges

The North Coast Ranges region extends from the southern Klamath Mountains to somewhat north of the San Francisco Bay (Figure 1.1). The region is actually composed of many smaller ranges oriented on roughly north-south axes, rising rather abruptly from the Pacific shoreline to elevations exceeding 2000 m (Schoenherr 1995:6–7). These ranges extend eastward some 50–80 km, where they gently disappear into the Central Valley. Rainfall in the North Coast Ranges is considerably diminished from levels in the Klamath Mountains, to as little as 100 cm/year in the southern reaches of the region, largely limited to the winter months. The celebrated Napa/Sonoma wine country is nestled within the inland slopes of the Coast Range region, attesting to the relatively mild, Mediterranean-like climate there. Many of the largest groves of the famed California redwoods are situated along the wetter zones of this region's coastal slopes.

The steep coastal terraces overlook treacherous coastlines and rough seas. While this effectively ruled out offshore exploitation of the sea, North Coast groups seasonally exploited the littoral zone for shellfish, nearshore fish, and sea mammals. Inland, the North Coast climate is, by California's standards, mostly wet and cool, and this climate supports rich and varied vegetation. Several river valleys provide lush riparian zones and limited anadromous fish runs. Rolling hills are dotted with large copses of acorn-rich oaks. When anthropologists have tried to define the "California culture area" (Heizer 1978: his Figure 1), among the archetypes of this adaptation were the groups of the southern North Coast Ranges, including especially the eastern Pomo, Yuki, Miwok, Wappo, and Patwin (Figure 1.2).

The Pomo typically maintained quite large, permanent winter villages, which were stocked with diverse stores gathered during wide-ranging but closely scheduled seasonal rounds. During the ethnohistoric era, the largest winter villages were home to a headperson with at least nominal authority over the local tribelet. These villages also hosted communal assemblies and ceremonies in large, communally built, semi-subterranean structures (Bean and Theodoratus 1978:293). There is compelling evidence from the later prehistoric era that resource availability at and around Clear Lake permitted virtually year-round Pomo village residence, larger overall village size, and networks of satellite communities (Hildebrandt 2007:85–86; White et al. 2002), suggesting hierarchical relationships among settlements. Furthermore, various Pomoan groups exercised monopolistic control over several critical commodities, including salt (Barrett 1908:239–244) and clam shell beads manufactured by specialists (Chase-Dunn and Mann 1998:85–86). In all, the purported political autonomy of tribelets, the suggestion of economic specialization and some centralized leadership, and aggregated residence, among other factors, create in the North Coast Ranges a fine laboratory for archaeological data to be marshaled to test models of emergent complexity.

San Francisco Bay

The San Francisco Bay is the largest estuarine system in California and was once considerably larger. As many as one billion cubic meters of silt sluiced their way down the Sacramento River during the Gold Rush, and purposeful filling of the bay has been a strategy for urban development for more than a century and a half. Extensive wetlands that once lined the bay's perimeter have been almost completely reclaimed and built on. It is difficult today to imagine the natural resources once held in and around the bay. While the seas roil outside the Golden Gate, the relatively calm bay waters and salt marshes were stocked with bay mussels, clam, and oyster, and navigation by reed canoe yielded a bounty of anadromous and resident fish, sea mammals, and migratory fowl. Short jaunts inland provided deer and, particularly, acorns and other gathered foodstuffs. When the Spanish arrived, the bay and its immediate environs supported large numbers of hunter-gatherers, including several Costanoan groups (Ramaytush, Chochenyo, Tamyen, Ohlone) as well as Coast and Bay Miwok, and perhaps Patwin. There is clear evidence, however, that population levels were still higher at one main juncture in prehistory (Lightfoot and Luby 2002; Luby et al. 2006; Milliken et al. 2007). Indeed, it appears that land-filling may not be just a modern phenomenon in the San Francisco Bay: there is evidence that that the famous bay area shell mound sites—Emeryville and West Berkeley to name just two—were purposefully constructed as conspicuous landmarks on the sociopolitical landscape. The decline of these political centers has been found to closely track patterns of overexploitation of critical prey species in the bay (Broughton 1994a, 1997, 1999, 2001). This observation alone, in view of the immense productivity assumed for the bay in prehistoric times, attests to high human population levels once sustained by the bay and its surrounding shores.

Central Coast

The Central Coast region is essentially a southern extension of the North Coast Ranges, extending south from the lower San Francisco Bay toward the northern Santa Barbara region (Figure 1.1). However, the Central Coast differs from the northern ranges in several key environmental respects, all of which hold significant implications for human adaptation. Perhaps the most salient difference is the more arid climate, much closer to a southern Mediterranean moisture regime, with smaller, more intermittent water courses. In general, these water courses apparently did little to encourage human exploitation. The northern Central Coast supported several bays, lagoons, and estuaries—notably Elkhorn Slough at Monterey Bay—and wetlands provided an abundance of tidal resources and migratory game to fairly mobile populations. The region was occupied by the southern groups of Costanoan/Ohlone and the Esselen and Salinan (Figure 1.2). The towering, steep cliffs of Big Sur south of Monterey overlook one of the most rugged stretches of the entire Pacific Coast, a place with severely limited access to the coast and its resources, lending this region its primarily terrestrial orientation. Perhaps because the Central Coast is bracketed by two regions that have garnered considerable anthropological and archaeological attention—the Santa Barbara Coast to the south and the San Francisco Bay to the north—the region remains somewhat overlooked and enigmatic in both the ethnographic and archaeological spheres. This situation has begun to be redressed in recent years through high-caliber CRM work and several notable discoveries, including firm evidence of early occupation near the southern coast (Breschini and Haversat 2004; Jones et al. 2007).

Central Valley/Delta

The expansive Central Valley of California is thought to have supported as much as one-third of California's native population at the time of historic contact (Rosenthal et. al 2007:149). Overall the valley is about 725 km long on a north-south axis and shows a latitudinal environmental gradient. Because this generality is reflected in human adaptations, archaeologists have seen fit to segregate this large feature into northern and southern regions, separated by the Sacramento/San Joaquin Delta (Figure 1.1). The northerly Sacramento Valley constitutes the upper one-third of the greater Central Valley. The Sacramento Valley is generally the cooler, better-watered portion of the Central Valley, including several major waterways (Sacramento, Feather, Yuba, American, and Cosumnes rivers) and heightened levels of rainfall and snow runoff. The plains and immediate foothills of the North Coast Ranges to the west and the Sierra Nevada to the east supported large stands of oak and plentiful game, amply exploited by the Interior Miwok, Patwin, Nisenan, Konkow, and Nomlaki (Figure 1.2). The Sacramento Valley is relatively narrow, at an average width of about 64 km, and centralized villages near the valley floor enjoyed easy access to valley grassland, delta marshes, riparian, and foothill-oak woodland regimes. Frequently, these village sites sat atop natural mounds and rises along watercourses, a response to spring flood levels.

The modern traveler through the parched San Joaquin Valley to the south will find it difficult to imagine that the San Joaquin River was once navigable by commercial vessels originating in the San Francisco Bay. The river and several large inland lakes have succumbed to the thirsts of modern agriculture, where farmers have found the land as productive as did the prehistoric hunter-gatherers. The San Joaquin Valley was dominated ethnographically by the Yokuts. Those in the southern San Joaquin Valley in particular were so intricately tied to the lakes, marshes, and sloughs that they were named *Tulareños* ("people of the tules") by Spanish explorers, after the reeds that permeate these water features. These wetlands provided game, migratory fowl, freshwater fish and shellfish, and of course tule reeds, which were put to use as building materials for houses, storage structures, boats, and baskets.

Sierra Nevada

The Sierra Nevada Range is also known as the *Range of Light*, so-named by naturalist John Muir around 1870. It essentially forms the spine of California, a steep, rugged, and picturesque obstacle to east-west travel. The Sierra range averages 65–80 km in width and is about 690 km long, extending from the Cascade Mountains in the north to the Tehachapi Mountains in the south (Figure 1.1). The Sierra boasts the highest elevation in the contiguous United States, Mt. Whitney at 4418 m (14,494'), as well as 12 other peaks that exceed 4267 m (14,000') in elevation. Usually when considering the Sierra Nevada, anthropologists are referring to the well-watered, relatively gentle western foothills and slopes, not to the alpine peaks or their eastern flanks that drop abruptly into the rain-shadowed Great Basin to the east. This is an analytical as well as a practical matter: the western foothills were home to large populations of indigenous peoples, all of whom were prototypically "California pattern" in their economies, meaning, in simplest terms, tribelets who were acorn focused, logistically organized, and utilized a broad spectrum of mammals and fish. These groups include (north to south) Foothill Maidu, Nisenan, Sierra Miwok, Monache, and Foothill Yokuts (Figure 1.2). Note that these groups generally have counterparts in the Central Valley. The sole exception are the Monache, whose nearest linguistic relatives reside in the Great Basin and are likely a relatively recent arrival to the area (Hull 2007:180). The eastern Sierra, on the other hand, was occupied by the Washo, Northern Paiute, and Owens Valley Paiute, groups more frequently considered to represent a Great Basin lifestyle and who made periodic albeit limited-use forays into the High Sierra.

Western Sierra foothill populations made extensive use of riparian and watershed habitats that ran from the high country to the Central Valley, wintering in the lower foothills and summering at higher elevations. Because of the steady climb from the valley floor to the high country, natives had access to a wide range of vegetation zones, from chaparral through oak woodland and into pine forest, each with its own seasonal bounty in vegetable and animal foods. In combination this varied environment provided security against shortfall in one or more habitat.

South Coast, Transverse Ranges, and Peninsular Ranges

The Santa Barbara coastal region, which for our purposes extends from the Central Coast to the Los Angeles Basin (Figure 1.1), is largely south-facing east of Point Conception and is thus semi-sheltered from the strongest westerly winds. The northern Channel Islands further protected much of the coast from rough oceanic swells (Figure 1.4). This relatively calm coastline was home to one of the state's most populous and politically complex groups, the Chumash. Although the Chumash maintained a robust inland presence, resources from the rocky shores, rich kelp forests, and minor estuaries along the coast provided the bulk of protein (in the form of shellfish, dozens of marine fish species, seabirds, and marine mammals) for the largest concentrations of Chumash. Of particular note, the Chumash were successful seafarers, an economic strategy that dates well into the prehistoric era. With the advent of the plank canoe, perhaps the most sophisticated watercraft in the New World (Arnold 2007), the Chumash traversed the Santa Barbara Channel with regularity and ease (Glassow et al. 2007). The plank

Figure 1.4. The northern Channel Islands: Morse Point, Santa Cruz Island, looking west toward Santa Rosa Island. Photo by Jeanne E. Arnold.

canoe permitted expansion of the diet to regularly include open-sea fish such as swordfish and large tuna (Arnold and Bernard 2005) and, significantly, fostered complex exchange systems between the northern Channel Islands and the mainland (Arnold and Graesch 2004:8–9). The Island Chumash were highly specialized, making millions of chert microdrills and shell beads, and the economy was governed by a shell bead currency that was used through much of southern California.

The Transverse Ranges are so-named for their generally east-west axis, an uncommon orientation for mountain ranges throughout North America, and otherwise unknown in California (Schoenherr 1995:8–9). These ranges include the Santa Monica and Santa Ynez mountains. Both ranges meet the sea within the Santa Barbara coastal region, and there is evidence that the northern Channel Islands are essentially extensions of the Santa Monica Mountains (Schoenherr et al. 1999:54–55). Depending on local topography, the coastal transverse ranges are home to stands of walnut and oak, a variety of seed-bearing species, and several species of mammals, including deer and rabbit. Reliable streams are rare beyond the year-round Santa Clara and Santa Ynez rivers and the smaller streams feeding the Goleta Slough and

Mugu Lagoon areas. For the most part, these mountains are poorly watered and chaparral-covered, a climax vegetation that is difficult to traverse.

We exclude a portion of the interior Transverse Ranges from the Santa Barbara Coast region, including them with the South Coast. Although technically these inland ranges to the southeast are physiographically similar to their coastal counterparts, they are significantly higher, more rugged, and wholly lacking in the mild climate associated with the coastal region. This is reflected as well in dramatic cultural differences.

The San Gabriel and San Bernardino mountain ranges in the interior are by far the largest of the Transverse Ranges, soaring to over 3050 m (10,000') to form the northern and eastern borders of the Los Angeles Basin. These ranges are invariably snow-capped in the winter. South-facing slopes of the San Gabriels and the San Bernadinos may receive as many as 100 cm of precipitation per year (Schoenherr 1995:9). However, at lower elevations these slopes are subject to intense evaporation rates and are thus essentially xeric, lending them a true Mediterranean climate. North-facing, rain-shadowed slopes retain moisture for a richer vegetation component. The result is a varied biotic component often separated by no more than a thin ridge line. Hunter-gatherers of the inland Transverse Ranges included Tataviam and Serrano (Figure 1.2), who exploited game, oak, and localized piñon pine over the rugged mountains and foothills.

The Peninsular Ranges are so designated because they are essentially the northernmost extent of the Baja California peninsula. These ranges form the southern boundary of the Los Angeles Basin and, as an archaeological convenience, the basin itself is usually considered to be allied with the Peninsular Ranges. The Los Angeles Basin was home to the Gabrielino, or as they are known today, the Tongva. The Tongva, like the Chumash, maintained a healthy inland as well as a coastal presence. Additionally, local inhabitants took to the sea well into prehistory in order to colonize the southern Channel Islands, including Santa Catalina and San Clemente (Byrd and Raab 2007). A vibrant island-mainland trade network was established by ca. A.D. 1400, notably centered on Santa Catalina steatite that was being supplied to coastal Chumash villages from Malibu to Santa Barbara, the northern islands, and beyond (Howard 2000).

The slopes of the Peninsular Ranges are dominated by sage, yucca, and spotty stands of live oaks near the coast. Yucca, agave, and mesquite trees are common farther inland. Mesquite, common in arid lands of southern California, provided an edible bean, eaten green or dried and stored in quantity. Mesquite rivaled the acorn in dietary importance. Population levels in the Peninsular Ranges were highest along the Pacific coast but considerably diminished from the levels achieved by the Tongva and Chumash to the north. Perhaps owing to the sheer traffic through the area by Spanish missionaries and chroniclers, ethnographic groups resident in the Peninsular Ranges are known by a variety of names, often associated with a named Catholic mission: Juaneño, Luiseño, and Diegeño. Today the Diegeño are known as the Kumeyaay, sometimes divided into the Tipai-Ipai (coastal and near-inland) and Kamia (inland) (Figure 1.2). They exploited the varied resources of some of the largest and richest estuaries on the west coast within the roughly 50 km from San Diego Bay to the north. Population sizes were limited almost solely by unreliability of fresh water sources.

Deserts

California is home to large parts of three major deserts: the Mojave Desert, the Colorado Desert, and the Great Basin (Figure 1.1). For earlier periods, before about A.D. 500, these regions essentially share culture histories and much of their culture-historical nomenclatures. But once native groups began to specialize and intensify (see Chapter 2), shared arid-lands adaptations began to be differentiated by the specific features that distinguish these three deserts (Figure 1.5).

The Mojave Desert is also known as the "high desert," with elevations generally about 1060 m (3500'). However, the Mojave Desert also includes Death Valley, a considerable portion of which is below sea level. The Mojave is lethally hot in the summer and brutally cold in the winter. What little precipitation there is falls in the winter months and evaporates quickly due to frequent strong and dry winds. Occasional snowfall in the northern Mojave evaporates in the wind before it melts into the soil. The dominant plant communities of the Mojave are creosote scrub and Joshua tree woodland (Vasek and Barbour 1995). These provinces yield little in the way of plant foods and only moderate populations of small game (jackrabbit, cottontail, desert tortoise). Widely scattered springs were the primary seasonal destinations throughout later prehistory (Sutton et al. 2007:231–232), and the ethnographic groups that plied the Mojave did so only seasonally, from base villages generally located in the surrounding foothills. These groups include the Kawaiisu, Vanyume/Serrano, Southern Paiute, and Shoshone (Figure

Figure 1.5. The Mojave Desert: view north toward the foothills of the Coso Mountains. Photo by Clarus J. Backes, Jr.

1.2). Although low population densities at contact meant little attention was paid to social territories (Zigmond 1986:398), there is some indication that productive territories were actively disputed at times in prehistory (Walsh 2010). Finally, the Mojave is home to numerous playa lakes that began to desiccate at the close of the Pleistocene. The ancient shores of these dry lakes have proved a propitious place to seek the earliest Californians.

The Colorado Desert is the "low desert," the California manifestation of the much larger Sonoran Desert. It is primarily confined to the Salton Slough, a large valley more than 50 m below sea level (Schoenherr 1995:14). Much of the lowest portion of the Slough is currently inundated by the Salton Sea, the consequence of an irrigation canal from the Colorado River that burst its channel in 1905. The Colorado is on average California's hottest desert. Annual precipitation is scant and primarily confined to the winter months. However, the Colorado Desert is one of the few places in California that witnesses regular summer thunder showers, at the fringe of the summer monsoonal flow that courses annually over the greater American Southwest. Most of this rainfall evaporates in short order or is lost to flash floods. But even so, these summer rains have distinct implications for incipient agricultural practices.

Creosote scrub forms the dominant vegetation regime in the Colorado Desert (Burk 1995), although springs, seeps, and sinks support stands of native palm and mesquite. Numerous hill slopes yield large patches of agave, and these were harvested for their roots by the Desert Cahuilla. As with the Mojave, occupation of the Colorado Desert at contact was largely seasonal and transitory, consisting largely of special-purpose sorties for plant foods such as agave and mesquite. However, the later prehistoric period in particular saw considerably more extended residence, owing to a *natural* inundation of the Salton Trough. This freshwater lake, known as Lake Cahuilla, cycled through several phases of inundation and desiccation between about A.D. 1200 and the late 1600s (Schaefer and Laylander 2007:250), which clearly held significant implications for prehistoric settlement patterns.

Finally, the Great Basin, not well represented in California, is a "cold desert" (Schoenherr 1995:11–12). Portions of Great Basin topography are found in the extreme northeastern corner of the state, but the clearest manifestation of the basin in California is in the Owens Valley, at the foot of the eastern Sierra (Figure 1.1). Owens Valley Paiute and Panamint Shoshone ranged seasonally from the valley floor through the foothills and to the peaks of the eastern Sierra as well as the Panamint and White mountains. They collected piñon nuts in large quantities and stored them for winter use at large, semi-permanent villages. Cooperative rabbit drives—often including residents from several villages—contributed most of the meat resources. The hunting of big game provided occasional windfalls but appears to have held a social significance well out of proportion to its actual contribution to the diet. Owens Lake, turned to salt flat by the water needs of Los Angeles in the early twentieth century, once provided fish, massive harvests of insect larva, and a significant draw for wild game and migratory fowl. Moreover, there is some indication that Owens Valley Paiute, in the Late Prehistoric era, cultivated wild plant foods to an extent that blurs the distinction between "protoagriculture" and "agriculture." For a small and seemingly insignificant corner of California, the Owens Valley has for decades provided fertile territory for ethnographers and archaeologists.

This brief tour of California in all its intricate environmental diversity sets the scene for understanding the enormous cultural, economic, technological, and even political heterogeneity that developed long after the first humans set foot on California soil late in the Pleistocene. With time, cycles of cold and heat, rising sea levels, and droughts, new challenges prompted various adaptations, innovations, and demographic shifts. The widely differing peoples across California shared at least one common thread: at the macroregional level, population grew significantly during those 13,000 years. These thriving populations met their most serious threat in the eighteenth and nineteenth centuries, when hundreds, then thousands, of strange men on horseback settled on the land, searching for souls to be saved, gold to be gleaned, and fertile lands to be sowed.

2

California's Culture History: 13,000 Years at the Continent's Edge

The past 25 years have seen some momentous and surprising discoveries in California's archaeological record, and regional models of culture history have been significantly revised. A few have been toppled entirely. Here we present a chronological sequence of cultural developments as currently understood. Because we are taking a statewide rather than a strictly regional approach, we emphasize that these developments were not necessarily expressed simultaneously everywhere, nor were most shifts sudden or abrupt. We select case studies that are illustrative and representative but may not fully characterize all subregional variations. We use as our chronological backdrop the series of climatic regimes from the Terminal Pleistocene through the Holocene. There is not unanimity concerning the transition dates for the Early, Middle, and Late Holocene periods, however, because paleoenvironmental models are as hard-pressed to characterize the entire state as are cultural models. For our purposes here, we adopt a hybrid scheme.

Pleistocene-Holocene Interface (pre-10,000 B.P.)

California's Paleoindian period is known in two general forms: firm radiocarbon evidence in the absence of diagnostic artifacts and diagnostic artifacts in the absence of reliable independent dates. Even so, the data clearly suggest that California's first inhabitants exploited a wide variety of niches and cannot be described simply as hunters of large mammals. Even more remarkably, we find that California's Paleoindians had an astute knowledge of seafaring, suggesting that they may have traveled a coastal route out of northeastern Asia. These two observations challenge a cherished belief about the peopling of the Americas: the model that posits big-game hunters following migratory herds over a midcontinental ice-free corridor. Indeed, for most of North America, the term "Paleoindian" evokes big-game hunting and is epitomized by the Clovis point. Either this archetype must be reexamined or California's Pleistocene hunter-gatherers require a new nomenclature. Whether a coastal route was the *first* route, the *only* route, or simply one of several routes into North America remains an open question. Whether Clovis-era sites without big game exist but are unrecognized elsewhere in North America is another open question. That these questions exist at all is a development of just the last few years.

The main challenge to existing models for the Pleistocene came from the Daisy Cave Site on San Miguel Island off the Santa Barbara coast (Figure 2.1). Daisy Cave shows intermittent occupation episodes spanning the Holocene, but its primary interest here is its earliest level, a thin soil horizon showing a small collection of flaked stone and shellfish remains. Shell samples and charred twigs have yielded seven radiocarbon dates that exceed 10,000 B.P. (Erlandson et al. 1996:361), including a date of 11,460 cal B.P. (Beta 52360) in secure association with chert flaking debris (Erlandson 1993). Elsewhere on San Miguel Island, as well as on other Channel Islands, enigmatic stone crescents have been recovered, and these are generally attributed to the Terminal Pleistocene-Early Holocene interface (Erlandson and Braje 2008a, 2008b). Although the function of these distinctive objects is unclear, one suggestion is that crescents served as transversely hafted projectile points used to hunt aquatic birds (Erlandson and Braje 2008a:187).

The island context of these early materials requires us to think about Paleoindians as coastal and even oceangoing foragers: the northern Channel Islands have been separated from the mainland since mid-Pleistocene times and likely were never closer than 7 km from the mainland at the last sea-level minimum some 18,000 years ago (Schoenherr et al. 1999:18, 58). Although truly long-distance, open-water navigation techniques have never been necessary to reach the closest Channel Islands, seaworthy craft most assuredly were. The Terminal Pleistocene occupation of San Miguel Island appears to represent ephemeral use of site locales such as Daisy Cave as bases from which to gather intertidal and nearshore marine resources.

The findings at Daisy Cave cast a new light on a previously known but skeptically received Pleistocene date for the Channel Islands. Human bone extracted in 1959 from a vertical canyon wall near Arlington Springs, Santa Rosa Island (Figure 2.1), was dated initially by stratigraphically associated charcoal to about 10,000 B.P. (Berger and Protsch 1989:59; Orr 1962). The find so strained the paradigm of the day that the date was largely ignored and attributed to an error in determining "association" between the charcoal and the bones. The Daisy Cave find rekindled interest in the Arlington bones, however, and direct assessment of the bones through AMS dating was performed, along with additional carbon samples from strata bracketing the find. These new analyses yielded a suite of dates showing that the original estimate was actually too conservative, and the find is currently thought to date between 12,000 and 13,000 B.P. (Johnson et al. 2000). The Arlington Springs adult male died *on an island* during the Terminal Pleistocene.

Another provocative Paleoindian find was made well inland, at Tule Lake, near the California-Oregon border (Figure 2.1). In this case, the surprise came not from the context of the find—in a rockshelter near the shore of an ancient lake—but from the associated faunal component. The Tule Lake site revealed a hearth feature with wood charcoal dated to 11,450 RCYBP (Beta 39545; Beaton 1991a:5). Fish bones were found in the hearth, along with undiagnostic, bifacially worked artifact fragments and chipped stone debris. Additional fish as well as waterfowl bones were recovered from beneath the hearth. The single radiocarbon assay from some10 m^3 of excavated deposits leaves room to question the reliability of the date. Still, the inhabitants of the Tule Lake site appear to have had as their dietary focus something other than large terrestrial mammals.

These radiometrically dated features failed to yield diagnostic artifacts. The converse is true for the diagnostic "early" stone tools recovered in California: not one has been recovered from a radiometrically dated context, nor have any been found unequivocally associated with extinct Pleistocene fauna. The primary diagnostic Paleoindian tool in California is the fluted Clovis point (Figure 2.2a), of which over 400 have been reported (Dillon 2002; Rondeau et al. 2007). Nearly all of these were recovered under less than ideal circumstances, however. Typically, fluted points have been recovered as isolated surface finds. More vexing still, most of California's fluted points have been discovered by private collectors, leaving associated contexts anecdotal at best (Wallace 1993a, 1993b).

Many of California's fluted points are aptly described as "Clovis-like," lacking the robust flute of Clovis points found elsewhere in North America (Justice 2002:70; Warren and Phagen 1988:129). Three locations in California have yielded Clovis or Clovis-like fluted points and other associated tools, such as crescents (Figure 2.2b), in appreciable numbers: Borax Lake,

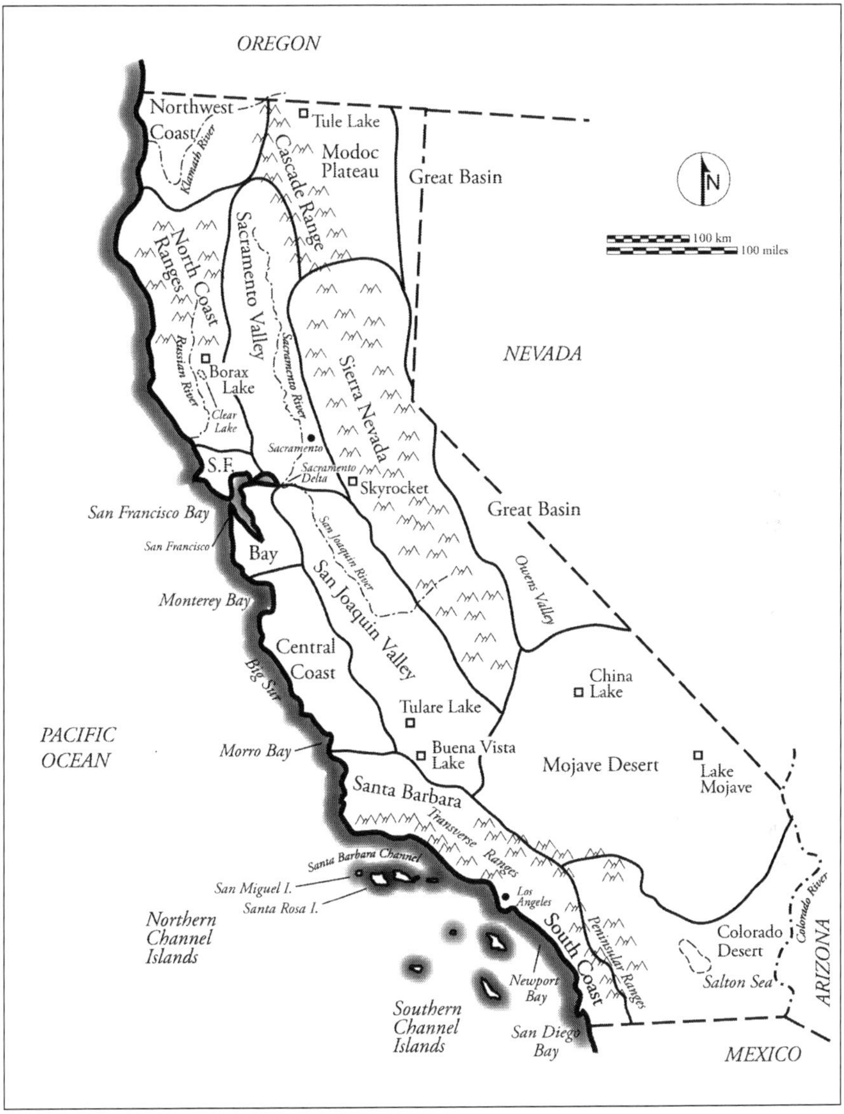

Figure 2.1. Selected early archaeological localities of California. Map by Clarus J. Backes, Jr.

China Lake, and Tulare Lake (the latter should not be confused with Tule Lake, discussed above). As we will see, there is every reason to accept these sites as representative of the Terminal Pleistocene-Holocene interface, but each is plagued by murky dates, equivocal context, or both.

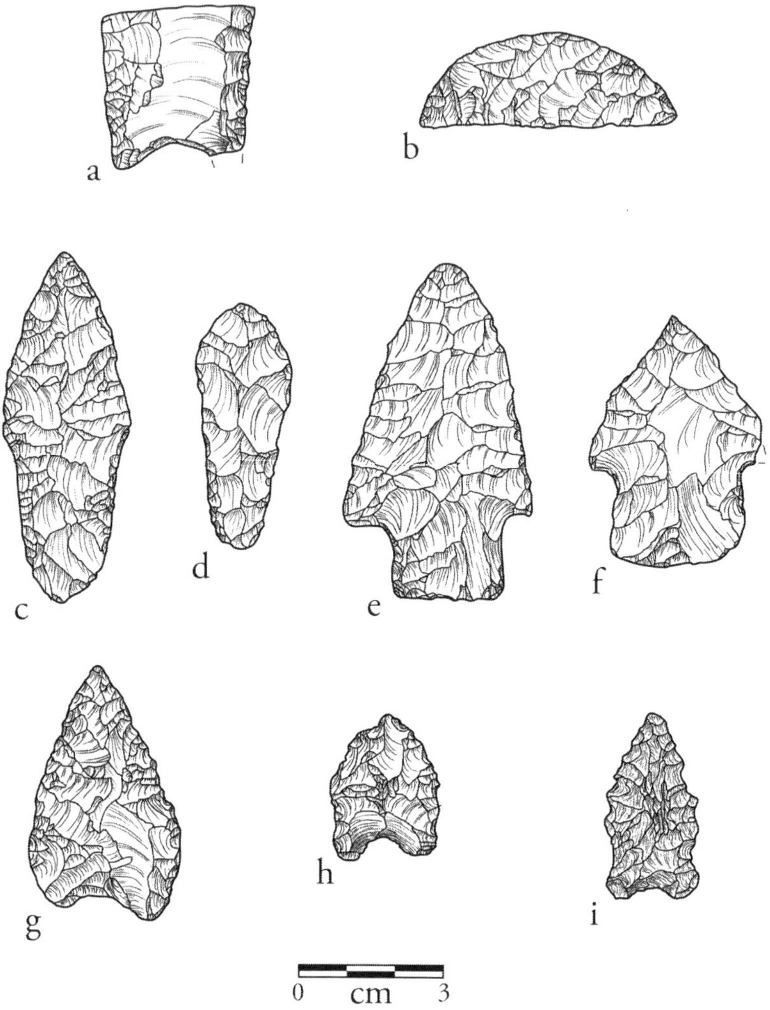

Figure 2.2. California projectile points, Terminal Pleistocene through Middle Holocene. a. Fluted point base, Lake County; b. Crescent, Santa Barbara County; c. Lake Mojave/Stemmed tradition variant, Kern County; d. Lake Mojave/Stemmed tradition variant, San Bernardino County; e. Borax Lake Wide-Stemmed, Lake County; f. Borax Lake Wide-Stemmed, Lake County; g. Concave base point, Kern County; h. Pinto Point variant, Riverside County; i. Pinto Point variant, Inyo County (all based on illustrations in Justice 2002). Illustration by Clarus J. Backes, Jr.

The Borax Lake site (Figure 2.1) is of particular interest because of the large number of obsidian points and crescents, which are amenable to direct chronological measurement. Obsidian hydration analysis has shown strong concordance between hydration rim values and typological assumptions: fluted points and crescents are consistently found with rim values at 10–12 microns or larger, while securely dated later diagnostics consistently yield smaller readings (Fredrickson and Origer 2002:162). Unfortunately, owing to vagaries in the obsidian hydration method, particularly for large rim readings, we cannot attach reliable absolute dates to these materials (Rondeau et al. 2007:68). Furthermore, the Borax Lake site has not revealed discrete chronological components that can be securely dated (Hildebrandt 2007:87). In short, while some of the Borax Lake materials are old, perhaps quite old, we are left wondering about absolute dates as well as about activities that may be associated with these finds.

The shoreline surrounding China Lake in the northern Mojave Desert has long been the focus of Paleoindian studies (Figure 2.1). At least 15 unequivocal fluted points have been found there, along with large numbers of basally thinned points, crescents, scrapers, and crude biface fragments (Basgall 2005; Dillon 2002:114; Giambastiani and Bullard 2010). Unfortunately, the vast majority of artifacts were recovered from surface contexts, lying atop deflated desert pavement. Fossil mammals have been found nearby, but given the deflated surface contexts, it is difficult to establish contemporaneity for any of the recovered materials. Although few scholars question the antiquity of the fluted points and other artifacts around China Lake, we cannot assign absolute dates to the points at this time nor can we derive firm inferences about their associated activities.

The plowed farmlands and washes surrounding extinct Tulare Lake in the San Joaquin Valley (Figure 2.1) have yielded a large percentage of the total number of Clovis or Clovis-like points reported for California (Dillon 2002). Whereas Tulare Lake has revealed a substantial number of fluted points, the actual number may be inflated by liberal inclusion of what are more accurately described as basally thinned, lanceolate points (Rondeau et al. 2007:68; Wilke 1991). In addition to fluted points, the margins of Tulare Lake have also revealed large quantities of crescents, eccentrics, and other artifacts considered diagnostic of the Pleistocene-Holocene interface. None, however, derives from a context that can be securely dated by independent means. Finally, the Tulare Lake region has yielded a wealth of fossil species, including Columbian Mammoth, sloth, and *Bison antiquus* (Fenenga 1991:13). Unfortunately, as is the case for other early sites, firm association of these animals with artifacts is elusive and reported only by private collectors. The Tulare Lake region holds considerable promise for furthering our understanding of Paleoindian activities in California. However, extreme disturbance to the surrounding farmlands and the zeal of artifact collectors acting on private lands conspire to dilute this potential.

Finally, although we have stated that firm association between Pleistocene artifacts and extinct fauna is lacking at most sites, two remarkable finds in the Mojave Desert may provide presumptive evidence for a relationship between humans and Pleistocene fauna. In the eastern Mojave, Whitley (1999) reports a petroglyph that bears a close resemblance to a camelid, perhaps a Pleistocene llama. In the northwestern Mojave, a pecked rock slab shows a quadruped with what appears to be a trunk and a pair of curved tusks suggestive of a Columbian mammoth or a mastodon (Kaldenberg 2005). Neither find is amenable at this time to direct dating, nor is either petroglyph securely associated with an artifact component, ancient or otherwise, and some caution over interpretation of these well-worn images is warranted. However, even granting artistic license to the rock artists, there are no modern mammals in North America that bear any likeness to those depicted in these unusual glyphs.

Early Holocene (10,000–7000 B.P.)

The Early Holocene, ca. 10,000–7000 B.P., is defined by warming temperatures and retreating ice sheets. Subalpine forests were replaced by more temperate pine, fir, and other conifer forests (West et al. 2007:19). Pine forests in turn shifted to oak savanna (Erlandson et al. 1996:369; La Jeunesse and Pryor 1998:31). Over the course of the Early Holocene, sea level rose about 45 m, to levels about 15 m lower than today (Masters and Aiello 2007:47). Pluvial lakes in the present desert regions continued to provide reliable water and associated habitat through much of the Early Holocene, but at levels diminished from Pleistocene times (Benson 2004). Tulare and China lakes continued to draw rain and snow-melt run-off from the Sierra Nevada, but these lakes, too, felt the pinch of Early Holocene drying trends. Still, longstanding interpretations of the Early Holocene favored a largely inland adaptation focused on exploiting large mammals around these shrinking lakes. Recent evidence suggests that we revise this model.

Among the most conspicuous Early Holocene type artifacts are Lake Mojave points (Figure 2.2c, d). These relatively large, stemmed points are considered a part of the broadly defined Great Basin stemmed point tradition, as a part of an adaptation known as the Western Pluvial Lakes Tradition (Beck and Jones 1997). The points were initially named for their discovery alongside ancient Lake Mojave (Figure 2.1). Most of our current knowledge of Lake Mojave sites derives from work carried out during the 1980s at Fort Irwin in the eastern Mojave Desert.

Lake Mojave stone tool assemblages have every appearance of an economy directed toward hunting large game. Large projectile points are accompanied by large bifacial knives, large, steep-edged scraping tools, and well-battered core-cobble tools (Basgall 2000a:127). Groundstone slabs are regular occurrences at Lake Mojave sites but do not occur in appreciable numbers at any single site (Sutton et al. 2007:237). Evidence for use wear is usually minimal. If a plant-processing industry existed, seed grinding played only a minor part. But there is other evidence for subsistence practices that go beyond big-game hunting. As the sample size of Early Holocene sites has grown, we have found Lake Mojave sites in a wide variety of environmental contexts, including lake shores, intermittent streams, springs, and marshes (Eerkens et al. 2007; Warren 1994). Significantly, faunal profiles and protein residue analyses of stone tools from excavated sites suggest that lagomorphs, rodents, and even reptiles played a significant—even dominant—role in the Lake Mojave diet (Basgall 1993, 2000a:127; Douglas et al. 1988; Sutton et al. 2007:237). In all, the Lake Mojave people are looking more and more like broad-spectrum hunter-gatherers.

Lake Mojave sites suggest a highly mobile, opportunistic subsistence regimen. Social units appear to have been small, and variation in the sizes of Lake Mojave sites appears to be a consequence of repeated visitation over hundreds of years and not a difference in site function or resident population size (Basgall 2000a:127). There is little variability in flaked stone tool assemblages from site to site, and many raw materials are represented, suggesting wide-ranging subsistence territories (Basgall 2000a, 2000b:6). Lake Mojave people surely emphasized big-game hunting in their tool kits but appear to have been diversified foragers in their day-to-day lives.

In some sense, the Early Holocene in California suffers the same problem that plagues the Paleoindian period: it has a large projectile point as its iconic artifact type, so sites naturally appear to focus on big game because it is a big-game hunting tool that dates the site in the first place. This big-game model resonates throughout the cultural region but is regularly toppled wherever substantial artifact assemblages and faunal records are obtained. For example, in the lower Central Valley the Early Holocene (Lower Archaic) is embodied by large, concave-based points as well as stemmed points (Figure 2.2c, d, g). However, the sole site excavated for this time frame in the region, near Buena Vista Lake (Figure 2.1), reveals a few fragments of large mammal (artiodactyl) within a faunal assemblage composed mainly of fish, waterfowl, and freshwater mussels (Hartzell 1992; Rosenthal et al. 2007:152). Near Honey Lake on the Modoc Plateau, freshwater shellfish, fish, and rabbits constitute the primary recovered fauna (McGuire 2007:170).

In the central Sierra foothills, groundstone became common beginning ca. 8000 B.P. (Moratto 2002:36–38). Along the Central Coast, Early Holocene sites occur in a wide variety of environmental contexts, and most reveal large numbers of millingstones, as well as a broad spectrum of faunal resources, including marine shell, fish, birds, and mammals of all sizes (Jones et al. 2007:137). Indeed, stable isotope analysis of human bone from the later stages of an Early Holocene component in Santa Cruz County suggests a diet consisting of about 75 percent marine foods, presumably shellfish (Newsome et al. 2004:1112). It is inconceivable that so high a dependence on marine resources was achieved overnight, and this analysis clearly reflects a dietary pattern developed deep in the Early Holocene.

Similarly, in the South Coast region, Early Holocene San Dieguito sites beginning about 9000 B.P. appear to show a broad-spectrum dietary regimen including fresh and salt water shellfish, small mammals, birds, and plant foods (Gallegos 1991). Projectile point style affinities with the Great Basin Stemmed Tradition, and in particular Lake Mojave points (Justice 2002:91), suggest that coastal San Dieguito populations arrived from the desert regions, presumably in search of improved foraging opportunities in the face of desiccating desert lakes. Finally, on San Miguel Island, the Daisy Cave site, first occupied during the terminal Pleistocene, shows increased occupation intensity throughout the Early Holocene (Erlandson et al. 1996:370, 2004:253; Rick et al. 2001). Among the tools recovered there are bone fish gorges, bipointed tools designed to hook fish in open water. The fish gorge suggests an industry far more complex than intertidal foraging for stranded fish.

We do not downplay the significance of hunting during the Early Holocene. Clearly, the manufacture of large projectile points, large bifaces, and other butchering tools had as their focus the taking of large game, presumably terrestrial mammals. But we do wish to illustrate that, as in the Pleistocene, subsistence strategies were considerably more varied than typical Early Holocene tool assemblages may imply. The importance of big game as a windfall in calories and protein, and perhaps even its value to the hunter in terms of social prestige, should not be underestimated. But neither should we characterize a hunter-gatherer group based on a single or limited number of iconic artifacts. Although much of California's Early Holocene is defined by thin basal deposits at a few scattered sites, or a handful of isolated diagnostic projectile points, by the end of the era virtually every subregion shows complex artifact assemblages of flaked and ground tools suggesting broad-spectrum hunting and gathering.

Middle Holocene (7000–4000 B.P.)

Climatic change in the Middle Holocene is difficult to encapsulate at the state-wide level, in part because the period represents a continuation of Early Holocene drying and warming, and this general trend was expressed differently across zones of California. Climatic data are more extensive for the Middle than Early Holocene and are not surprisingly more contradictory at the inter-regional level. In all, the Middle Holocene was warmer and dryer than the Early Holocene and also warmer and dryer than today (Benson 2004; Davis 1999; Kennett 2005:66; Koehler et al. 2005; Masters and Aiello 2007; Pope et al. 2004; West et al. 2007). The Middle Holocene saw final desiccation of the desert lakes and a greatly diminished rate of sea-level rise. Lowered sea surface temperatures correlated with lower levels of rainfall in both coastal and inland contexts. Mediterranean conditions characteristic of southern California today may have extended well into northern California (West 1993:232).

Population decline is measured for some regions during the Middle Holocene. For instance, in the North Coast Ranges, Middle Holocene sites are relatively rare and uniformly small (Hildebrandt 2007:91; Kennedy 2005). Some debate exists about whether this observation is real or illusory. Some attribute the decline in site numbers to erosion anomalies that have selectively affected mid-Holocene sites (White at al. 2002) as well as difficulties assigning sites to this time frame (Hildebrandt 2007:91). While these factors may be at play, it is more likely that Middle Holocene populations stopped using certain locations because of diminishing productivity (Hildebrandt and Levulett 1997), a pattern that is seen elsewhere in the state as well. Declining site frequency is observed in the Santa Barbara region from the terminal Early Holocene through the first half of the Middle Holocene, ca. 8500–6500 B.P., and the pattern appears to be attributable to decline in both marine and terrestrial productivity (Erlandson 1997:106; Glassow et al. 1988:72, 2007:196; Kennett 2005:66). Middle Holocene populations in the Mojave Desert began to decline as early as 6500 B.P., and a virtual occupation hiatus is suggested for ca. 5000–4000 B.P. (Sutton et al 2007:241).

Many Middle Holocene sites are characterized by large quantities of stone milling tools. In combination, manos and metates are often the majority tool type. Projectile points began to show more variety in their forms. Certain stemmed projectile points took on a "shouldered" appearance, as in Borax Lake Wide-stemmed points from the northern coastal regions (Figure 2.2e, f). In more southerly regions, particularly in the deserts, projectile points decreased in frequency and in size, as can be seen in the appearance of Pinto points (Figure 2.2h, i). These developments along with faunal profiles suggest a clear emphasis on small prey species, probably taken opportunistically during gathering forays (McGuire and Hildebrandt 1994:48–49). The implication from artifact assemblages is that Middle Holocene hunter-gatherers placed increased emphasis on plant foods, but this interpretation could misread the evidence if earlier forms of grinding equipment are not preserved or are otherwise difficult to identify as plant processing tools. However, recall that stone metates made their first appearance during the Early Holocene, so the actual technological innovation clearly was pre-Middle Holocene. More likely, we are seeing a genuine dietary shift during this era toward stationary resources such as plants and shellfish. From the sheer numbers of grinding tools at many Middle Holocene sites—unsurpassed in earlier or later times—and concurrent decreases in numbers of flaked stone tools (especially projectile points and bifaces), it is reasonable to conclude that much of California witnessed a true "Millingstone Horizon" that placed primary dietary focus on plant food processing (Fitzgerald and Jones 1999; Glassow 1997a:76–79; Jones et al. 2007; McGuire and Hildebrandt 1994; Masters and Gallegos 1997). Still, it is likely that the earliest dates of heavy reliance on milling gear and associated plants varied notably around California, and it is simply not yet clear when the fully entrenched adaptation began.

Although some regional populations appear to have declined, the increasingly arid conditions of the Middle Holocene proved to be an exhilarating condition for California's native oaks (e.g., West 1993:229). Evidence for moderate acorn exploitation may date to as early as 8500 B.P. near Clear Lake in the North Coast Ranges (White et al 2002; Wohlgemuth 2004). The Skyrocket site in the northern San Joaquin Valley (Figure 2.1) has yielded some evidence for very early plant exploitation—including perhaps acorns—as early as 7000–8000 B.P. in the form of rudimentary ground stone tools (Bieling et al. 1996; La Jeunesse and Pryor 1998:30). But for most of California, acorns likely remained a secondary resource, or survival food, at such an early date. Nutritious and easy to gather in great quantity, acorns require intensive processing, primarily the leaching of tannins, to make them edible (see Ortiz 1991). Early evidence for acorn exploitation is largely circumstantial, in the form of increased occurrences of cobble-modified mortars and pestles (Gamble and King 1997:67; cf. Glassow et al. 2007:197). The earliest mortars and pestles appeared in appreciable numbers between about 6000 and 5000 B.P. (Erlandson and Colten 1991:7; Glassow 1997b:152; Glassow et al. 2007:197; Hildebrandt 2007:91; Hull 2007:189; Jones and Klar 2007:305; Jones et al. 2007:138; Rosenthal et al. 2007:155). Perhaps climatic downturns led to the initial widespread use of the acorn, but once begun, acorn exploitation profoundly affected the social and economic trajectories of most of California's native groups.

By the close of the Middle Holocene, some Californians began to organize logistically. In the Sacramento Delta (Figure 2.1) the earliest Windmiller sites indicate the onset of intensive subsistence procurement strategies and extended occupation at stable home bases (Rosenthal et al. 2007:153–154). Windmiller sites (named for the type site located on the Windmiller farm) are generally found near ancient marshes and riparian zones, atop natural levees, ridges, and mounds that rise above flood levels of rivers emptying into the Delta. Perhaps the oldest Windmiller site is the Blossom Mound, a village site on an ancient channel of the Mokelumne River. Extended residence by a relatively large population is suggested by stone and bone tool assemblages as well as by a wealth of non-utilitarian items crafted of shell, antler, bone, and stone (Ragir 1972). Local resources are well represented in the faunal assemblage, including small mammals, waterfowl, and fish, suggesting multi-seasonal residence. Crude mortars and pestles, as well as artiodactyl bones, suggest that Blossom's residents journeyed into the Sierra foothills in search of acorns and game, since neither of these resources would have been common in the Middle Holocene Delta. Windmiller sites are particularly noteworthy for their extensive cemeteries. This is significant because formal burial grounds seem to suggest a sense of permanence, a sense of "home." Formal cemeteries of this scope are lacking in pre-Windmiller times.

It appears that the pattern of logistical residence with scheduled resource collection forays developed in the later years of the Middle Holocene. We see a concomitant increase in exploitation of the acorn, a resource that stores supremely well (Ortiz 1991:45–48) and can be transported some distance to be processed. This Middle Holocene development cascaded into acorn dependence during the Late Holocene.

Late Holocene (4000 B.P.–present)

The Late Holocene in California is far too complicated—and the archaeological record too rich—to encapsulate in any simple way, other than to trace general themes. Important developments of the period are: (1) widespread population growth, despite local abandonment of selected regions; (2) increased sedentism and logistical organization; (3) intensive resource collection, often resulting in declining productivity of the local resource base; (4) increased emphasis on exclusive territories; (5) development of regional exchange networks; and (6) emergence of complex political systems in some areas. All but this last change appear to have occurred, to one degree or another, throughout the California cultural region.

The Late Holocene essentially brought to an end the extended dry period, ushering in a cooler and wetter climatic regime. By about 1950 B.P. the climate had leveled-off to roughly the conditions familiar today (West et al. 2007:25). The ocean assumed its present level, inland pluvial lakes and marshes largely vanished, and various regions took on the biotic patterns visible in the present day. But this grand scheme masks oscillating periods of multi-year drought and cooler wetter conditions that are visible at the local level (Davis 1999; Masters and Aiello 2007:40; Schimmelmann et al. 2003; Stine 1994). Although oscillations—particularly droughts—affected the lives of hunter-gatherers, most did not prompt discernable adaptive change in the archaeological record.

One particularly severe and extended drought may provide an exception. Although not yet fully understood, the Medieval Climatic Anomaly (MCA) appears to have been a mostly hot, dry period that endured over most of California for about 500 years, ca. 1150 to 650 B.P. (Gardner 2006; Graumlich 1993:253; Jones and Kennett 1999; West et al. 2007:17). The MCA was of sufficient strength and duration to have stimulated significant sociocultural and technological responses over multiple generations in some regions. For instance, the San Francisco Bay appears to have been dramatically impacted by the MCA. Although rising water may have obscured some older bay area sites, during the Late Holocene the bay area witnessed its first dramatic population growth, beginning about 2500 B.P. This led to a "golden age" in the bay area, in which hundreds of mounds dotted the bay shores (Lightfoot and Luby 2002:263). Population appears to have peaked at about 950 B.P., followed by a rapid decline (Broughton 1999:32-33; Jones 1992:12; Milliken and Bennyhoff 1993:383). Jack Broughton has securely tied depopulation of the San Francisco Bay at that time to human overexploitation of resources (Broughton 1994a, 1997, 1999, 2001; Broughton et al. 2007). The local resources simply could not sustain high population levels with a food base already taxed by MCA-era drought cycles.

Abandonments of one scale or another are not uncommon during the MCA (Jones et al. 1999). For instance, portions of the western Sierra foothills appear to have been virtually abandoned throughout the MCA between about 750 and 500 B.P. (Hull 2007:188; Hull and Moratto 1999). The western Mojave Desert "Rose Spring" period witnessed rapid population growth between about 1750 and 1150 B.P. (Gardner 2002, 2006; Sutton et al. 2007:241–242), only to see population sizes dwindle steadily thereafter, concomitant with the MCA. Overpredation may be a causal factor in the Rose Spring decline (Sutton et al. 2007:242), but once again of a resource base undoubtedly stressed by the MCA. There is also evidence for settlement disruption along the Central Coast during the MCA (Jones and Ferneau 2002:229), generally in the form of fewer and smaller sites. In the North Coast Range region, "Berkeley Pattern" sites, characterized by sedentary villages until about 1150 B.P., gave way to "Augustine Pattern" sites revealing increased mobility and special-purpose sites characterized by short-term residence (Dowdall 2002:295; Hildebrandt 2007:94–95). It is impossible to ignore the role of the MCA in these social adjustments.

But adjustments they were. *People* survived, perhaps elsewhere, and perhaps by slightly different means, but the MCA resulted only in minor dips in population growth at the statewide level (Jones 2002:8). At the end of the MCA most native Californians returned to pre-MCA lifeways, which brings us to the second broad trend during the Late Holocene: the development of semi-permanent (multi-seasonal) and permanent (year-round) villages. Incipient village life emerged at the close of the Middle Horizon among the Windmiller of the Delta. By the end of the first millennium of the Late Holocene, residential villages were commonplace in most regions of California and were typically occupied by multiple family groups throughout the late fall and winter. These village sites indicate a broad range of activities: they are characterized by a range of utilitarian and non-utilitarian artifacts, specialized activity areas including ceremonial spaces and cemeteries, and evidence for extra-local resources.

In the Central Coast region, shells from some nearshore sites indicate year-round residence (Jones et al. 2008). Since acorns were also a part of the diet, a dedicated foray party must have ventured inland for acorns in the fall, leaving behind a remnant population. The same study suggests that semi-sedentary *inland* populations carried out coastal forays in search of shellfish in the summer. In the Owens Valley of eastern California, foragers roamed freely across large expanses of land until about 3200 B.P., when growing regional population size began to restrict annual ranges. By about 1350 B.P., population growth and territorial restrictions had conspired to generate a "processors" lifestyle, where work parties scheduled seasonal visits to known, productive resource patches. These patches were exploited systematically and fully, with an eye toward generating surplus for storage at semi-sedentary valley-floor villages (Bettinger 1999). A study in the North Coast Ranges took a creative approach to suggest the presence of sedentary villages (Hildebrandt and Hayes 1993). Specialized hunting sites in the North Coast Range uplands, beginning ca. 3400 B.P., were seen as distinct from earlier forager camps in the vicinity. This led to the inference of increased sedentism—although actual village sites have yet to be discovered—simply because a logistically located village site is the logical destination for resources collected during such specialized forays (see also Hildebrandt 2007:96). In each case, there was a shift from the forager's practice of moving consumers to resources to the collector's practice of moving resources to consumers.

Extra-local, logistical forays became increasingly important as the Late Holocene progressed. The evidence includes decreased productivity of immediately available resources, a consequence of the high population density of village locales (Broughton 1994b). Sedentism near San Francisco Bay, as we have seen, resulted in local resource depletion so severe that steep population decline was the ultimate result. On the northern Channel Islands during the Late Holocene, intensive village-level exploitation of molluscan species on Santa Rosa Island (Braje et al. 2007) and San Miguel Island (Erlandson et al. 2008) led to localized deflation of prey species productivity (size and numbers) and ultimately shifts to higher-cost resources. Climatic instability may have further stressed resource productivity in the Channel Islands (Kennett 2005; Munns and Arnold 2002). Finally, as previously noted, people at Late Holocene Rose Spring sites in the Mojave Desert thrived in sedentary circumstances, ca. 1750–1150 B.P., only to disperse in the face of local resource depletions presumed to be at least a partial result of overpredation by humans (Sutton et al. 2007:242).

The theme of Late Holocene population aggregation and semi-sedentary village life correlates strongly with resource depletions and increases in the cost of collecting resources at the local level. Whether resource depletion was a consequence of human overpredation, microenvironmental change, or both, is worthy of investigation on a case-by-case basis (Perry 2004; Wake and Simons 2000). But no matter the primary cause, resource depletion was a serious matter. In certain extreme cases, such as in the San Francisco Bay, resource depletion correlated directly with social collapse and population dispersal. But in the vast majority of cases, technological or social responses served to ameliorate many of the negative aspects of high human population density in the Late Holocene. One obvious technological breakthrough of the Late Holocene was the introduction of the bow and arrow between 1750 and 1350 B.P. (Bettinger et al. 2006; Sutton et al. 2007:241). Fishing gear became more elaborated along the southern coast, including the introduction of circular shell fishhooks. Resource collection during the Late Holocene became both more intensive and extensive.

Another technological response took the form of resource management, of which there were many forms (Anderson 2005; Bendix 2002; Blackburn and Anderson 1993; Parker 2002; Weigel 1993). A particularly noteworthy means of stimulating higher natural plant food yields was the systematic burning of large tracts of grassland and climax chaparral in order to encourage growth of annual edibles in the spring. This procedure had the added effect of attracting game animals to new growth areas (Anderson 2005:137). There are difficulties in attributing ancient fires to purposeful human agency (Parker 2002), but the pervasive practice of burning in the ethnographic present suggests some antiquity to the practice. In addition to burning, selective pruning, sowing, and transplanting of wild seeds is well documented ethnographically. Unfortunately, these leave no signature in the archaeological record. But judicious harvesting was not limited to plant foods alone. A recent study suggests that coastal mussels were selectively harvested after about 650 B.P. along the northern coast, perhaps at the risk of short-term efficiency, but at a benefit to long-term productivity (Whitaker 2008). We do not know when these kinds of ecological manipulation started, but such practices appear widespread in association with Late Holocene sedentism.

One noteworthy example of "tending the wild" is found in the Owens Valley, where wild plant and grass growth was encouraged by small irrigation channels, rain runoff diversion features, and check dams (Lawton et al. 1993). The practice is well documented in the ethnographic and historic records and of a scope that would suggest some antiquity to the practice. However, prehistoric indicators for the practice have yet to be confirmed, primarily because stone diversion walls and check dams are very difficult to date. Evidence for true agriculture in prehistoric California—involving domesticated plants—is limited to the far southeastern desert, particularly along the Colorado River, and is equally controversial (Schaefer and Laylander 2007:253–254). No agricultural features or tools are known from prehistoric contexts, and carbonized seeds (maize, squash) known from archaeological contexts may be trade items. But, as in the Owens Valley, the practice at the time of European contact was highly developed and suggests long familiarity with the technology.

One social correlate of increased sedentism is increased attention to distinctive territories. Whereas specific territorial boundaries are difficult to reconstruct, one way that a strong sense of territoriality may be inferred is through observations of increased interpersonal violence. Although not rampant, violence in California was widespread. In virtually all cases it correlated to some degree with territoriality and/or subsistence stress (Kennett and Kennett 2000; Lambert 2002:216–219). The greater San Francisco Bay area experienced widespread violence throughout its "golden age." Cemetery excavations reveal healed fractures, embedded points, puncture wounds, trophy-taking of body parts, and evidence for scalping (Grady et al. 2001; Hylkema 2002:260; Milliken et al. 2007:113-114). Windmiller villages in the Delta show clear evidence for trophy-taking among the graves dated to the earliest Late Holocene (Ragir 1972:112).

Along the Santa Barbara coast, evidence for systematic violence takes the form of skeletal pathologies (Lambert 1994, 1997, 2002:217) as well as inferences derived from the locations of permanent villages, some of which may have been selected for defensive reasons (Kennett 1998). A grim consequence of the widespread use of the bow and arrow along the Santa Barbara coast is found in an increased occurrence of puncture wounds (Kennett and Kennett 2000:390; Lambert 1994). Although burial data are scanty for the desert regions, intense competition among neighboring villages has been inferred by the abandonment of large tracts of land thought to represent buffer zones among Mojave Desert villages (Allen 1998:74) and by vandalism and substitution of rock art elements within these buffer zones (Walsh 2010). The correlation between violence and territorial sedentism seems clear.

A further correlate with increased sedentism and territoriality appears to be found in Late Holocene evidence for complex trade networks. Perhaps the most readily identifiable objects of exchange are obsidian and shell beads, particularly because each may be unambiguously identified as nonlocal to a given region, and each holds chronological promise (through obsidian hydration, AMS dating, or bead-type seriation). In the Owens Valley, nonlocal obsidian is abundant at sites dated to 3200–1350 B.P., followed by almost exclusive use of only local sources until about 650 B.P. (Basgall and Delacorte 2003; Eerkens and Spurling 2008). This same pattern is evident in the Mojave Desert to the south (Gilreath and Hildebrandt 1997:183) and in the Yosemite region to the west (Hull 2002, 2005).

The exchange of beads from Pacific Coast sources appears to have followed a different trajectory. Hughes and colleagues (Bennyhoff and Hughes 1987:161; Hughes and Milliken 2007:266) have argued that shell beads and other shell ornaments presumably derived from the central coast and territories north of San Francisco Bay appear most frequently in eastern California and the Great Basin starting at the beginning of the Late Holocene, from about 4000 to 2150 B.P. Such long-range trade in beads declined steadily thereafter, until about 1250 B.P., when once again long-distance exchange of shell beads increased through about 450 B.P. Relatively few shell beads from the central coast and Bay crossed the Sierra after 450 B.P., a pattern that is not easy to explain. Archaeologists have not detected major cultural disruptions during the circum-450 B.P. era on the central coast, in the Great Basin, or in intermediate lands that likely served as exchange conduits. Newer data suggest a quite different scenario: that long-distance exchange *increased* during the later part of the Late Holocene in the Owens Valley (Eerkens et al. 2008), including the expanded acquisition and use of shell beads primarily from southern coast sources (Eerkens et al. 2005).

Recent investigations identify more precisely the points of origin for beads found in eastern California and Great Basin contexts, and the results may help to resolve this issue. The chemical "sourcing" of shells used to manufacture beads and ornaments shows considerable promise, and preliminary results indicate that far more of the beads found in the Great Basin may derive from the southern California coast and the Channel Islands than expected, perhaps even more than came from central coast sources, undermining long-standing assumptions (Eerkens et al. 2005). The greater distances and different intermediary routes that are entailed in a southern California supply chain could account in part for the late pre-contact decline in consumption of beads in the Great Basin. Certainly within the Channel Islands region it appears that exchange practices became more locally focused and involved much less importation of lithic materials from long distances after about 700 B.P. (Arnold et al. 2001:124–125), so it stands to reason that there may have been lower numbers of exported beads as well. Very intensive production of beads at specialized villages on the Channel Islands accounted for expanded use of beads within southern California by ca. 750 B.P., and certain bead types came to be used as a formal currency around that time. Possibly some of these bead types became too expensive for far-distant consumers to acquire.

Looking at California as a whole, it is difficult to ignore the concordance between some of these shifts in long-distance movement of goods and the Medieval Climatic Anomaly (MCA). Obsidian exchange networks appear to have broken down at or about the onset of the MCA, ca. 1150 B.P. It is not possible at this time to determine whether this may have resulted from population decline and dispersal, thus breaking down established trade routes, or whether social groups simply became more insular as a consequence of environmental stress.

A final characteristic of the Late Holocene is the development of politically complex societies in parts of California. Shifting dietary emphases arose throughout the last few thousand years along the coast and on the Channel Islands near Santa Barbara, and resource productivity intermittently waned with droughts, fluctuating oceanic currents, and intensive exploitation by increasingly sedentary populations (Arnold 2001; Erlandson et al. 2008:2149; Kennett 2005). Climatic downturns likely played some, albeit limited, roles in cultural changes in that region. Most of the region's archaeologists do not see paleoclimate as determinative. Technological developments, such as new watercraft, as well as emergent integrative ritual organizations and new economic interdependencies were also quite important in political evolution and the eventual rise of more complex polities.

Beginning about 750–800 B.P., several thousand villagers living on the coasts of the three largest northern Channel Islands developed an effective monopoly over shell bead manufacture and control over access to island quarries with blocky cherts suitable for the mass-manufacture of bead-making microdrills (Arnold 2004; Arnold and Graesch 2001; Arnold and Munns 1994; Glassow et al. 2007; Preziosi 2001). Indicators of wealth-based status differentiation, which continued largely unabated into the early colonial era, emerged in domestic contexts and burial populations (Arnold 2001; Graesch 2004; Lambert 1994; Noah 2005). Certain laborious-to-make bead types became standards of value, or currency, used in formal transactions throughout coastal southern California, as later documented by the Spaniards and detailed ethnographic accounts (Arnold 2001).

Craft specializations flourished as social and political complexity escalated, and a craft guild associated with the construction and operation of rare and costly oceangoing plank canoes allowed emerging elites, through ownership of the canoes, to control the distribution of prized beads and many other goods. Plank canoes were the only viable means for getting shell beads to a lucrative market on the mainland and to get needed plant food resources to the protein-rich but relatively plant-poor islands; this disparity was particularly acute during extended droughts, such as during the MCA. Chumash political complexity was apparently a relatively rapid development (Arnold 1992), spurred in part by a swift reorganization of labor to accommodate specialized manufacturing practices and the culmination of a long period of refinement of the plank canoe at more or less the same juncture (Arnold 2007). The Island Chumash—and other Chumash subgroups in the Santa Barbara Channel area—operated as simple chiefdoms for several centuries.

Differing levels of political complexity may be inferred for other regions, particularly in places where resources were unequally distributed and productive locations could be monopolized. In the upper Sacramento Valley and Sacramento Delta regions, for instance, particularly productive fishing locations saw the founding of quite large villages, central places surrounded by satellite hamlets (White 2003). Additionally, these villages show differences in the disposition of the dead, including disparities in the nature and amount of grave goods, suggesting status distinctions among individuals (Rosenthal et al. 2007:157–158). In the San Francisco Bay, distinct polities are clearly suggested by conspicuous mounds and mound clusters (Luby et al. 2006). These mounds served not only as cemeteries, but also as political and ceremonial centers, mixing residential and ritual activities (Lightfoot 1997:139; Lightfoot and Luby 2002). Although this form of elaborate landscaping is usually accompanied by marked social inequality (Sassaman 2004), there are conflicting signals in the archaeological record of the San Francisco Bay. Specifically, grave goods from upper-strata burials interred during the peak years of mound visibility show *less* distinction among individuals than those buried much earlier, at the basal levels of mounds (Luby and Gruber 1999:101).

For now, we have every reason to believe that the San Francisco Bay of about a millennium ago saw some form of politically and ceremonially complex social organization. We also observe firm evidence for marked inequality among individuals in the Sacramento Valley and Delta, but it is not yet possible to define those systems in more specific terms. For much of California, the question remains not, "How complex were they?" but rather, "How were they complex?"

In concluding we stress that this brisk tour through 13,000 years of California's rich prehistory is topical in approach, and we have chosen examples to further that approach. Any broadly stated rule about California's prehistoric development can be disconfirmed by at least one counterexample somewhere in the greater cultural region. This is one reason that practically every subregion of the state has its own esoteric jargon, its own projectile point or bead typology, and its own developmental history. When archaeology was in its infancy in the state, Alfred Kroeber (1925:926) wrote, "the correlation of the findings of archaeology and ethnology is that not only the general Californian culture area, but even its subdivisions or provinces, were determined a long time ago and have ever since maintained themselves with relatively little change." Kroeber was quite wrong about stasis in California's prehistory when he made this assertion close to 90 years ago. But then most archaeologists just a few decades ago could not have predicted the early strata at Daisy Cave, imagined the Lake Mojave as broad-spectrum foragers, or envisioned the complex political organization that now seems evident along coastal Santa Barbara.

3

Northwest Coast Economies in Northern California

Within the northernmost 160 km (100 mi) of the California coast, at latitudes north of Cape Mendocino, people whose adaptations resonated with those of the classic Northwest Coast culture area lived along great river systems amid dense redwood and fir-spruce forests. Pockets of oaks in drier portions of the interior provided ample acorns, deer and elk roamed, and the rivers teemed with salmon and steelhead as well as sturgeon. Scattered offshore rocks, remnants of ancient coastal ridges, supported marine mammal rookeries that seasonally drew the most northerly groups, including the Tolowa, several miles onto the ocean in their redwood dugout canoes.

At contact, at least eight tribal groups were part of this traditional culture area, including the best-known Tolowa, Yurok, Karok, Hupa, and Wiyot (Figure 3.1). Much like their counterparts in the Pacific Northwest Coast region of Washington and British Columbia (Ames and Maschner 1999; Matson and Coupland 1995; Sobel et al. 2006), they lived in redwood plank houses and had delayed-return economies characterized by large-scale storage of dried salmon and plant foods, in this case acorns. Good-sized groups numbering in the dozens to hundreds lived together in favorable locales, and they were somewhat more sedentary than most Northwest groups, clustering in fairly permanent settlements situated along major rivers such as the Klamath and Trinity or on the coast at the mouths of these rivers. Although it is not widely acknowledged, the renowned coastal groups throughout much of the Northwest Coast (e.g., the Nuu-chah-nulth and Kwakwaka'wakw of Vancouver Island and neighbors on the B.C. mainland coast) were actually not sedentary but semi-sedentary, moving their entire households and most of their house planks and contents at least twice per year to follow resources. The northwestern California groups for the most part stayed in their villages

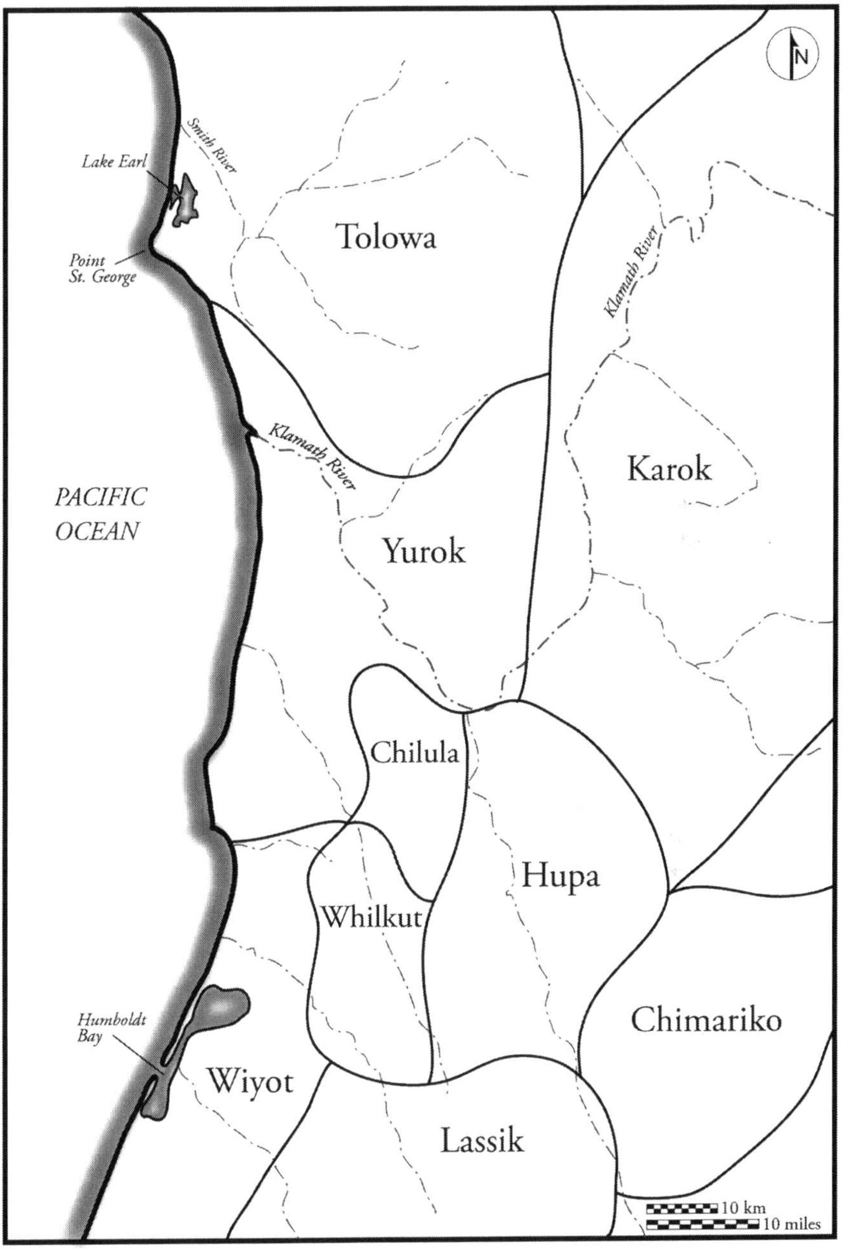

Figure 3.1. Northwest Coast ethnographic groups. Map by Clarus J. Backes, Jr.

nine to ten months of the year and shifted to camp near communal fish weirs or by the most productive acorn groves during the late summer/early autumn months, returning often to their villages with basketloads of dried fish and nuts for winter storage (Gould 1978:130).

Northwestern Californian economies at contact were governed by dentalium currency and strong principles of property ownership that included resource areas (such as oak groves, fishing pools and eddies, and offshore rocks), houses, ceremonial obsidian bifaces, and dugout canoes for river travel and oceanic forays. Villagers communally owned beaches and the rights to butcher and distribute whales that might wash up there. Wealth accumulations and ritual wealth displays were a primary pathway to modest levels of political power, which in this region did not appear to rise to the level of chieftainship. The most frequently described leaders were men in prominent families who inherited wealth from elders, and shamans, who were often women or transvestite males. The rich men had no formal authority, however. Ethnographer Philip Drucker (1937a:244) wrote regarding the Tolowa rich household head: "If his kinsmen did his bidding it was out of respect for his wealth and his personality." So we see that these nominal leaders could not fully command the labor of their own kinspeople, much less non-kin in their villages.

Although slavery was present in this region, it was limited in scale and a minor phenomenon. Northern California slaves were not captives of raids or warfare, as was the case in the Northwest Coast proper (Donald 1997); rather, they were generally poor adults who could not pay off a debt, often for having uttered damaging insults or affronting the honor of a richer man (Drucker 1937a:250).

Other material culture indicators of the Northwest culture connection are bone harpoons associated with marine mammal hunting and ocean fishing as well as antler wedges and bell-shaped stone mauls associated with extensive woodworking tasks such as house-plank splitting and dugout canoe making. This region exhibits modest influences from the south as well. The 16 to 20 tribal groups who lived south and east of Cape Mendocino but still north of San Francisco Bay included the well-known Miwok and several Pomo subgroups, most of whom shared a terrestrial rather than a maritime or riverine economic orientation. A rich mix of acorns, berries, deer, elk, and anadromous fish such as salmon stimulated a pattern of semi-mobile to largely sedentary living and a strong focus on the art of making fine basketry for storage and other functions. Influences due to contact with these groups filtered into the diets and material assemblages of the more southerly northwestern California groups.

The first documented encounters between these groups and Euroamericans occurred during the early nineteenth century. Explorer Jedediah Smith traveled among the Tolowa in June of 1828 and made cursory observations about their trading and haggling acumen in his journal (Pilling 1978). A stream of ethnographers, primarily from Berkeley, began to descend on northern and central California during the 1910s and 1920s and captured substantial information on the region's disappearing lifeways. We next examine the archaeological record and then return to discuss a few significant material characteristics—those with notable implications for archaeology—of two of the region's important groups, the Yurok and the Tolowa.

Archaeological Explorations in Northwestern California

Although considerably more archaeological research has been conducted in this part of California during the last 20 years than in all of the preceding century, we are still limited in what we know about early adaptations. The scattered late Pleistocene fluted points and crescents known from sites a couple of hundred miles south, near Clear Lake, have no counterparts in the far northwest. The earliest people to occupy northwestern California are represented by a few early Holocene-era inland sites in the Trinity River/Pilot Ridge area at the southeastern margin of this region (Hildebrandt 2007:87). This cultural manifestation is known as the Borax Lake Pattern (8000–2500 cal B.C.), first evident at roughly 10,000 cal B.P. Excavations at HUM–573, located just above 1230 m (4,000'), revealed a well-preserved 8,000-year-old house floor with a significant assemblage of milling tools and chert and obsidian bifaces (Fitzgerald and Hildebrandt 2002), making it one of the older houses identified in the northern half of California. The early Borax Lake phase is presumed to reflect a settlement-subsistence system with significant residential mobility, manifested by sites in both higher-elevation mountain locales and riverine settings that yield fairly complete artifact assemblages, including large, wide-stemmed points and milling gear. More fieldwork is needed to locate other early sites and more fully elucidate how people used this rugged landscape.

The following Mendocino Pattern (ca. 4500–1500 B.P. [2500 cal B.C.–A.D. 500]) is characterized by new point (dart) styles and reduced residential mobility. Sites in the mountains may be the remains of short-term hunting camps used by residents of village sites situated in the lower elevations along the major rivers, supported by salmon and acorn harvests. Semi-sedentary villages composed of multiple redwood plank houses may have been first established along the region's rivers about three millennia ago. Recent work at sites on the Smith River near the Oregon border indicates that simple plank houses there may date as early as cal 3100 B.P. (Hildebrandt 2007; Tushingham 2005, 2009). Tushingham (2009) set out to document when intensive foraging/collecting systems focused on salmon fishing and acorn processing first emerged in northwestern California, using data from five sites in the Smith River watershed. Her excavations reveal a long chronological sequence with four main components, featuring the region's earliest semi-subterranean redwood plank houses. She shows that residential stability increased in the region as reliance on acorns expanded more than 3,000 years ago, but almost two full millennia passed before intensive mass-harvesting and storage strategies and largely sedentary plank-house villages were established locally (Tushingham 2009:281–283).

However, there is no evidence of human occupation directly on the shorelines of the north coast even as late as 2500 B.P., which has led many scholars to speculate that early sites have been lost to sea-level rise or other preservation problems. Subsidence linked to earthquakes in the Cascadia subduction zone possibly led to the loss of some early peri-coastal sites in northern Oregon and Washington (Minor and Grant 1996). But geomorphic studies show that parts of the northern California coast have actually been rising a few meters per millennium, meaning that archaeologists have traversed and inspected at least some quite old land forms without finding sites (Hildebrandt 2007:95–96; Hildebrandt and Levulett 2002). Thus, rising seas have not inundated major stretches of the northern California coastline and do not account for the rarity of early coastal sites, although it remains possible that tsunamis have destroyed coastal deposits. So it appears that local settlement patterns largely reflect the foraging decisions of early populations. Diverse resources in the interior, Hildebrandt and Levulett (1997, 2002) argue, were plenty rich enough to keep people well-fed and inland-based until the last couple of millennia.

The assertion that the north coast began to be lightly used from ca. 2,500–1,500 years ago is confirmed by a suite of obsidian hydration and radiocarbon data from several sites (Hildebrandt and Levulett 2002:306–308).

The important stratified Point St. George site (DNO–11) has a lower component that appears not earlier than ca. 2260 B.P. (uncalibrated; the calibrated date would presumably be younger). It was probably a lithic workshop and temporary camp for collecting chert, not a coastal food-extraction locale (Gould 1978:135). Subsistence was still terrestrially oriented there and at a Humboldt Bay coastal site (HUM–351) to the south that is no older than 2400–2500 B.P. [500 cal B.C.] (Hildebrandt 2007:92; Hildebrandt and Levulett 2002:309–310). These were seasonal encampments by people not yet pursuing coastal resources.

The first village sites of any size on the coast that reflect a marine dietary focus date to after 950 B.P., according to multiple sources. Between Humboldt Bay and the Oregon border, we have excavation data from five major sites that have yielded the remains of redwood houses (planks or timbers were found at three of these sites), dugout canoes, and/or marine foods. These sites are the upper component at Point St. George (DNO-11; Gould 1966a); the Stone Lagoon site (HUM-129; work done by Milburn and colleagues in the 1970s); Patrick's Point (HUM-118) and Trinidad (HUM-169) (Elsasser and Heizer 1966); and Gunther Island in Humboldt Bay (HUM-67; first excavated by Loud in the 1910s; Elsasser and Heizer 1964).

The upper component at Point St. George dates to the last 500 years before contact. Evidence for a house was recovered along with artifacts similar to Gunther Island assemblages (Gould 1978:136; see also Gould 1966b). The mammalian faunal remains recovered from several sites in the region, dominated by marine mammal specimens (>70 percent), support the supposition that sea-oriented technologies in the north accurately reflect a pronounced maritime economy north of Humboldt Bay (Hildebrandt and Levulett 2002:314–315).

Northwest California sites exhibit a new proliferation of people and of artifact types associated with the archaeologically defined Gunther Pattern after 1,500 years ago. These assemblages include Gunther barbed points and other stone projectile types used as tips of marine mammal and fish harpoons; pestles, hammerstones, and notched net sinkers (for fish, duck nets); bowl-shaped steatite grease catchers, zoomorphic polished stone clubs, and polished stone adze handles; elk antler wedges for splitting redwood; antler harpoons; and an array of bone gorges, awls, needles, and flakers (Hildebrandt and Levulett 2002:310–313). Hildebrandt and others have suggested that the nearby offshore rocks found a few miles from the northernmost coasts stimulated the development of the ancient version of the Tolowa dugout canoe to procure sea mammals and oceanic fish. Interested readers can revisit a lively debate about marine mammal exploitation and its relationship to the invention and adoption of boating technologies in various parts of California by reading Hildebrandt and Jones (1992), Lyman (1995), and Colten and Arnold (1998).

Social differentiation is evident in Gunther Pattern cemeteries. The cemetery area of the Gunther Island site yielded more than 60 huge obsidian ceremonial bifaces (25 to 50 cm long) of precisely the kinds used within the colonial era as part of the White Deerskin Dance. Of course we can only speculate about their use in pre-contact contexts. Also common in the burials were antler wedges, zoomorphic clubs, adze handles, flanged pestles, dentalium beads, Olivella beads, and abalone ornaments (Hildebrandt and Levulett 2002:313). X-ray fluorescence analysis shows that many of the big obsidian bifaces found at sites in northwestern California are from distant sources and of distinctive colors such as red or mottled red and black volcanic glass (recorded sources include Glass Buttes and Warner Mountains), obviously adding to their intrinsic value (Hughes 1978), while obsidian projectile points are frequently from local sources (Hildebrandt and Levulett 2002:315).

In this phase we find clear signs of sedentism, considerable marine mammal and fish hunting and netting (harpoons, clubs, net sinkers), intensive plant processing (pestles, mauls), and the inferred use of oceangoing canoes. Also found are well-defined redwood houses, some with clay floors and small stone patios, and woodworking tools such as chisels, wedges, and mauls. North of Humboldt Bay there was more emphasis on wealth accumulation, ownership of resource areas, sedentism, and social ranking (Hildebrandt and Levulett 2002:314–315). This latter "adaptive mode" was limited to the areas later occupied by the Tolowa, Yurok, and Wiyot. Tushingham (2009:293) argues that at about 1250 B.P., Gunther-era social units in ancient Tolowa territory along the Smith River laid claim to optimal resource areas and became more fixed on the landscape while defending these patches. They were mass-harvesting acorns and salmon, employing new bulk storage strategies, and establishing modest-sized plank-house villages, and although populations grew larger and more affluent, complex political structures did not develop, in part because co-resident group size remained small. Her results may lend some credence to a migration model first advanced by Bennyhoff (1950), elaborated in unpublished papers by Kenneth Whistler, and supported by recent linguistic research (Golla 2007). The model proposes that people from the Northwest Coast arrived in Tolowa territory around 1250 B.P., stimulating much more intensified salmon harvesting practices and favoring year-round residence at fixed locations in order to secure premium fishing locales. She describes the local political economy as nonetheless remaining small-scale, village-focused, and culturally resistant to higher-level labor demands in the face of this purported migration because of a tenacious ethos of individual and family-level (rather than corporate) resource ownership (Tushingham 2009:295–296).

South of Humboldt Bay, the post–1500 B.P. era is labeled the Late period. Thirteen sites yield artifacts that differ in notable ways from those north of the bay. Clearly this is a zone where the material culture signals an ecological and cultural transition from the Northwest orientation to the North Coast Ranges (see Chapter 1), part of the more prototypical classic California oak- woodland adaptation. This is where groups such as the Southern Wiyot, Mattole, Nongatl, and Sinkyone lived at the time of Euroamerican contact. Signs of extensive woodworking, permanent houses, and a marine focus are largely absent in these territories. The large ceremonial bifaces and stone harpoon tips prevalent to the north are absent. On the other hand, small bone tools are common, and clam disk and Olivella beads turn up frequently in burials (Hildebrandt and Levulett 2002:313). Deer and acorns dominated in a terrestrially focused economy. Tribelet organization with village leaders predominated. The major obsidian sources at Clear Lake and Annadel farther to the south supplied much of the material for local tool making and trade.

The Yurok: The Great Fish Dam and Riverine Village Organization

One of the first cultural features that young ethnographer T. T. Waterman chose to record after he began his fieldwork among the Yurok was the building of the Kepel fish dam. The so-called dam was actually a great, communally constructed tribal fish weir built annually along a populous part of the Klamath River, and the raw materials to build the weir were collected from throughout upper Yurok territory. Its construction was marked by a series of impressive ceremonies (Waterman 1920:246). This topic was an appropriate choice by Waterman because salmon fishing and the construction of the weir were both salient organizing foci of Yurok life and culture. This one activity brought together great pools of labor, provided many social opportunities, reinforced important ritual prescriptions, and supplied enough fish to support Yurok households for many months. Our understanding of the archaeological features we see in this region is notably enhanced by observing how these activities were organized and which technological objects were instrumental in carrying them out.

The Yurok lived along the lower 57 km (36 mi) of the Klamath River, from roughly the point where the Trinity River empties into the Klamath in southeastern Yurok territory to the Pacific (Figure 3.2). They also controlled about 67 km (42 mi) of coastline. Most of the main "private holdings" of families (owned places where they collected key resources) were within a few miles of the river and coast. Linguistically, there were two dialects—the river people and the coast people—and the former were numerically dominant.

The Kepel fish weir was built each year for the massive early summer salmon harvest. Several hundred Yurok from up and down the Klamath gathered and camped in the towns of *Ke'pel* and *Sa"a* (Waterman and Kroeber 1938:54). In the very strong current, the construction took some engineering skill and was very labor intensive, with much coordination of effort. The weir was shored with larger poles to counter the force of the current. The weir's thousands of stakes were driven into the gravel river bottom. It was positioned at a place where the river is wide and fairly shallow and where natural fishing places (eddies, pools) were few. Individual fishing could still go on at these productive pools, but *Ke'pel* was the perfect place for the large-scale activities associated with the weir. Yurok people who were interviewed stated that the rationale for this location was that trial and error produced just the "right" spot. The feature extended fully across the river, with only the narrowest of openings, much too small for a fish to pass through. The long face of the weir encompassed 10 traps, or pens, where the fish concentrated as they struggled to pass through. They funneled into these pens and were then netted and taken to the river banks for butchering. It was said that the salmon filled pens as quickly as the Yurok could empty them.

Many rituals were practiced in connection with building and use of the weir, starting with the strict avoidance of the "first salmon" to arrive and a taboo-removing ceremony at the mouth of the river (Waterman and Kroeber 1938:52). Events surrounding the weir were choreographed such that it took precisely10 days to build, then it was used for precisely 10 days, then it was rapidly removed. The Yurok of course had to allow sufficient numbers of

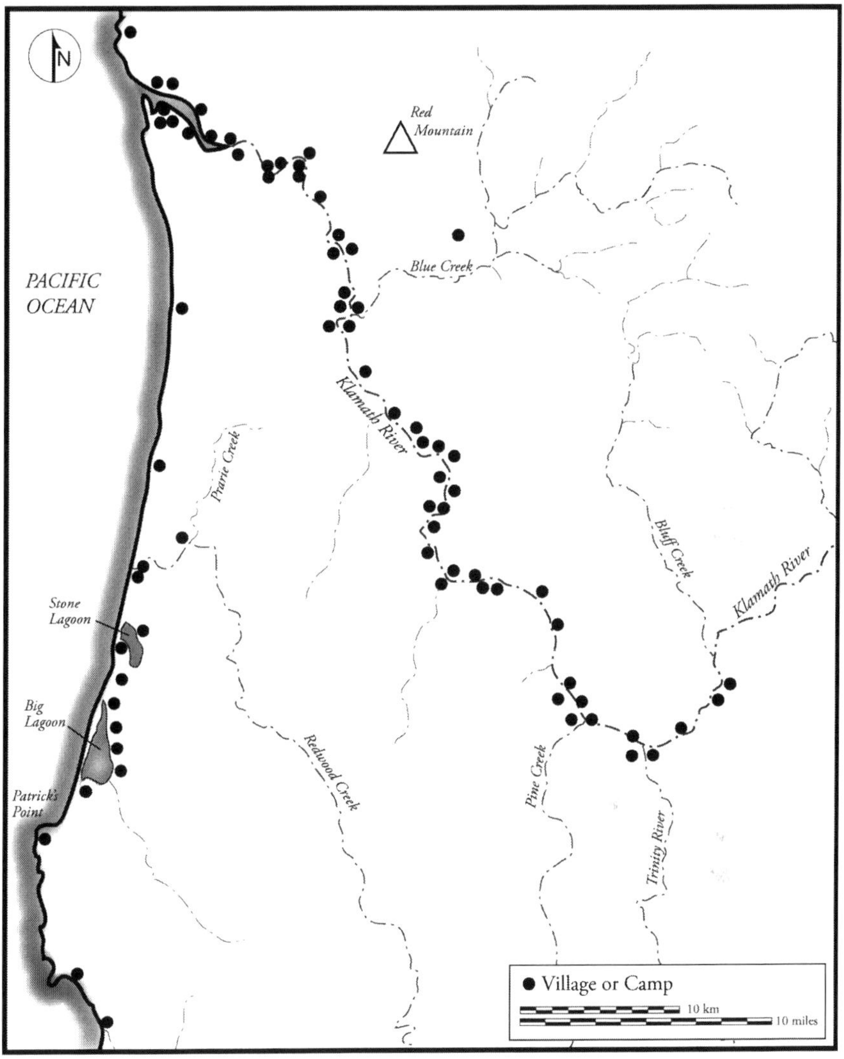

Figure 3.2. Pre- and post-contact Yurok villages (not all occupied coterminously), with clear focus along the Klamath River. Map by Clarus J. Backes, Jr. Adapted from Pilling (1978:139).

fish to pass through for upstream harvests by other groups. The person in charge of the ritual linked with the building and use phases was a shaman who possessed the necessary medicine to oversee it all. There was also a stake-maker who managed many of the necessary resources; both positions were held by members of single families for many years. Stake cutters followed ritual procedures and commenced work at the same time throughout Yurok territory. They used fir trees exclusively, shaping stakes with mauls and elk-horn wedges (Waterman and Kroeber 1938:54). On the sixth day of the 10-day period, weir assembly would begin, employing about 70 men. Builders used flat stone pounders to drive the stakes into the river bed, proceeding simultaneously from both sides of the river to meet in the middle, with the "V" shape pointing upstream. The weir was always finished by the tenth day.

Settlement was in what Waterman (1920:200–205) called "towns." The communities ranged from 6 to 25 redwood plank houses, usually situated at about 30 m (100') above the river on old river terraces (Figure 3.3). The Klamath River can rise annually as much as 22 m (70'), so such positioning was crucial to avoid catastrophic destruction. A particularly bad winter flood in1862 nonetheless wiped out several villages. Most settlements were on the south-facing north bank, with its patches of grass and oaks (and fewer conifers), allowing for better sun exposure. All larger villages were outside the redwood timber belt, presumably for similar reasons, and a few other large Yurok villages could be found at the mouth of the Klamath and other rivers near lagoons and estuaries. A good deal of this information is essential in interpreting the region's still-expanding archaeological record.

Waterman (1920:208–214) also reported that the Yurok gave names to their substantial houses. When a family was prosperous and had numerous descendants, they built additional houses but all kept the one name. Names were largely informal and positionally descriptive, but the names also were remembered and held meaning for descendants. Some were related to historical people or events (e.g., *lo"oliL* = dam-builder's house). Others reflected locational information (*regwona'* = at the end; *wo'gu* = in the middle) or nearby landscape features (*he'Lqau* = back from the river; *wo'nau* = uphill), while still others referred to size (*mekwoma'* = biggest) or the natural environment (*sa'sip* = wild honeysuckle).

Although they largely stayed in one village for most of the year, the Yurok had a strongly developed sense of property ownership that strictly preserved families' food resource rights through the seasons and across the tribal territory. Their many private holdings could be found at great distances from their homes, throughout the river corridors. Most were fishing places, acorn places, and snaring places. Fishing occurred via traps/weirs, seines/nets (up to 30 m long), dip nets, hook-and-line, and bipointed har-

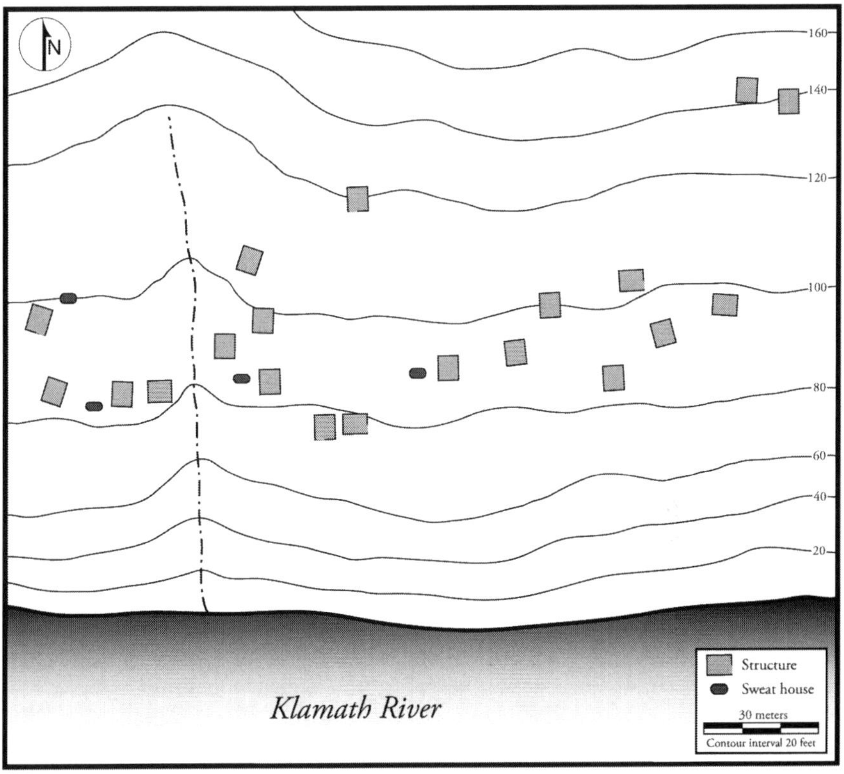

Figure 3.3. Yurok village plan (Mu-rek). Map by Clarus J. Backes, Jr. Adapted from Waterman (1920:Map18).

poons (Waterman 1920:218–222). The prime fishing places were at eddies or backwaters where salmon congregate; these could be sold at any time, their value depending on their recent yields. Such places could be owned by as many as 10 entities, and used on alternating days and varying river levels. Beach rights (including offshore rocks) were held by groups rather than individuals, and acorn places of up to a few acres in size were apparently owned by families. Narrow snaring places where game passed through gullies or moved toward water were strictly private property. Waterman (1920:225) shows about 25 distinct resource extraction places owned by one family, stretching across the whole length of Yurok territory. Property was not necessarily handed down to children; that which did was usually passed through females.

The Tolowa : A Coastal Economy

Most of the estimated 2,000 Tolowa (Figure 3.4) lived in one of eight good-sized villages, each housing as many as 300 people, that dotted the far north coast in places such as Crescent Bay and Lake Earl (Drucker 1937a; Gould 1978:128, 130). These settlements were occupied for roughly 10 months of the year and were largely vacated during late summer through early fall, when residents left to collect salmon and acorns in the interior. Like the Yurok, they constructed a major fish weir annually. Theirs was about 6 km up the Smith River, where they camped collectively for a few weeks during the late summer to catch and dry salmon for winter (Drucker 1937a:232). Many short visits to the home villages occurred during those months as residents returned periodically with dried fish and nuts for winter storage. Dried salmon was one of many products filling rows of storage baskets lined up in every well-run house. The Smith River was the principal river system in Tolowa territory, and although it supported reasonably good runs of salmon, it had far fewer salmon and eels than the Klamath River to the south. This more depauperate riverine fauna at least partially explains the strong coastal orientation of the Tolowa. Dense forests of redwood, cedar, Douglas fir, spruce, pine abounded near the coastal strip, with up to 50 cm (20") of rain monthly in the winter. Deer, elk, and plant foods could be taken in many places, and fish, mollusks, and sea mammals could be exploited on the coast. The settlements inland/upstream were minor.

Each village of these Athapascan-speaking people was a largely independent economic unit (Drucker 1937a). Individuals or families clearly owned key food resource spots such as upriver fishing places, oak groves, and the rights to go first to the sea lion rocks off Point St. George. Such rights were inherited (Drucker 1937a:243). Settlements collectively owned beaches and associated whale-butchering rights.

Tolowa houses were square or rectangular, about 4 or 5 m on each side, and made of redwood planks with a pitched roof (Figure 3.5). In the interior, an area measuring about 3 m per side was excavated to roughly 1 m deep, creating two levels of living floor. The entrance door on one end was low and circular. Houses of the rich were named, but not most other houses. Recently, Tushingham (2005:14) has reported the discovery and excavation of a burned contact-era structure, interpreted as a sweathouse, with redwood plank floor remnants and a slab-lined hearth at a site along the Smith River.

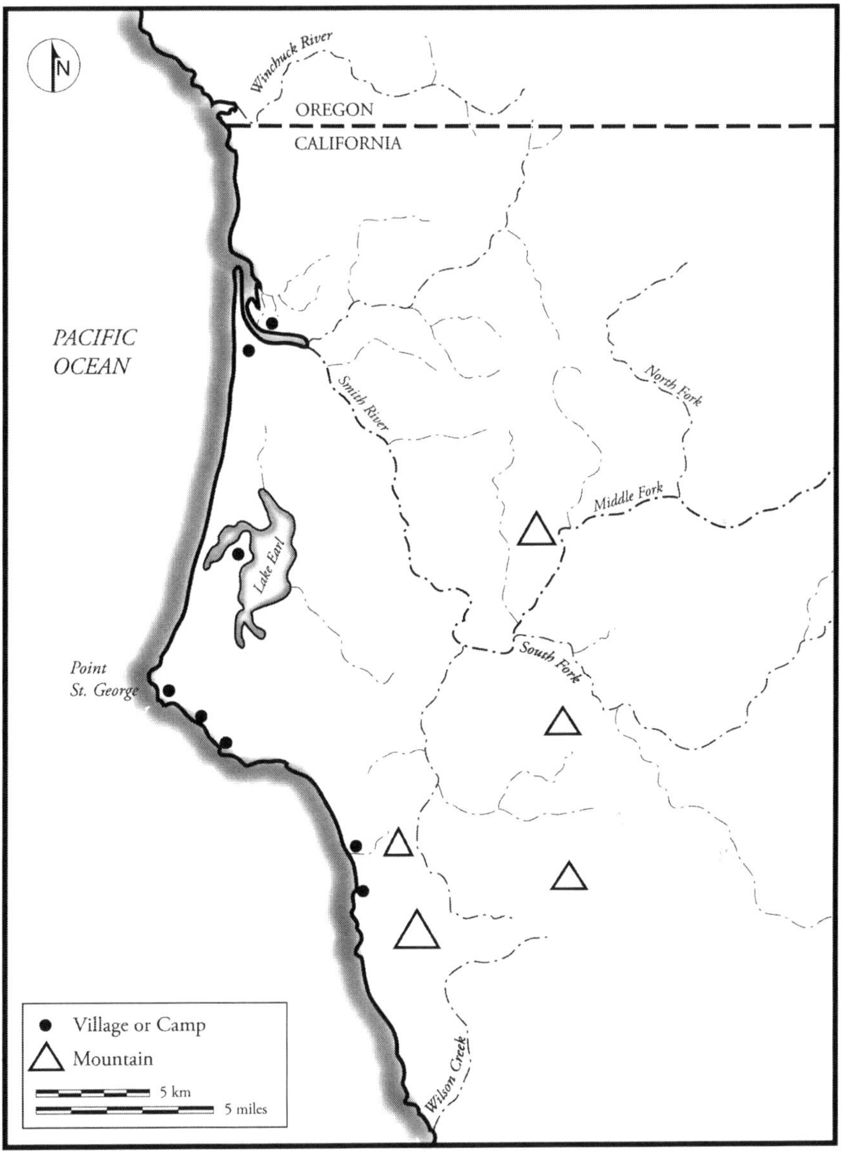

Figure 3.4. Principal recorded villages of the Tolowa. Map by Clarus J. Backes, Jr. Adapted from Gould (1978:128).

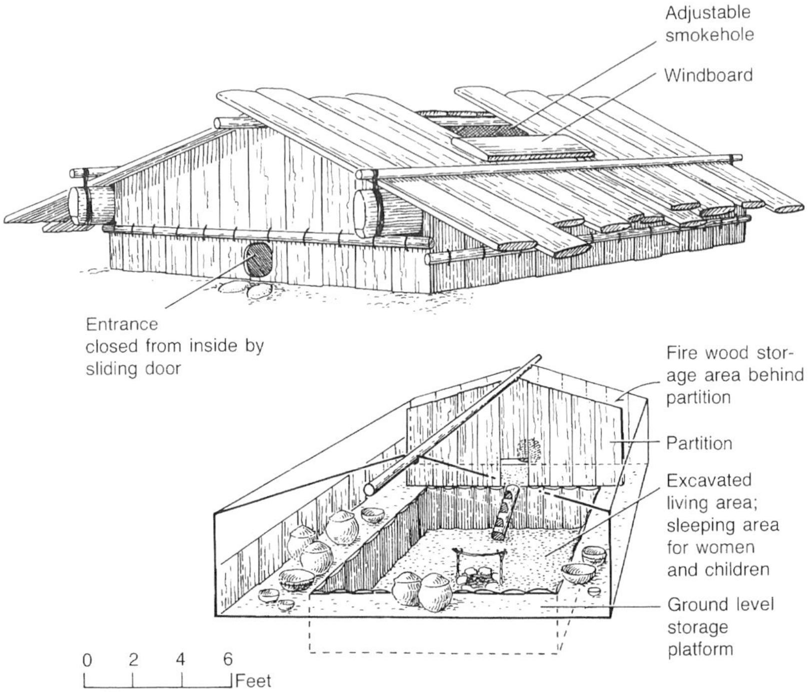

Figure 3.5. Redwood plank house of the Tolowa (from Gould 1978:131). Used with the permission of the Department of Anthropology, National Museum of Natural History, Smithsonian Institution.

She has also excavated portions of other Late (Gunther Pattern) semi-subterranean plank-house structures during the course of her dissertation research, showing that inland occupation was more substantial than previously believed (Tushingham 2009:283).

The Tolowa made large redwood dugout canoes that were as long as 13 m and up to 3 m wide. They employed the dugouts to hunt at sea lion rookeries on rocks situated offshore, and there is faunal evidence for such watercraft and harpooning technology (Figure 3.6) in the pre-contact era as well (Hildebrandt and Jones 1992). Drucker (1937a:237) notes that the large canoes were called "5-men boats," and they also built narrower, shallower river canoes. Other fine woodworking products included carved paddles, stools, and troughs.

Gould (1978) argues that politically, the Tolowa did not have chiefs or exhibit sharp social stratification. Considerable trade, ceremonial interac-

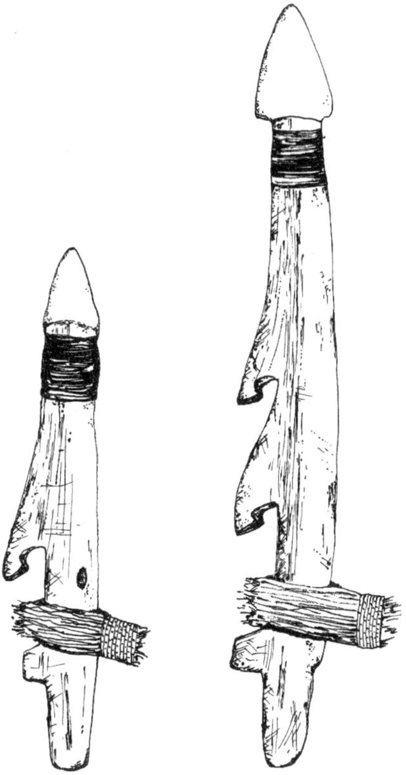

Figure 3.6. Northwest harpoons and harpoon heads. Left, Yurok single-barb sea-lion harpoon; center, Tolowa sea-lion harpoon; right, bilaterally barbed harpoon head, archaeological specimen. Illustration by Jeanne E. Arnold. Adapted from Gifford (1940: 233, 237).

tion, and intermarriage occurred with neighboring tribes (Yurok, Karok, Hupa, Tututni), but no one controlled access to these transactions. Headmen accrued and displayed wealth, consisting of large obsidian bifaces, red-headed woodpecker scalps, and strings of dentalium beads (Gould 1966b). The rich men had no formal authority, however (Drucker 1937a).There were no potlatches or destructions of property among the Tolowa; rich men sought to enhance honor and prestige through maintenance of respect (ensuring that others always treated them respectfully). They routinely avenged any affronts and insults and worked hard to retain and display their wealth (Drucker 1937a:251). Having the respect of others was paramount.

The labor of a wife or wives (some rich men had multiple wives) and of daughters (and the future value for bride price income) was a primary economic engine for Tolowa society (Gould 1978:132–133).

The Tolowa used money made from *Dentalium* shells from the distant Northwest Coast sources around Vancouver Island. As was true elsewhere in the region, large shells were extremely valuable, and shorter shells less so. Shells were strung in counts of ten, and value was assigned based on the total length of the string. Currency could be used to hire services, pay damages, or buy objects or information, but they were not usually used to buy foods. According to Drucker (1937a:241), most people had "trifling amounts," and most dentalia circulated among a few wealthy Tolowa men and their descendants. With few exceptions, the poor could not become wealthy since money was strictly inherited. A few people made money by means of their skills in some special crafts (such as canoe making), but there was not enough demand to make them rich. Thus, two clear classes of Tolowa people co-existed (Drucker 1937a:242). They also had material "treasure" in the form of red woodpecker scalps, huge obsidian bifaces, and women's dance regalia that were used in rituals and wealth displays. Gould (1978:132) downplays the distinction between dentalium as currency and the other artifacts as "treasures," calling them all treasures. At the same time, Gould notes that plenty of currency transactions with dentalia occurred, and a lot of haggling occurred over bride-price payments. Gould also sees more pathways to wealth through manipulation and trade than did Drucker, who argued that wealth simply had to be inherited.

Summary

The native groups of northwestern California developed distinctive regional traditions starting some 1,500 to 2,000 years ago that reflect a Northwest Coast affinity and heritage with a clear local twist. Whereas a number of the characteristics of these ancient cultures (and their contact-era counterparts) can be readily identified as similar to those of Washington or British Columbia—a reliance on massive salmon runs, good-sized villages of redwood plank houses (cedar on the Northwest Coast), most settlements positioned along the rivers and coasts, extensive woodworking technologies, large dugout canoes, and the use of dentalium shell money —others clearly are northwest Californian. Distinctively Californian elements include a heavy reliance on acorns, large obsidian bifaces as wealth and status indicators, abundant shell beads and ornaments, minimal use of slaves, small-scale political institutions (often lineage-only or village-only authority within loosely connected tribelets), small-scale household labor organization, and the absence of potlatches.

Some—although certainly not all—of the cultural differences within the greater Northwest culture area may be linked to well-documented variations from south to the far north coast (Alaska) in the seasonality of Pacific salmon runs at varying latitudes. Years ago, Schalk (1977) correctly asserted that (until modern overfishing devastated these populations) various spawning salmonid fish species were available nearly year round south of 45 degrees north latitude (including all of California), although Tushingham (2009:27) makes it clear that there were distinct spring and fall "pulses" in the salmon runs (chinook, coho, chum, steelhead) and among the estuary-based cutthroat along the Smith River. But these pulses were not brief; they overlapped across species and lasted for many months, and the Smith, Klamath, and Trinity rivers witnessed major fall *and* spring runs of king (chinook) salmon, allowing small labor units to fairly steadily harvest the catches with efficiency. Within the core Northwest Coast culture area to the north, the fish runs were much more abbreviated—mostly during late summer into fall —and required different labor organization and storage strategies (see Matson and Coupland 1995). From late fall to early spring, runs were generally absent. In the far north (>60 degrees north latitude; Kenai Peninsula of Alaska), fish runs of three weeks or fewer, solely in midsummer, characterized most river systems and again had some impacts on settlement, subsistence, and economic organization. But patterns of resource ownership, the ways people reckon kinship, technological resources, and other variables are of course also crucial in accounting for cultural differences.

Today, many of the ethnographically recorded attributes of groups such as the Yurok and Tolowa are being used by archaeologists to generate specific expectations for the archaeological record, particularly those that are likely to be visible under average or above-average preservation conditions. First, in deposits dating after 2000 B.P., archaeologists are locating sites that reflect the region's dominant settlement patterns, one reflecting a coastal adaptation and the other with a strong riverine economic focus. Recorded observations about the elevation and other determinants of community placement above the major rivers aid in finding interior Yurok and Tolowa sites, for instance (see Tushingham 2005). Second, seasonal encampments (late summer/early fall) may be identified at places that were once near good fish weir locations and productive acorn groves. Third, archaeologists are documenting multi-house communities with square or rectangular plank house footprints (with or without subterranean floors) and sweat houses. Later sites may reveal dentalia, obsidian tools and ceremonial bifaces, harpoons, projectile points, net spacers, shell and mammal remains, and woodworking tools. Contact-era sites occasionally yield preserved redwood plank floors. Clearly, however, systematic archaeological exploration of this important region is still modest in scale compared to many areas of California, and much more field research is warranted.

4

San Francisco Bay: California's Mound Builders

The most postcard-perfect panorama of the San Francisco Bay utterly fails to capture the culture area as it has come to be defined by archaeologists. The "bay area" we speak about reaches well beyond the immediate bay waters and its associated shores, extending to Bodega Bay in the north, Monterey Bay to the south, and eastward to the marshes of the Sacramento River (Figure 4.1). While the actual area covered by this broad cultural region is not especially large by California's standards, this territory carries with it immense environmental diversity, including bay/estuary, salt marsh, coastal sands, tidal zones, grassland, oak woodland, lacustrine shores, and riparian forest. As a consequence of this variation the cultural region shows tremendous technological and economic diversity in all time frames. Each of these adaptations has come to be graced with its own specific cultural, chronological, and geographic designations by local archaeologists. For this reason, even specialists characterize the cultural sequence scheme of the greater bay area as an intricate "nightmare of detail" (Milliken et al. 2007:105).

Still, there are good ethnohistoric and linguistic reasons to retain this inclusive definition of the San Francisco Bay cultural region. At contact as many as eight cultural groups or subgroups laid claim to portions of the area that directly abut the bay shores (Figure 4.1). Several of these ethnographic groups maintained territorial claims well inland during the colonial era, and it makes no anthropological sense to truncate these closely related tribelets at arbitrary distances from the bay. These peoples include several groups subsumed under the antiquated name "Costanoan" (now Ohlone), including Chochenyo in the east bay, Ramaytush in the west bay, Karkin in the northeastern bay, and Tamyen and Awaswas in the southern bay. Coast Miwok

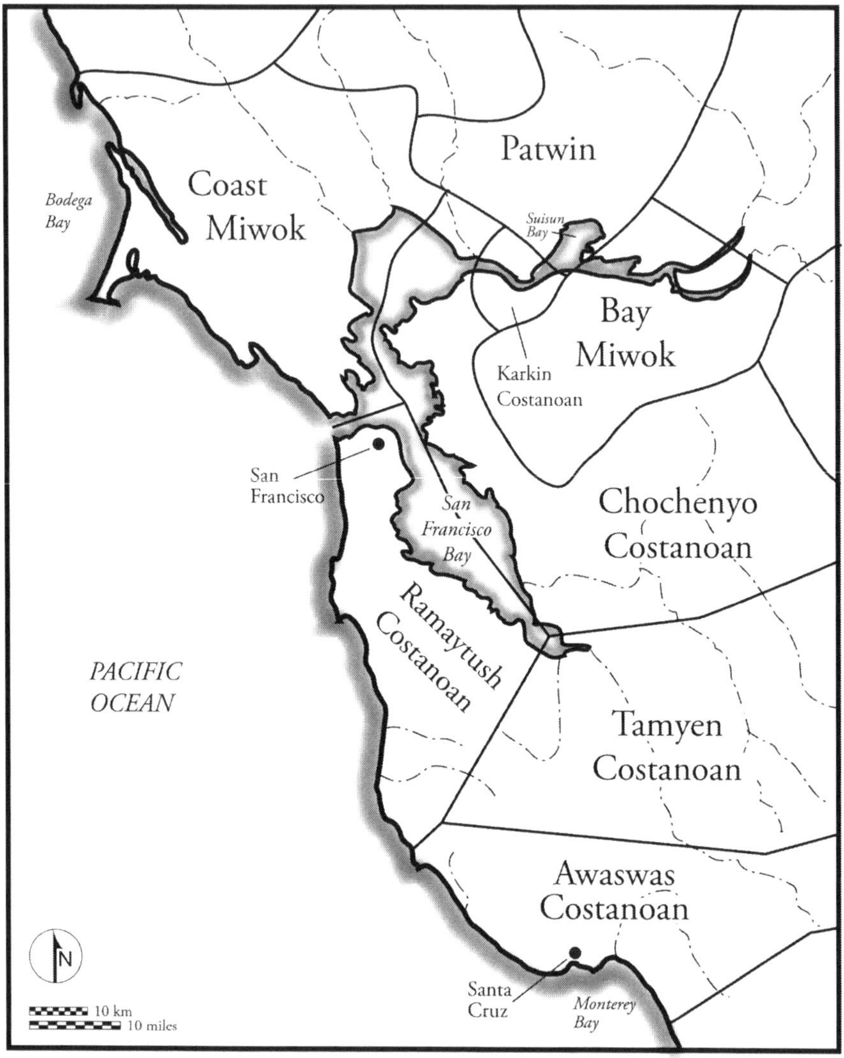

Figure 4.1. San Francisco Bay area ethnographic groups. Map by Clarus J. Backes, Jr.

ranged over the northern bay, and Bay Miwok and Patwin territories abutted the Suisun Bay/Sacramento River juncture. Furthermore, these diverse linguistic groups plied rather similar lifestyles that revolved around semipermanent villages and seasonal exploitation of a variety of resources. No matter the language spoken, the economies of the area depended first and foremost on the acorn. When the San Francisco Bay cultural region was first drawn, there was no reason to suspect that social, economic, and political homogeneity did not extend well into the past.

This assumption held sway despite the huge, abandoned shell mounds that ring the bay, particularly its eastern shore. These mounds are unique in California and appear to elude ethnographic memory, yet were viewed as simple (if extraordinarily large) kitchen middens. The mounds seemed out of keeping with the native adaptation noted in the historic and ethnographic records only in terms of scale. After a century of dedicated archaeological examination of these mounds, however, we have come to believe that the mounds reflect a social, economic, and political phenomenon that is without analogue in the greater bay area and may indeed be unique in all of North America (Arnold et al. 2004:35; Luby et al. 2006:196). In this chapter we distill the prehistoric cultural sequence of the San Francisco Bay to its barest essence in order to focus on the unusual and fascinating social developments that flowered at and around these mounds at the midpoint of the known prehistoric sequence, approximately 2450–950 B.P.

Archaeological Research in the San Francisco Bay Area

The earliest systematic archaeological work in the region—and some of the most important and formative methodological research in the history of America archaeology—focused on the conspicuous shell mounds along the flat tidal shores of the San Francisco Bay. Largely through the efforts of Nels Nelson, at least 425 mounded sites were recorded during the first decade of the twentieth century (Nelson 1909). Of great interest to early archaeologists were the impressive and extensive stratigraphic profiles of these mounded sites, some ranging to nearly 10 m above the ground surface and as many as 6 m *below* the modern surface (Luby et al. 2006:194). It is no surprise that stratigraphic study of the mounds proved to be the focus of all early investigations and may well have inspired Nelson's subsequent pioneering efforts to control for stratigraphic superposition of artifacts (Kowta 2000).

Throughout the twentieth century these stratigraphic profiles and their changing artifact inventories provided the backbone of all subsequent reconstruction of bay area prehistory. Reports on mounds such as Emeryville (Schenck 1926; Uhle 1907), West Berkeley (Wallace and Lathrap 1975), Ellis Landing (Nelson 1910), Fernandez (Davis 1960), the Stege Mounds (Loud 1924), University Village (Gerow 1968), and Patterson (Bickel 1981; Davis and Treganza 1959) still have considerable utility (Figure 4.2). These

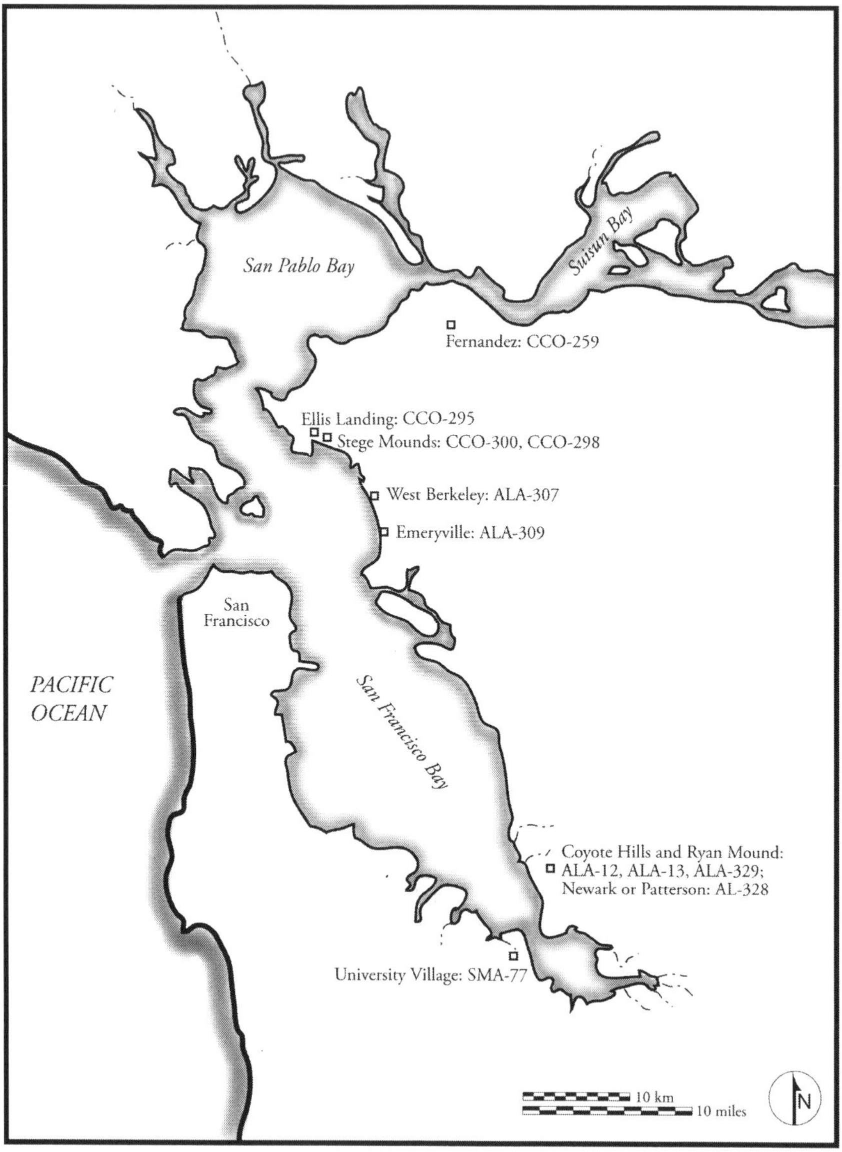

Figure 4.2. Selected shell mound sites, San Francisco Bay area. Map by Clarus J. Backes, Jr.

are required reading for regional scholars, not least because the artifact typologies and stratigraphic seriations derived from these mounds continue to drive the culture historical reconstruction of the region. As if to underscore this point, Broughton (1996) has edited and published Nelson's 1906 manuscript detailing excavations at the Emeryville Mound, not just for its merit as an historical curiosity, but as a valuable addition to the corpus of bay area data. It is fortunate indeed that the quality of these early investigations stood out for their day and thus continue to be worthy of scholarly attention, since the ravages of twentieth-century development severely impacted the bay-shore mounds, and *none* of the larger mounds have intact deposits remaining today.

From the earliest investigations of the bay mounds, archaeologists noticed several enigmatic phenomena. Perhaps foremost among these were apparently intact features in the matrices of what were otherwise thought of as thick layers of discarded shell and bone consistent with classic kitchen middens. Most notable among these features were human burials, both singly and in groups, and intact house floors, household hearths, and large, presumed ceremonial fire pits and ash lenses. Occasionally, archaeologists found the remains of purposefully interred raptors and condors and caches of artifacts including large points and charmstones. These intact features seemed entirely out of keeping with the expectations for a "trash midden." Nevertheless, by and large, the mounds consisted of what appeared to be unconsolidated domestic waste, especially animal bone and, in most cases, stupendous quantities of shell, particularly of bay-dwelling shellfish including bay mussel (*Mytilus edulis*), bent-nosed clam (*Macoma nasuta*), and oyster (*Ostrea lurida*). Archaeologists were also perplexed by the remarkably low densities of artifacts in the mounds of domestic debris and by lenses of sterile soil that occasionally alternated with the more greasy midden soils of the largest mounds (Figure 4.3).

Each of these phenomena was explained for decades in keeping with the tenacious belief that the bay mounds were in fact kitchen middens. Scholars reasoned that the midden soils provided easy digging for interment of the dead above high-tide lines, and house floors and other features were simply later manifestations of site reoccupation. Low artifact densities reflected elementary toolkits geared toward a rich resource base that posed few challenges to either collection or preparation. Sterile soils were deposited by periodic flooding or represent occupational hiatuses.

During the 1990s, these enigmatic intact features were confronted from a wholly differing perspective (e.g., Lightfoot 1997). They came to be viewed not as inconvenient elements that interfered with our understanding of the mounds but as fundamentally important building blocks within a complex

Figure 4.3. Emeryville Shellmound, San Francisco Bay. A view of the open trench on the western side in 1902. The full height of this massive mound exceeded 12 m. Photo from Uhle (1907:Plate 5).

mix of ceremonial, domestic, and residential space. This new perspective represented an interpretive shift of seismic proportions. It suggested that the intact features are just what they appear to be, at stratigraphic levels commensurate with the timing of their construction rather than later intrusions. Sterile soils were purposefully carried to mound locations for the express purpose of *building* mounded space, and low artifact densities resulted from dilution of the mound artifact component by the addition of sterile soil and debris. "Full service" village activities commingled with the deposition of midden debris, and purposefully so (Luby et al. 2006:196). Below we explore the great bay area mounds and the impact of these new interpretations in greater depth within the context of the full regional sequence.

Early Holocene (10,000–7000 B.P.) and Middle Holocene (7000–4000 B.P.)

Very little is known about human populations in the immediate bay area prior to 4000 B.P. Several putatively ancient finds have tantalized archaeologists over the years, notably the BART skeleton (Bickel 1978). The BART male was recovered during subterranean construction of the eponymous Bay Area Rapid Transit tube at a depth of 22 m below present ground surface (and 14 m below the estimated surface at the beginning of the Gold Rush). Depth of the find created quite a stir, but a subsequent radiocarbon assay revealed the bones to be roughly 5,000 years old. Other inhumations that created initial excitement, such as the Sunnyvale skeleton and the Stanford I and Stanford II skeletons, met similar fates upon closer examination (Bickel 1978). To date, the BART male is the earliest human burial encountered in the region.

Virtually every other major estuarine environment in California has yielded significant evidence for human habitation and exploitation well in excess of the 4000 B.P. terminal Middle Holocene (Jones 1992:4). But the paucity of Early and Middle Holocene data in the San Francisco Bay area is almost certainly tied to inundation caused by rising sea level and to steady sedimentation that conceals older materials (Rosenthal and Meyer 2004). Early Holocene sea-level rise was quite rapid, averaging perhaps 2 cm/year from approximately 9500 to 8000 B.P. (Atwater et al. 1979). Owing to the gently sloping terrain of what is now the bay floor, even a centimeter or two in sea-level rise resulted in localized shore advance that exceeded 30 m/year (Atwater et al. 1977:11). By the Middle Holocene sea-level rise had slowed considerably, but the flat terrain nevertheless permitted steady inundation of large tracts of land. Dating to the terminus of the Middle Holocene, the earliest unambiguous near-bay archaeological materials appear in the form of the basal strata of large, mostly Late Holocene shell mounds. These basal strata are in many cases up to 6 m below current sea level (Broughton 1999:32; Lightfoot 1997:138).

Some clues to Middle Holocene adaptations are provided by a handful of sites near—but never precisely *on*—the bay shore (Lightfoot 1997:138).

Sites dated to as early as 5500 B.P. evince a mammalian fauna that is exclusively terrestrial. Small amounts of bones from migratory water birds, a few mollusk shells, and a few fish bones suggest limited exploitation of the estuarine environment. Small numbers of milling stones suggest that these were temporary, multipurpose encampments that facilitated the collection and transport of resources to more permanent settlements inland. It is possible that vast tracts surrounding the bay shore were treated as a marginal environment, with impassable mud flats and tidal marshlands impeding systematic exploitation.

Fully terrestrial late-Middle Holocene sites within the greater San Francisco Bay cultural region suggest an adaptation in keeping with much of California's Middle Holocene Millingstone adaptation. This phase is characterized by manos and metates as the primary grinding equipment and large stemmed points suggesting a focus on large terrestrial mammal species (Fitzgerald 1993:100; Fitzgerald and Jones 1999). As early as 4500 B.P., milling equipment began to take the form of crude cobble-type mortars and pestles, and scholars infer increased dependence on the acorn as a dietary staple by the Middle/Late Holocene transition. Toward the close of the Middle Holocene, the region—in particular the east bay—began to take on a character entirely its own.

Late Holocene (4000 B.P. to Historic Contact)

LOWER BERKELEY PATTERN (4000–2500 B.P.). Occupation and expansion of what were to become the largest mound sites in the immediate bay-shore area began at about the close of the Middle Holocene, a time frame synonymously referred to as the Middle Archaic or Early period for the greater bay area, and the Lower Berkeley Pattern along the bay shore (Milliken et al. 2007:104). The bay-shore manifestation of the era is typified by flexed inhumations at the basal levels of what were to become the largest mounds along the shore (Luby 2004:22). Although many of these burials are accompanied by grave goods, these usually consist of only a few ornamental artifacts, possibly worn at the time of interment rather than "offerings" *per se*. A dusting of red ocher appears to be the primary mode through which certain burials were distinguished. Artifact assemblages include crude mortars and pestles—to the near exclusion of manos and metates—and perforated charmstones, grooved stone net weights, large stemmed projectile points, rectangular beads and pendants of a variety of shell types (mussel, abalone, clam), and an assortment of bone tools. Mammal hunting shows a clear terrestrial focus, and occupation of the mound sites was probably seasonal (Arnold et al. 2004:33).

Sea-level rise had slowed by this time, making residential construction right on the shore more practical. But the bay waters did not completely cease to creep vertically, hence the submerged basal strata of numerous mounds (Broughton 1999:32; Lightfoot 1997:138; Nelson 1909:329–330). Notable among these partially submerged mounds are the Emeryville, West Berkeley, and Ellis Landing mounds, the basal levels of which have been dated to the initial Late Holocene (Bickel 1978:10; Broughton 1999:32). Near-shore residence was ideally suited to exploitation of estuarine localities, particularly for water birds, fish, and shellfish, which suggests the use of tule rafts. Foot traffic may have been difficult over surrounding salt marshes and mudflats (Lightfoot 1997:139). In any case, the convenience of immediate access to bay resources apparently outweighed the threat of slowly encroaching high tide lines.

But encroach these waters did, imperceptibly at the annual level perhaps but certainly noticeable from one generation to the next. Residents of these dozens of early mound sites—including the Emeryville, West Berkeley, and Ellis Landing mounds—did not simply relocate to higher ground in order to stay above the high-tide line, a pattern typical of prehistoric shoreline adaptations elsewhere in the world (see Lightfoot et al. 1987). Instead, the inhabitants chose to *construct* higher and higher ground. Large amounts of rock, sand, and clay were trundled to mound sites—undoubtedly in burden baskets—to augment the natural accrual of domestic debris (Nelson 1909:335). In the process of slowly elevating the mounds, ceremonial spaces originally at or near the surface, including human burials, ritual interments of raptors and other large birds, and caches of artifacts, were slowly buried deeper and deeper beneath newly constructed living surfaces (Figure 4.4).

Earth moving would not seem to be the least-cost solution to slowly encroaching tidal waters. The region's scholars offer a plausible explanation: where once archaeologists saw these mounds as vast accumulations of generations of domestic refuse, we now see purposeful mound building for the singular purpose of maintaining residential and ceremonial activities directly atop ancestral sacred spaces, forging an unambiguous bond between the living and the dead (Lightfoot 1997:139; Lightfoot and Luby 2002; Luby 2004; Luby and Gruber 1999). They suggest that corporate group member-

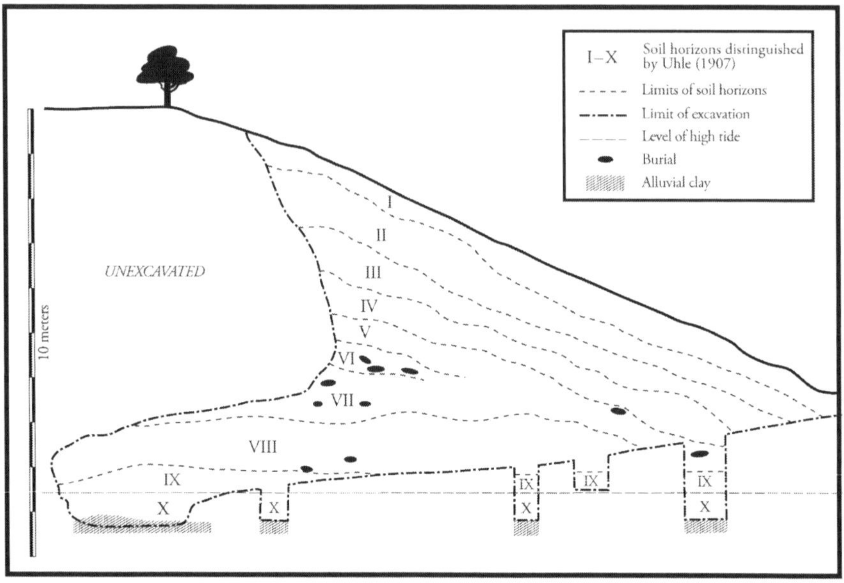

Figure 4.4. Emeryville Shellmound profile. Maximum mound height from upper slope to the alluvial clay was about 9.2 m (no scale in original). Full height was estimated at 12.2 m before the mound surface was graded for construction of a pavilion (Schenck 1926:161). The solid black features are burials. Illustration by Clarus J. Backes, Jr. Adapted from Uhle (1907:Plate 4, Figure 2).

ship, and the use rights such membership implied, was proclaimed by the presence of direct ancestors immediately under house and hearth. The corporate nature of the hierarchical structure is hinted at by large, hard-packed clay surfaces with multiple post molds suggestive of communal ceremonial houses (Lightfoot 1997:136–137; Wallace and Lathrap 1975:44). Moreover, the largest mounds provided elevated residential locations that were surely visible to each other over the flat bay shore, particularly at night when multiple household fires burned or ceremonial fires roared. This may have reiterated "territorial rights to nearby land and estuarine resources by claiming genealogical relations to their ancestors buried in the mounded villages" (Lightfoot 1997:139). As we shall see, population growth in and around the bay was to place increasing value on claims of use rights and access to bay resources.

UPPER BERKELEY PATTERN (2500–1000 B.P.). As the Late Holocene progressed to the Upper Berkeley Pattern (also Upper Archaic or Middle

Period; Milliken et al. 2007:104) at approximately 2500–1000 B.P., the San Francisco Bay entered its "Golden Age" of shell mound communities (Lightfoot and Luby 2002). Existing mounds grew in size and new mounds were founded as population steadily increased. Mound clusters consisted of four to six mounds, with the oldest sites closest to the bay waters (Luby et al. 2006:196). There appears to have been a site hierarchy based on mound size and on site location with respect to proximity to the bay shore. During the Lower Berkeley, mounds were spaced around the bay shore an average distance of about 3.2 km; by the Upper Berkeley, mound (or mound cluster) spacing had decreased to approximately 2.1 km between nearest neighbors (Lightfoot 1997:140).

Although the tops of most of the larger mounds were sheared off during the modern era due to agriculture, construction, or the mining of the midden contents for use as phosphate-rich garden compost, the large Ellis Landing mound (Figure 4.2) was left largely intact until well into the twentieth century. There, Nelson (1910) recorded numerous house depressions at the very top of the mound. There is no reason to believe that Ellis Landing was unique in this regard among the bay's large mounds. Villages constructed atop shell mounds have small-scale counterparts elsewhere in California on the Santa Barbara Channel Islands (e.g., the Prisoners Harbor site and about 20 other contact-era Chumash villages situated on low shell mounds on the islands; Arnold 2001), but in terms of function and scale the bay mounds appear to represent a very rare phenomenon in North America (Luby et al. 2006:196). William Marquardt (2004), Ken Sassaman and David Anderson (2004), and colleagues discuss shellmound sites in Florida and the greater Southeast, some from quite early periods, but these were generally quite different from the bay mounds in function, character, and size.

Faunal profiles suggest that mound sites were occupied year-round during the Upper Berkeley. For the first time, marine resources including sea mammals, waterfowl, and fish appeared in significant quantities. Beads and other ornamental goods underwent rapid and dramatic stylistic change for the first time, and new forms of ornamental shell and bone objects appeared (Milliken et al. 2007:115). Grooved netsinkers disappeared from most site assemblages while barbless fish spears appeared, suggesting a change in fishing technology, target species, or sizes of preferred species. Perhaps most significantly, burial patterns—never terribly elaborate—became still less so, leading Luby (2004) to suggest a trend away from publicly expressed social inequality and toward corporate egalitarianism. One might rephrase this as status measured at the village level, reckoned through village membership and verified by direct descent from bay-shore pioneers buried immediately underfoot.

As the Late Holocene progressed through the Upper Berkeley Golden Age, we find that priority of place and access to the bay was to become of immense importance, as population continued to rise despite the dwindling supply of natural resources. Broughton (1994a, 1997, 1999, 2001) has observed declines in the numbers of terrestrial mammals—the presumed preferred species—and increased use of bay-marine resources, including sea mammals, fish, and water birds. From this he has inferred overexploitation of terrestrial mammals and increased reliance on higher-cost marine resources. Moreover, he observes across-the-board declines in body sizes for all vertebrate species, both terrestrial and marine, and suggests that this is a clear sign of overpredation in the immediate bay area (Broughton 1999:55–57, 65–66, 69; Broughton et al. 2007; see also Hildebrandt and Jones 1992:383; Zogg 1998). Although Broughton's studies draw primarily from a single mound (Emeryville), a survey of 11 bay area sites tends to confirm the conclusion that overpredation significantly impacted the bay area resource base (Simons 1992:88). Nevertheless, we must cautiously add that, considering the numbers of mounds that once dotted the bay shore, postulated adverse human impacts on the environment are drawn from a quite small sample of sites. Many of the sites that contributed to the sample—*particularly* Emeryville—were excavated using decades-old collection protocols (e.g., one-quarter inch screens where screens were used at all).

The Upper Berkeley also saw a peak in regional violence. Burial data have revealed evidence for "nightstick" fractures to forearms as well as other healed fractures, apparent trophy-taking (heads, hands), puncture wounds and embedded points, and evidence for scalping (Grady et al. 2001; Hylkema 2002:260; Keeley 1996:91; Lambert 2002:216; Milliken et al. 2007:113–114; Wiberg 1988:22). There are firm indications that overpopulation rendered dwindling resource bases more and more worth fighting over. There is also evidence for a spread of Central Valley cultural traits into the east bay, expressed in certain bead types and in the practice of extended burial; this was the so-called Meganos intrusion (Bennyhoff 1994a; Wiberg 1988). A short-lived phenomenon, the disruption was confined to the Upper Berkeley era, after which Meganos traits appear to have returned to exclusively Central Valley locales (Bennyhoff 1994a:87). The timing of the Meganos intrusion corresponds with this increase in interpersonal violence throughout the bay area and is difficult to dismiss. The combination of resource stress, immigration, and the threat of interpersonal violence may have further encouraged mound building as ostentatious shows of power and proclamations of legitimate claims to bay area lands. Increasing mound size during the Upper Berkeley can no longer be attributed solely to the threat of rising tidal waters.

AUGUSTINE PATTERN (1000 B.P.–HISTORIC CONTACT). The Augustine Pattern in the greater bay area is alternatively known as the Late, Emeryville A, or Emergent period (Milliken et al. 2007:104). Founding of new sites on or near the bay shore declined dramatically, while inland portions of the greater bay area saw the establishment of a profusion of sites (Jones 1992:13). The Emergent designation derives from the inland Augustine tendency toward increased village sedentism, greater dependence on the acorn as a dietary staple, facilities for mass storage of acorns, and the development of finely wrought ornaments of shell and stone that were often interred in graves (Fredrickson 1973; Milliken et al. 2007:116–117). Augustine burials are distinguished from Upper Berkeley graves by occasional whole or partial cremation (Fredrickson 1994). Mortuary wealth items appear disproportionately in certain single graves, suggestive of individual status ascription (Hylkema 2002:261–262). Among these presumed wealth items are large obsidian and chert knives, elaborately flanged steatite pipes, unperforated charmstones, immense quantities of beads, and very large and finely sculpted stone mortars (Bellifemine 1997; Hylkema 2002:258; Milliken et al. 2007:110). These large mortars frequently have elaborate recurved rims with walls so thin that the functional designation mortar appears inappropriate (Walsh 2007:141, 144). Occasionally, such mortars are inverted over flexed burials or partial cremations. All of these grave goods, and in particular ornamental stone mortars, represent substantial labor efforts, and their removal from circulation among the living suggests "surplus time and specialized labor" available to replenish the supply of wealth items (Milliken et al. 2007:110).

There also appears to be a shift in the nature of exchange networks (Lightfoot and Luby 2002:280). In particular, obsidian source analyses suggest firm dependence on Napa Valley sources, where previously the source locations had a more stochastic character, deriving from all points of the compass including the far reaches of northern California and the eastern Sierra Nevada. While the timing varies slightly from place to place outside the greater bay area, the Augustine Pattern of sedentism, acorn storage, and wealth ascription is recognized (and so-named) as far north as Shasta County (Golla 2007:77) and the greater Northwest Coast region (Hildebrandt 2007:94–95).

The one place where the Augustine Pattern is poorly expressed is directly along the bay shore. The great mounds of the east bay were either abandoned entirely or came to see only sporadic use as burial or ritual grounds during the early Augustine, ca. 1000 to 450 B.P. (Lightfoot and Luby 2002:271–272, 277; Milliken et al. 2007:107). Residence—and certainly year-round residence—directly atop these ceremonial spaces appears to have ceased, and the Golden Age of the mounds along San Francisco Bay was over.

There are several competing but not necessarily mutually exclusive explanations for the abandonment of bay-shore mounds. Environmental degradation, and in particular drought related to the Medieval Climatic Anomaly (MCA), may have altered the availability of drinking water sources at near-bay locations. Indeed, most sites founded during this period *anywhere* near the bay are found at least several kilometers inland, along freshwater streams (Lightfoot and Luby 2002:272). The MCA may have further disrupted sedimentation rates and thus affected salinity levels of the bay waters, which, combined with sea-level rise, may have changed the population dynamics of nearshore resources, especially shellfish (Ingram 1998:108). When we factor in probable overpredation beginning in the Upper Berkeley, particularly of mammal species, we may suggest that the bay lost a good portion of its capacity to support a substantial hunter-gatherer population. Moreover, these populations were faced with elevated levels of violence, probably exacerbated by increasing competition over dwindling resources.

A second scenario for bay-shore abandonment follows directly from the first: declining carrying capacity on and near the bay shore encouraged sweeping change in the nature of the overall subsistence-settlement system. As bay resources declined and inland resources increased in significance, populations located themselves farther inland to accommodate a more dispersed seasonal round (Lightfoot and Luby 2002:279). Indeed, Broughton (1999:54) noted increases in the exploitation of terrestrial mammals at the Emeryville Mound just prior to its abandonment. This does not suggest wholesale abandonment of the bay as a resource collection zone, of course.

Of the mounded villages that remained occupied through the Augustine period, perhaps the best known is the Fernandez Mound (Figure 4.2), a mound featuring copious amounts of shell despite its location about 7 km from the bay shore (Davis 1960:11). Thus, we should not equate abandonment of the mounds with permanent withdrawal from the bay; rather, we should view such shifts as a clear sign of the increased importance of inland resources. Unfortunately, we cannot fully explore the nature of Augustine use of the bay because small, limited-use sites along the bay shore may have very little archaeological visibility due to subsequent sedimentation. But it does appear that large-scale, fulltime use of the bay shore declined dramatically in favor of inland resource patches.

A third scenario suggests that immigrants from the north and east, people fully established in the Augustine cultural pattern, began to arrive, usurp, and defend valuable interior resource patches (Bennyhoff 1994a:83; Lightfoot and Luby 2002:279). With the increased significance of these same interior resources to the mound dwellers, the necessity to strike up residence near critical resources and defend them from newcomers may have overridden their long-standing concerns with defending ancestral places on the bay shore.

The shift in emphasis from shellfish to acorns as a dietary staple may have had the far-reaching effect of creating an economy more and more reliant on a readily storable commodity—Augustine-like acorn exploitation (an idea first proposed by Gould [1964:152]). The acorn economy may have coincided with the advent of a more individual orientation to wealth accumulation, as suggested by Augustine burial lots, in contrast to the ancestor-centered corporate status identities and less pronounced wealth and status markers in burials that coincided with tenacious residence atop Upper Berkeley mounds.

The Past and Future of the Mound Cultures

The San Francisco Bay area continues to be a challenging place to conduct archaeological research. It may involve wading through troves of published reports, unpublished notes, and gray literature manuscripts; rooting through extensive materials warehoused in various museums and storage facilities; gleaning the tailings of bulldozers past; or scurrying ahead of bulldozers present. Fortunately, the region currently enjoys an elegant melding of academic interests and CRM enterprises (see Luby et al. 2006). One result of that has been an intensity of study that may be unmatched anywhere in California, and this has led to a shift in the way that archaeologists view the enigmatic mounds that dot the shores of the San Francisco, San Pablo, and Suisun bays.

Until 1997, these mounds were seen as piles of domestic refuse, rich in culture-historical data and testimony to large populations exploiting a fertile natural landscape. Certain mysteries vexed archaeologists, in particular the presence of intact features within the mound matrices, including residential and ceremonial spaces and burial plots. By turning this puzzle upside down, the region's archaeologists have come to a startling conclusion: the features are not incidental or later components of the mounds, they are the reason the mounds exist at all. By continuous accretion of residential space above ancestral features and above the ancestors themselves, the mounds conveyed deep-rooted ancestral rights to the bay. They served as prominent, unambiguous claims on each of the social, economic, and political landscapes. Mound residence provided proof of priority of place, and it is quite possible that as a measure of the antiquity of a group's lineage, the size and/or height of the mound mattered.

The shift from Upper Berkeley bay mound occupation to the inland, terrestrially oriented Augustine Pattern appears to represent an utter collapse of the great mound system. If mound residence once provided status and insured access to the bounty of the bay, it came to be an anchor lodged too near a set of depleted resources and too far from plentiful alternatives, in particular a prime, storable resource, the acorn. When the bay waters provided primary subsistence, favorable locations along the bay shore allowed continuity of village location, and mound sites grew and grew. As the bay resources dwindled, and inland locations increased in their significance, residential locations took on a more dispersed character: there were innumerable large groves of oaks toward the interior, but only one bay.

The mounds appear to have retained some symbolic importance during the Augustine, however, including their continued use as burial grounds. By inference, lineage association must have maintained some level of significance. Nevertheless, the Augustine saw a complete shift in residential locations and settlement patterns, economic practices, and basic political structure and the expression of wealth. This Augustine Pattern was clearly successful, if only measured by its widespread appearance in the archaeological record (Hildebrandt 2007). The Augustine Pattern is essentially what the Spaniards first saw when they entered the bay area to stay, after A.D. 1769 (Hylkema 2002:257–258; Milliken 1995).

Several unresolved questions await the attention of archaeologists. Perhaps first among these is the need to further refine our understanding of the nature of hierarchy and social inequality at the mound sites. Burial data provide our firmest suggestion that Upper Berkeley mound dwellers expressed relatively non-hierarchical ideals in treatment of the dead (Luby 1992, 2004). From this we derive our strongest suggestion of corporate status as the driving political structure at the mounds. This logical conclusion, however, does not carry the full force of the scientific method, and we do not yet know whether the trappings of wealth or status were absorbed by the living, destroyed during some stage of the burial process, or simply go unrecognized in the archaeological present.

A second question concerns evidence for feasting at the mounds, which exists in the form of ash lenses and large hearth features suggestive of ceremonial fires. We are unsure whether these were a part of burial ceremonies for the newly departed or focused on honoring those ancestors long dead (Luby and Gruber 1999:101). Furthermore we cannot as yet determine whether these ceremonies were intra- or inter-mound affairs. It will be interesting to explore whether feasting at the mounds—as a part of the burial process or not—reflects competitions among aggrandizing mound dwellers or celebrations of alliances, truces, or shared dates on the ceremonial calendar.

Another interesting question for the Golden Age directly confronts relationships among the mound populations. Were these residents at various mounds confederated or allied through blood or marriage? Were they in uneasy coalitions, with peace kept by an arms race that took the form of population aggregation or mound clustering or building higher mounds? Or were the mound dwellers openly antagonistic toward one another? Violence appears to have been common, but we are unsure whether hostilities were expressed mound-to-mound or between mound dwellers and inland populations viewed as interlopers trying to share in the bounty of the bay.

We are confident that these questions will find whole or partial solutions. A sense of collegiality between academics and CRM practitioners characterizes the bay area, and both sectors of the archaeological community enjoy largely amicable relations with local Native American populations. It appears that reanalysis of extant collections—including perhaps DNA analysis of selected burial populations—may further our understanding of inter-mound relationships as well as our understanding of the links between the mounds and the inland populations of the greater bay area.

5

The Classic California Lifeway: Acorn-Based Economies of Central California

Central California is a vast, low-elevation territory in the heart of the state and includes the entire Central Valley and the lower foothills of the Sierra Nevada (Lightfoot and Parrish 2009:185). The Sacramento and San Joaquin rivers drain the north and south ends of the great valley, respectively, and the Sacramento-San Joaquin Delta constitutes an expansive marshy zone in the middle that connects the valley with the greater San Francisco Bay to the west. Major cultural groups in the region were the Wintu, Yana, Nomlaki, Maidu, Patwin, Pomo, Wappo, Konkow, and Nisenan in the north and the Miwok and Yokuts in the south (Figure 5.1). Several Pomo subgroups straddled the physiographic boundary between the western Central Valley and the North Coast Range province, and we include the eastern Pomo groups and their southeastern Coast Range lands in this chapter because of certain shared ecological features and adaptations. The Berkeley Pattern is the name given to the culturally similar adaptation found in much of the northern valley, Delta, and Pomo territory after about 2500 B.P., and the Augustine Pattern is the name for the shared cultural features in the same areas after 1400–1500 B.P.

In many ways these adaptations represent the prototypical California lifeway. Alfred Kroeber (1925) introduced the concept of the "tribelet" as the quintessential form of political organization in California. The term "tribelet" reflects in part the relative size of the autonomous political unit and carries no intent to depreciate the significance of native social or political organization. Each California tribelet or "village community" typically consisted of 100 to 200 people (rarely, as many as 500) under the authority of one or several village-level leaders and independent with respect to neighboring sociopolitical units. According to Kroeber, numerous tribelets may have

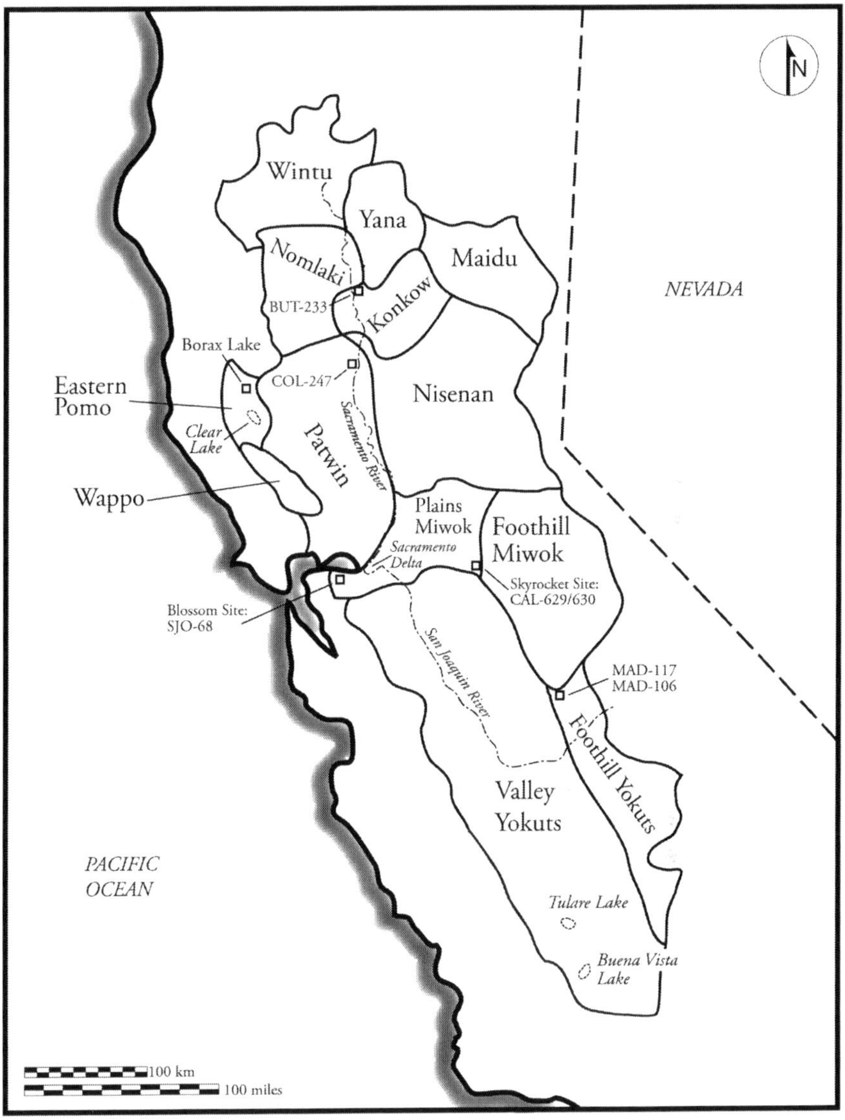

Figure 5.1. Central Valley ethnographic groups and selected archaeological localities. Map by Clarus J. Backes, Jr.

shared a single linguistic idiom. Only among the Yokuts of the San Joaquin Valley and adjacent foothills were true "tribes" suggested by a large population sharing both linguistic and sociopolitical boundaries (Kroeber 1925:474). Formal chiefdoms were reportedly absent in the central region

Figure 5.2. Village on the Sacramento River, Konkow territory; note the many barrel-shaped acorn granaries. Illustration by Henry B. Brown, ca. 1853, "Chino village near Monroeville, California." Used with the permission of the John Carter Brown Library at Brown University.

although, as we shall see, wealth and status played an important role at various times and places during the region's culture history.

People living in central California found a plentiful subsistence base in acorns and small seeds, complemented by an array of protein sources such as deer, rabbit, elk, migratory waterfowl, resident freshwater fish, and anadromous fish on seasonal spawning "runs" from the ocean to the headwaters of freshwater streams. Villages and hamlets consisted of semi-subterranean, wood-framed, earth-covered roundhouses (sometimes roofed with wood only), occupied most of the year (Figure 5.2), and people forayed logistically from these residential bases for staples such as acorns during the autumn at oak-rich localities at the fringes of the valley and in the foothills. Spawning steelhead and salmon kept people close to the rivers for short spans during spring or summer months. The expansive marshes of the Sacramento Delta, southern valley lakes and marshes, and other well-watered areas attracted great flocks of migratory birds that were exploited in key seasons. Occasionally, severe droughts impacted many of these resources.

Figure 5.3. Typical California stone mortar and pestle. Scale = 30 cm. Photo by Renee Fraser.

For decades, it was proposed that the region's smaller and more mobile Early and Middle Holocene populations lived by collecting a suite of resources much like this, except that they relied largely on small seeds and did not yet exploit acorns. This assumption emerged from the Early to Middle Holocene material record across much of California that is dominated by manos (hand stones) and large metates and milling slabs of coarse rock such as sandstone and granite. These shallow grinding tools, found at thousands of early sites, are superior processors of hard seeds but are not overly effective in pounding acorns. Acorn processing can be conducted more efficiently with a deeper, more bowl-shaped vessel such as the mortar and an elongated pounding tool such as the pestle (Figure 5.3). For years, dating of grinding tool complexes indicated that the first mortar and pestle technology was developed at a relatively late juncture, perhaps three to four millennia ago in many parts of California (e.g., Basgall 1987). It was thought, therefore, that a long-lasting seed-based plant diet was supplanted by an emphasis on laborious-to-process acorns only after the first mortar and pestle technology was developed.

Hildebrandt (2007), Wohlgemuth (2004), and White et al. (2002) now suggest that acorns may have become important in ancient Native Californian economies much earlier. Assemblages containing pestles and acorn macrofossils from the Clear Lake region place them before 7000 B.P. (Hildebrandt 2007:90), and Early Holocene paleobotanical assemblages with abundant acorn remnants from the Sierra foothills and near the Delta indicate that acorns were at least a moderately significant resource for millennia before the Late Holocene. In some parts of the region, mortar and pestle technology, albeit in low frequencies, apparently coexisted with metates and manos. In places such as Clear Lake, people may have partially leached acorn crops by treating them with clays from the natural wetlands in ways that allowed ordinary milling stones to be used for the production of edible acorn products. The investigations at Clear Lake by White and colleagues (2002) involved extensive geoarchaeological exploration to sample well-preserved seed and bone assemblages as old as 9,000 years. They show that intensive use of acorns began at least 7,000 years ago, together with consumption of fish, seeds, and other resources, and was associated with nearly exclusive use of manos and metates until 2000 B.P. Rosenthal et al. (2007:155) summarize the evidence from at least eight Central Valley botanical assemblages dating to roughly 6000 B.P.; these all yielded acorn remnants, some in association with mortars and pestles, some not. Hildebrandt (2007:96) suggests that we may be able to link costly-to-make mortars and pestles with acorn use by largely sedentary populations and expediently made manos and metates with acorn processing by contemporaneous but more mobile populations. Clearly, whether or not all of these interpretations are correct, there is increasingly compelling evidence that many central California groups used acorns from quite an early date.

The overall richness of the food base was augmented by the development of secure storage facilities such as aboveground granaries for acorns, which allowed people to hold them for one to two years. Long-term storage precipitated the emergence of delayed-return economies and semi-sedentism among many of the central groups, perhaps as early as the terminus of the Millingstone (or Middle Archaic) period (ca. 8000–4000 B.P.). Attempts to reconstruct the gender dynamics of the region's early periods—all seemingly dominated by plant-processing activities—stimulated provocative discussions during the mid-1990s. Because Millingstone sites exhibit abundant milling equipment and the great majority of sites yield very few hunting tools (e.g., projectile points), interpreting milling tools as women's tools would make most sites of this era solely "women's sites." McGuire and Hildebrandt (1994) stress the unlikelihood of this scenario and suggest that women and men collected and processed staples such as seeds, game, and shellfish during the Millingstone period in male-female (not female-only) task groups. They contend that heightened aridity precipitated food stresses that required dependable, broad-based subsistence strategies to be practiced by everyone in the group. They point as well to an absence of gender-based differences in Millingstone-era burial goods, which reflects a minimum of gender polarity in the division of labor.

In places such as the Sierra foothills, where acorns were a premium local resource and assumed great importance, subsequent periods witnessed a sharp differentiation of men's and women's subsistence roles. Jackson (1991) argues that women began to invest in making and using bedrock mortars for their acorn processing where suitable bedrock was situated near productive oak groves. Some of the bedrock mortar sites that were developed were very large and permitted substantial communal acorn processing (Figure 5.4). It has been argued that groups experiencing population pressure in many parts of California turned to acorns as a staple during major climatic downturns, since the labor expenditures associated with processing acorn flour were quite high (Basgall 1987). But as we have seen, acorns were actually collected at much earlier dates, leaving archaeologists to further debate the causes and kinds of cultural changes that are embodied in the apparent growth in acorn processing activities around 4,000 years ago.

Early Developments in the Pomo/Sacramento Valley Region

Pomo. The earliest site known in the Pomo territories is Borax Lake, where dozens of Clovis-like fluted obsidian points have been recovered that date to the Pleistocene/Holocene transition (before 10,000 B.P.), based on obsidian hydration readings (Hildebrandt 2007:87). Despite multiple investigations at the site, these tools remain unassociated with fauna or other important artifact types, and there are no early counterparts to this site elsewhere in the northern valley/ southeastern Coast Range area. The next few thousand

Figure 5.4. Large bedrock mortar concentration, Indian Grinding Rock State Historic Park, central California. Photo by Michael J. Moratto.

years are sparsely represented by a few sites with Holocene-era Borax Lake wide-stemmed points, a controversial locus or two, and the sites at Clear Lake with the millingstones and acorn remnants (see above discussion). Erosion has obliterated a span of more than three full millennia at Clear Lake (White et al. 2002).

After ca. 2500 B.P. and lasting about one millennium, the "Berkeley Pattern" is a phase that represents the region's greatest population densities and maximal sedentism. The economy was built on a dietary foundation of salmon and other fish, acorns, and large game. Substantial middens and well-defined house floors yield fishing implements, bone tool industries, mortars and pestles, and significant local production of obsidian bifaces from the Borax Lake source (Hildebrandt 2007:93). Bifaces and shell beads were exchanged widely. Historically, the Pomo were important bead makers, but it is not clear where beads of this era were manufactured. This cultural tradition clearly extended into the southern Sacramento Valley and Delta.

A trend toward greater residential mobility and smaller community size (with semi-sedentism in certain zones) emerged with the Augustine Pattern (post–1400 B.P.). Artifact assemblages include several new artifact types such as Olivella and clam disk beads, magnesite cylinders, "banjo" abalone ornaments, bird bone whistles, flanged steatite pipes, and small "rattlesnake corner-notched" points (Hildebrandt 2007:94). The finished clam disk beads are found at sites throughout the area, and it has been suggested that they were used as a money form in north-central California. Sites dating to the last couple of centuries before contact and situated near the juncture of the Coast Ranges and western Sacramento Valley have yielded clam shell bead-making by-products and bead blanks. These sites are located within nineteenth-century Patwin territory, but, we suggest, possibly were eastern Pomo lands during the late pre-contact era. Ethnographic accounts clearly identify male "money makers" who focused on clam bead making among the Clear Lake Pomo, and although various specialists are noted among the Patwin, clam bead making is not among them (Gifford 1926; Loeb 1926; McKern 1922). So-called functional families of the Patwin held virtual monopolies on the manufacture of salt, arrow points, drums, and headdresses, but we are not aware of archaeological evidence for unusual concentrations of these activities at Sacramento Valley sites. Although many Augustine Pattern groups appear to have had social ranking, this era is presumed by local archaeologists to mark an overall decline in population aggregation and political complexity.

The historic Clear Lake Pomo economy supported other male occupational specialists, including stone-drill makers, shamans and doctors, and net makers. The women were great basket weavers and invested substantial labor in an array of functional baskets as well as fine feather baskets (Kroeber 1925:245), although they would not be considered specialists since virtually all women engaged in the craft. Some basket aficionados herald the Pomo as the world's most skilled basket makers. The archaeological record reveals at least a several thousand-year history of basketry use in the region. Although we would not dispute the acclaim justifiably given to the Pomo for their dazzling basketry, it is fair to say that *all* of the California groups who used baskets and trays extensively for cooking, carrying, processing, storing, and games were superb weavers and were extraordinarily adept at tending and manipulating the native plants they needed to make these important vessels. They practiced pruning, clearing, controlled burning, specific digging techniques, and selective harvesting to maximize yields of usable of willow, redbud, sedges, and more. From the striking burden baskets, cradles, and cooking baskets of the Paiute and Washo to the storage baskets, gambling trays, hats, and water bottles of the dozens of other groups throughout the state, one of the most remarkable pre- and post-contact material traditions of California was its functional yet spectacular basketry (Figure 5.5). Most Californian groups were quite familiar with ceramics, and a few groups in the eastern deserts, near Baja California, and in scattered other areas made simple pottery, but most chose not to.

Sacramento Valley. The core of the Central Valley province used to contain many "mound" sites located on natural levees and other higher ground near the rivers, but virtually all of these sites were destroyed by early farming, canals, and agribusiness projects. Most of the region's later Pleistocene and Early and Middle Holocene land surfaces, particularly those likely to have been loci of human activity, have been buried by rapid sedimentation. Very high rates of alluviation continue to affect the potential to explore the archaeological record in this vast basin, and the problem of lost data has been compounded by a dearth of sustained research over the last 20 years (Rosenthal et al. 2007).

In the northern valley, the earliest periods (Paleoindian and Early Archaic; before 7500 B.P.) remain unrepresented by stratified sites. Only a few isolated artifacts with limited chronological potential have been recovered. During the Middle Archaic, as rising sea levels pushed waters in from San

Figure 5.5. Typical basket of the Yokuts of the San Joaquin Valley, central California. Basket #YO-4F-12. Photo used with the permission of the Santa Barbara Museum of Natural History.

Francisco Bay and created the Delta and its vast wetlands, a few camps yielding toolkits linked with pine nut and acorn processing appeared in the foothills east of the Delta, but not in the Sacramento Valley. So-called Middle Archaic "Valley tradition" sites are the first well-documented occupation of the Sacramento River area, including components at COL–247 and BUT–233 that date to the later phases of the Middle Archaic (roughly after 4500 B.P.). Growing residential stability is indicated by food remains from all seasons (nuts, seeds, elk, deer, pronghorn, rodents, rabbits, fish, waterfowl) and a wide array of artifact types. Small villages were situated along the river, and logistical organization and wide-ranging trade systems brought many goods into the residential bases, including obsidian from several sources east of the Sierra, the North Coast Ranges, and the Cascades. Greg White (2003) has documented that the small populations present in the Sacramento Valley at the time used leaf-shaped, contracting-stem, and corner-notched spear points; various core tools; fishing gear; basketry; shell beads and ornaments; elk-horn tools; and manos at the type site COL–247.

Just to the south, the Windmiller Pattern is an expression of this same tradition in the Delta and the San Joaquin Valley (see below).

With the onset of cooler and wetter Late Holocene climatic conditions, the Berkeley Pattern (starting ca. 2600 B.P.) was marked by more sharply drawn distinctions among neighboring sociopolitical units. Populations three to five times higher than those of the preceding period settled into large villages supported by mass capture and/or processing of seasonally abundant resources such as salmon, rabbits, acorns, and deer (White 2003). Elaboration of bone tools and ornaments, ground stone plummets, shell beads, and mortar-pestle technologies emerged (Rosenthal et al. 2007:156). House floors, flexed burials, hearths, and rock-lined ovens appear at many sites, and contrasting burial postures and artifact styles mark local cultural-political identities.

The Augustine Pattern is well represented in the Sacramento-Delta region after ca. 1400–1000 B.P. A much more comprehensive archaeological record is available for this period, and cultural traditions that appear to be directly ancestral to the groups present at contact emerged in various subregions (Rosenthal et al. 2007). The bow and arrow spread throughout northern California. Larger communities were established near newly constructed fish weirs along the river, and hamlets and smaller villages were located on tributaries. Artifact assemblages are much like those of contemporaneous eastern Pomo sites: bird bone whistles, soapstone pipes, banjo abalone ornaments, Olivella rectangular and lipped beads, clam disk beads, magnesite cylinders, mortars and pestles, several kinds of fishing gear, and small arrow points. In the lower Sacramento Valley, local potters made Cosumnes brownware (Johnson 1990) and fashioned clay balls used in cooking. Obsidian bifaces that had been finished near source areas in preceding periods began to be finished at the sites where they were used throughout the region. Most burials were tightly flexed and bodies interred in burned grave pits, and cremations were the norm for high-status individuals.

Archaeologists have excavated Augustine house floors at a number of sites, primarily outside the heavily sedimented Delta area (Rosenthal et al. 2007:158). Populations grew substantially during this period, and abundant floral and faunal evidence verifies heavy reliance on acorns, pine nuts, large grass seeds, hard seeds, and manzanita, as well as diverse fish, mammal, and bird populations (Broughton 1994b; White 2003; Wohlgemuth 2004). Plant foods and fish became far more important than had been the case previously, and debates are ongoing regarding the best explanation for a clear spike in the acquisition of artiodactyls (deer, elk) during this period relative to small game when optimal foraging and diet-breadth models would suggest the opposite (Rosenthal et al. 2007:162–163). People were more densely packed on the landscape, turning increasingly to mass-food capture techniques (weirs, nets, communal hunts). Skeletal pathologies observed in substantial cemetery populations (mostly excavated years ago) indicate that nutritional stress accelerated during the last millennium across much of central California. Winter villages contained as many as several hundred persons.

Riddell (1993) has analyzed several pre-contact structures in the Maidu territories that he interprets as semi-subterranean earth-covered lodges (compare Konkow village, Figure 5.2). These may have functioned in political and religious activities, possibly as sweathouses or communal ceremonial structures, which were common in the north valley and lower foothill area. The presence of these structures in particular villages suggests to him a system of political-religious central places with satellite villages whose inhabitants attended activities in the "capitals." Riddell also theorizes that the larger Maidu houses were the homes of village leaders.

A major challenge for archaeologists working in northern California, with its myriad and tightly packed cultural groups, is the definition of cultural boundaries in the past and their relationship to historic-era territories of known groups. This is relevant of course for NAGPRA issues as well as more general cultural historical questions. Lightfoot and Martinez (1995) assess group boundary construction and interpretations for the archaeology of northern California, where obsidian sourcing has often played a role. Chemical characterization of obsidian source localities is of some utility in delineating prehistoric boundaries of tribelet organization (typically one to a few villages), according to Fredrickson (1996). He argues that tribelets may be visible in the archaeological record but reminds archaeologists that language does not equal ethnicity, and ethnicity may not be reflected in artifact styles. Another study of artifacts with implications for understanding ethnicity arose from the infamous case of Ishi, the "last of his tribe" of the Yahi band of the Yana. Ishi spent years alone and in hiding after his people were decimated by disease and bounty hunting during the post-Gold Rush years in northern California. He stumbled into the town of Oroville, some 60 miles north of Sacramento, in 1911 when he was near starvation. Ishi was taken to the Museum at San Francisco's Golden Gate

Park and, under the care and oversight of Alfred Kroeber, he provided ethnological and linguistic information and displayed his tool-making abilities to the public for several years, until his death from tuberculosis in 1916 (Heizer and Kroeber 1979; Kroeber 1969). Shackley's (2000) recent analysis of Ishi's projectile points indicates that he adopted a hybrid Wintu-Nomlaki knapping style as he grew up in a disrupted, amalgamated cultural environment during the 1800s. Ishi's biological ancestry may have included Wintu-Nomlaki as well as Yahi, even though he self-identified only as the latter.

The Sacramento Delta, San Joaquin Valley, and Southern Sierra Nevada Foothills

OVERVIEW. The division of California's Great Central valley into northern (Sacramento) and southern (San Joaquin) sectors is traditionally drawn at the Sacramento River Delta, some 40 miles to the south of the state capitol. The Delta shows cultural affinities with both the lower (San Joaquin) and upper (Sacramento) valleys as well as the San Francisco Bay area at various points in its prehistory. However, its earliest well-documented prehistory—the Windmiller, discussed shortly—has much in common with the San Joaquin Valley alone, and so we conflate the regions here (see Bennyhoff 1994a, 1994b; Rosenthal et al. 2007). Furthermore, both the Delta and San Joaquin Valley natives had close cultural ties to people to their immediate east, essentially linguistic relatives in the western Sierra Nevada foothills (Hull 2007:180, Fig. 12.2). Each of these regions—the Delta, Valley, and Foothills—exemplifies in later prehistory the acorn-based economy that is part and parcel of the "California Pattern" (Figure 5.1).

Population estimates made for aboriginal California are debatable (Anderson 2005:34), but in relative terms at least, it has been estimated that the total population for the combined Delta, San Joaquin Valley, and adjacent Sierra foothills exceeded that of any other geographic province in California (Cook 1978:91). Although population densities never approached those of selected regions along the Pacific Coast, by even conservative estimates the Delta-Valley-Foothill region far exceeded mean population densities of hunter-gatherers worldwide (Kelly 1995:222–226). This provides testimony to the rich mosaic of riverine, lacustrine, wetland, and oak woodland resources present and the potential for populations to flourish under the acorn-based economy witnessed at the time of European contact.

In the historic era the Delta was home to Plains Miwok (also, Miwuk), who fished the rivers for salmon, sturgeon, and lampreys with throw nets, dip nets, hook and line, and two-pronged spears (Levy 1978:404). The plains to the immediate east of the Delta held large populations of tule elk and antelope, while forays farther east to the Sierra Nevada foothills yielded deer, plant foods, and especially large quantities of acorns.

The San Joaquin Valley was home to Valley Yokuts (Figure 5.1). The Valley Yokuts are often divided roughly into Northern and Southern Yokuts subgroups (Rosenthal et al. 2007:149), but the salient differences between the two essentially reflect critical differences in the respective local environments. In the north, people fished and exploited the rich riparian wetlands along the sluggish San Joaquin River, while those in the south acquired foods from lacustrine shores and associated marshlands. The Northern Valley Yokuts are not well known ethnographically (Wallace 1978:462), owing to their proximity to missions and gold fields. Those who were not forced to relocate to a mission in the eighteenth century were mercilessly displaced by gold miners and other settlers in the mid-nineteenth century. Southern Yokuts fared better because Spanish missionary efforts in the south were comparatively unenthusiastic, precious metals were scarce, and the forbidding marshy wetlands characteristic of the area discouraged significant Euro-American settlement until quite late in the nineteenth century.

The Sierra foothills east of the Delta were home to the Foothill (or Sierra) Miwok (Levy 1978:400), and the Foothill Yokuts lived east of the San Joaquin Valley (Spier 1978). During the historic era these groups lived along tributaries that emptied Sierra snowmelt into the delta and valley. Although more seasonally variable than the permanent Sacramento and San Joaquin rivers, these tributaries provided foothill groups with aquatic resources. The riparian habitat was rich in plant foods and a prime attractant to terrestrial game, which provided the prime protein source for foothill groups. Oaks, generally sparse in the Valley and Delta regions, appear in abundance over the rolling foothills. Linguistic evidence for the Yokuts Valley and Foothill subgroups suggests a rather late divergence, on the order of 1,000 to 1,500 years ago (Golla 2007:76), so lumping them here in a survey of regional prehistory is not a mere expedience. As we range deeper into prehistory the distinction between Foothill and Valley/Delta cultural regions virtually disappears, and there is some suggestion that one and the same people were exploiting both valley and foothill localities (Chartkoff 1990). In particular, for much of prehistory, "special purpose" sites including bedrock milling stations that targeted acorns and sites showing emphases on hunting activities dominate the archaeological record (Arnold et al. 2004:41–42; Fredrickson 1997:295; Jackson 1991; Rosenthal et al. 2007:152). This suggests that the foothills were used primarily as seasonal destinations for logistically organized Delta and Valley villagers.

CHRONOLOGY. Although the full chronological spectrum is present in the Sacramento Delta-San Joaquin Valley-Sierra Foothill region when considered as a whole, no single subregion shows an unbroken, undisturbed, and unambiguous prehistoric sequence. In the northern San Joaquin and the Delta, natural flooding, massive earthmoving associated with hydraulic mining practices at the close of the Gold Rush, and extensive agribusiness have taken an enormous toll on the archaeological record, obscuring or destroying much of what we must assume to have been a rich and ancient archaeological record. But somewhat perversely, massive agribusiness in the southern reaches of the San Joaquin Valley has proved to be a boon to studies of the terminal Pleistocene in the southern Valley. The modern quest for both arable land and water for irrigation has led to drainage of ancient lakes Tulare and Buena Vista (Figure 5.1), exposing deeply buried and very ancient remains. These same agricultural enterprises, however, have taken a heavy toll on the later archaeological record, as surface soils have been thoroughly churned and displaced. Much of our work on later prehistoric sites is conducted in the "plow zone." Foothill regions have suffered from natural erosion as well as from accelerated rates of erosion due to mining. Today the foothills are primarily used as grazing lands, rather than farms, which exacts a somewhat lesser toll on the later prehistoric record.

Overall, cultural succession in the region is poorly understood in its precise timing, not least because chronologies were developed through relative dating of artifact styles, burial postures, and the like (Rosenthal et al. 2007:150). Many of these typological efforts were made decades ago, and there have been few attempts to evaluate and update these chronological markers through absolute dating. The reader must try to follow as we leapfrog from place to place in search of firm dates in order to piece together the development of acorn-based economies of the Delta-San Joaquin-Foothill regions at the close of the prehistoric era.

Almost all of the evidence from the Pleistocene/Holocene transition in the southern Central Valley derives from the Tulare Lake region in the central San Joaquin Valley (Wallace and Riddell 1991, 1993). The lake (now drained) and its ancient shoreline has yielded more reports of fluted projectile points than the remainder of the state *combined* (Dillon 2002; Hopkins 1991). However, many of these purported "fluted" points have been questioned on several grounds (Rondeau 2009). First, many appear to be more aptly described as "basally thinned," and not fluted per se (Rondeau et al. 2007). Second, it must be noted that many points are better termed "Clovis-like," leaving some room for ambiguity regarding their utility as clear time markers for the Clovis Pleistocene. Since many reports of fluted specimens are essentially anecdotal accounts from private collectors, the failure of some specimens to withstand professional scrutiny casts doubt on much of the anecdotal evidence from Tulare Lake, which unfortunately represents a significant portion of what has been recovered of possible Terminal Pleistocene age there (Fenenga 1991:11; Wallace 1993a, 1993b). Few archaeologists doubt that Tulare Lake was the scene of very ancient human activities, and extinct megafauna derived from its shorelines clearly cast the lakeshore as a Pleistocene landscape (Fenenga 1991:12). But tying humans to megafauna or other clear Pleistocene markers has proved elusive. It will be rewarding when a Clovis or "Clovis-like" point is finally discovered during the course of a professional archaeological examination. With any luck, it will be embedded in a *Bison antiquus* rib.

The Skyrocket site (CA-CAL-629/630), located in the Sierra foothills east of Stockton (Figure 5.1), shows an intact and extensive stratigraphic profile, the earliest levels of which have been attributed to the Terminal Pleistocene-Early Holocene or "Lower Archaic" transition (Bieling et al. 1996; La Jeunesse and Pryor 1998; Rosenthal et al. 2007:152). A radiocarbon date suggests a basal date for the deposit in excess of 10,000 B.P., and a single fluted point is reported, although the latter was recovered in a stratigraphic context containing later, stemmed projectile points and may have been "scavenged" by Lower Archaic residents (Bieling et al. 1996:4; La Jeunesse and Pryor 1998:30). The radiocarbon age of the Skyrocket site remains intriguing and is not disputed, but human activities of that era have proved difficult to document unequivocally.

The Lower Archaic, ca. 10,000–7500 B.P., is represented primarily by isolated finds of chipped crescents and stemmed projectile points resembling Lake Mojave and Borax Lake wide-stemmed variants. Most of these finds are centered on Tulare Lake (Fenenga 1992) and a more southerly extinct lake,

Buena Vista Lake (Hartzell 1992. See also Figure 5.1). Lower Archaic finds are plagued by private collecting and questionable provenience. In a rare exception to this, archaeologists recovered a small artifact assemblage including a stemmed point fragment, several crescents, debitage, and an atlatl spur from KER-116 near Buena Vista Lake (Fredrickson and Grossman 1977; Hartzell 1992). The deposit also yielded a human cranial fragment as well as a small faunal component, including freshwater shell, fish, waterfowl, and a few artiodactyl bones. Freshwater mussel shell yielded a radiocarbon date in excess of 8350 B.P. No milling tools or other evidence for exploitation of plants is known for the site (Rosenthal et al. 2007:151–152). Scholars may have until recently largely ignored the role of plant foods in the Lower Archaic diet, but we must remember that our time markers consist largely of hunting points. When we find a site such as KER-116 in an undisturbed context, we find firm evidence for a mixed diet. Nevertheless, it appears that the acorn-based economy was still a long way off during the Lower Archaic.

The Skyrocket site may be a propitious place to explore the nature of plant food exploitation during the Lower Archaic (Bieling et al. 1996). A stone "platform" feature was discovered that may have been constructed to provide a dry surface for occupation and exploitation of marshy ground, dated to 7000–8000 B.P. (La Jeunesse and Pryor 1998:30). The feature matrix reveals a number of stemmed projectile points and, significantly, more than 250 milling stone slabs and hand stones. However, the platform also reveals a few later point varieties, including Pinto points, so the dating of the feature is ambiguous. If the grinding tools are associated with the stemmed points, and not the later varieties, it appears that we have a quite early emphasis on plant food exploitation at the site.

The local Middle Archaic spans the time frame from 7500 to 2500 B.P. (Rosenthal et al. 2007:152) and thus encompasses the entire Middle Holocene (7000–4000 B.P.) and part of the Late Holocene (4000 B.P.–present). The early Middle Archaic is poorly represented in the San Joaquin Valley and Sacramento Delta regions. The lone example of the time frame is, however, a wealthy source of information regarding the era. Basal levels of the Blossom site (SJO–68; see Figure 5.1) date to 5000–6000 B.P., serving as the earliest example of the Windmiller Pattern in the Delta region (Ragir 1972). Blossom was occupied for approximately 1,500 years and reveals a rich array of artifacts, many of which were recovered in direct or close association with more than 150 burials (although not all burials date to the Middle Archaic). The earliest artifacts include a wide variety of charmstones, shell and bone ornaments, shell beads, projectile points, other stone tools, bone and antler tools, and enigmatic objects of baked clay, including many that may have functioned as surrogate cooking stones in the stone-poor Delta. Of particular interest here, the site yielded significant numbers of milling stones, including many crude cobble mortars and more expertly crafted specimens. Mortars occur throughout the vertical deposit, representing the entire occupation history of the site, including its deepest Middle Archaic levels. Because the use of stone mortars in the interior is likely tied to the processing of fleshy seeds and nuts, including acorns, it may be argued that the Blossom Site represents the earliest artifactual evidence for the onset of the economic importance of the acorn in the Delta region (Rosenthal et al. 2007:155), and acorn exploitation using other tools may have been earlier still.

It is worth noting that mortars at Blossom greatly outnumber pestles (Ragir 1972:98). Although there is no direct evidence, this disproportion may suggest that pestles were made from perishable materials such as wood (recall that the Delta is generally stone poor). If so, we are reminded that the shortage of plant-processing tools from earlier sites in the Central Valley may be attributed to the use of perishable milling equipment.

The Windmiller Pattern appears to have expanded rapidly after ca. 3800 B.P. in the Delta and San Joaquin Valley, enduring until ca. 2700 B.P., or virtually the entire Middle Archaic (Bennyhoff 1994a, 1994b; Rosenthal et al. 2007:155). Faunal profiles from Delta and northern San Joaquin Valley sites suggest a trend toward year-round village occupations and increasingly circumscribed territorial ranges (Arnold et al. 2004:41; Broughton 1994b). New fishing technologies included fish gorges, compound hooks, and several types of spear, revealing strong reliance on freshwater and anadromous fish. Faunal profiles suggest extensive exploitation of rivers, riparian forest, marshes, foothills, and grasslands (Rosenthal et al. 2007:155).

Of particular interest from Middle Archaic Windmiller sites are burial data that suggest distinctions in individual wealth, as measured by the kinds and numbers of objects included as grave goods. Because differences in the presumed wealth of certain graves cross-cut both age and gender categories, some scholars propose the emergence of ascribed status, while others suggest that the evidence is consistent with achieved status differences (Moratto 1984). With the combination of increased population size (more and larger sites), inferred differences in individual status (burial goods), and circumscribed territories (faunal profiles), it is reasonable to associate the Windmiller with a storage-based economy, a common correlate of growing political complexity (Beaton 1991b). As the preeminent storable commodity available to Central Valley culture groups, acorns began to change the cultural landscape.

Middle Archaic locations in the Sierra foothills, including the Skyrocket site, reveal more intensive exploitation of acorns in the botanical profiles as well as in the artifact assemblages, which include expedient pounding, chopping, and milling stones (Rosenthal et al. 2007:153; Wohlgemuth 2004). Food procurement and processing tools are abundant, including projectile points, but there are few ornaments or maintenance tools such as bone awls (Rosenthal et al. 2007:153). In stark contrast, contemporary Valley and Delta locations show a full range of both utilitarian and non-utilitarian artifacts, suggesting that foothill sites were functionally specific, special-purpose sites, presumably seasonal destinations for logistically oriented villages located in the Valley and Delta.

Upper Archaic (2500–850 B.P.) sites in the Delta region appear to shift toward affinity with the Berkeley Pattern, in keeping with trends observed in the Sacramento Valley and the San Francisco Bay area. Windmiller-type sites continue throughout the Upper Archaic in the San Joaquin Valley, however, as suggested by the continuation of extended burial posture (Bennyhoff 1994a, 1994b). The Berkeley and Windmiller patterns appear to be further distinguished on the basis of trade routes used to obtain obsidian: San Joaquin Valley Windmiller sites enjoyed a flourishing trade for obsidian biface blanks from east of the Sierra crest, including sources at Coso, Bodie Hills, and Casa Diablo. Berkeley Pattern sites appear to have obtained most of their obsidian from more northerly sources, especially Borax Lake and various Napa Valley sources (Rosenthal et al. 2007:157). We can infer that territorial distinctions between the Miwok and the Yokuts may have emerged at this time.

Upper Archaic sites are less common than Middle Archaic sites (Rosenthal et al. 2007:156–157), but those we see tend to be large, aggregated villages. It is difficult to dismiss the timing of this demographic shift, which corresponds roughly to the Medieval Climatic Anomaly (MCA) at ca. 1150–650 B.P. (West et al. 2007:17). The MCA had dire ecological consequences, and those who remained in the valley appear to have adopted a highly structured, seasonal system of resource exploitation based at well-watered locations. Although artifact assemblages suggest that acorn exploitation increased significantly in the valley during this time, an overall decline in the numbers of archaeological sites is evident in the oak-rich foothills (Moratto 2002:40–41). Clearly, drought conditions of the MCA increased the lure of the San Joaquin and Sacramento rivers, as well as Tulare and Buena Vista lakes and associated marshlands. Foothill regions, for the most part, held their primary attraction in the fall alone, when acorns ripened and game animals returned from their summer migrations to the high Sierra.

Certain foothill locations *were* occupied by relatively substantial populations, however, and so the foothills should not be dismissed as mere hinterlands. Settlements were located along permanent streams that feed the valley floor from sources high in the Sierra. Among these are MAD-117 and MAD-106, located along the Chowchilla River (Figure 5.1). The two sites yielded a substantial corpus of burial data possibly indicating heritable status differentiation beginning in the terminal Upper Archaic. King (1978:243) and Moratto (1972, 1984:316–323) make the case for status ascription in the burial population from ca. 1700–1100 B.P. Although they have minor differences of opinion concerning the precise timing and persistence of non-egalitarian political organization, their findings are based on the sorts and numbers of burial offerings that cross-cut age and gender categories, differences in burial posture, and spatial segregation of the presumed "higher status" interments. Status ascription appears to wax and wane, reflecting some variation in local prosperity, particularly as suggested by numbers of exotic goods (e.g. shell ornaments). The period of lowest prosperity, the Raymond Phase (1650–450 B.P.), is when the evidence for status differentiation is weakest, and we see elevated levels of violence and "chronic cycles of occupation and abandonment" (Moratto 1984:319). The Raymond Phase coincides with the MCA, leading us to ask, did social structure change during the Raymond Phase, or is the archaeological signature affected by demographic shifts associated with the MCA drought? In any case it appears that during favorable periods, wealth-based status differences characterized parts of the Sierra foothills.

The Emergent period (850 B.P.–historic) marked the close of the MCA and witnessed a rapid surge in regional populations. Many archaeological sites can be tied to specific social groups known ethnographically (Arnold et al. 2004:41; Moratto 2002:42–43; Rosenthal et al. 2007:157). The period corresponds to the Augustine Pattern of the Sacramento Valley and San

Francisco Bay and included such innovations as the bow and arrow, harpoon-like compound spears, and a vast array of ornamental objects of bone and shell, soapstone pipes, bone whistles, and finely crafted mortars and pestles. Burial data suggest broad differences in individual status at Valley and Delta sites, particularly in the nature and frequency of grave furnishings, which included large numbers of goods (Bennyhoff and Fredrickson 1994; Milliken and Bennyhoff 1993). The foothill sites MAD-117 and MAD-106 saw a resurgence of occupation and renewed evidence for social differentiation (King 1978:232). Large villages were established along the Delta, often mounded to maintain elevation above the flood plain. The San Joaquin River and its tributaries similarly saw community growth, although on a smaller scale (Rosenthal et al. 2007:158). The classic California adaptation, with its heavy dependence on the acorn as a plant staple, was certainly fully developed by or before this time throughout the region.

We note the clear dominance of the mortar and pestle over all other forms of grinding tools by the Emergent Period and see it as reasonable to assume that the additional costs of mortar and pestle manufacture—compared to the mano and metate—represent a significant leap in the importance of the acorn to the diet and, presumably, to changes in other facets of native life. These likely included scheduling priorities more rigorously tied to the harvest of acorns, reorganization of labor, increased territoriality, and greater social inequalities. Differences in the distribution of wealth among individuals—whether tied to ascribed differences in status, achieved differences in wealth, or both—permit some inference that there existed a storage-based economy, which was almost certainly focused on massive acorn exploitation (e.g., Basgall 1987; Beaton 1991b). What we *do not* have for the Delta, Valley, and Foothill cultural subregions is an appreciable amount of direct evidence for prehistoric acorn storage itself.

The historic and ethnographic records may provide us with a clue to this gaping hole in the archaeological record. Both historic and ethnographic sources record large granaries built for the specific purpose of storing abundant quantities of acorns. Many of these were quite elaborately constructed to protect against the elements as well as vermin. However, granaries were constructed of wickerwork or tule thatch, which do not preserve well. Moreover, granaries were often constructed directly on the ground or slightly raised above the ground and supported by one to four posts (Latta 1977:400–401; Levy 1978:405; Powers 1976 [1874]:Figure 32). These leave at best a meager footprint in the archaeological record. Large wickerwork storage bins were also constructed atop boulders or in the forks of trees (Anderson 2005:259; Latta 1977:400; Powers 1976 [1874]:351), in which case we expect no archaeological trace. Finally, perhaps the most common form of acorn storage made use of large baskets woven specifically for the purpose (Levy 1978:406). Food storage baskets were typically kept in houses and would rarely have been left behind when a house was abandoned. For all of these storage options, weak archaeological signatures would be expected even amid a thriving acorn-driven economy.

There is clear and ample evidence for continuity between the historic acorn-based economy and prehistoric practices (Hull 2002). We can be certain that this uniquely Californian emphasis began to prevail deep in the past. Efforts to flesh out its origin and development over time are reliant largely on the character of stone milling technology, tests geared toward identifying delayed-return economies, and archaeobotanical studies. We applaud these investigations, which have turned the clock back on the use of the acorn in California, and we look forward to more widespread analyses of these types. Although hunter-gatherer-fishers maintained substantially higher population densities at selected places along the Pacific coast, the great majority of California's native people pursued economic livelihoods in the interior that revolved around the acorn.

6

Money Makers and Oceangoing Traders of Southern California

From many vantage points along the arid coast of southern California between Point Conception and San Diego, it is possible to glimpse one or more of the eight California Channel Islands (Figure 6.1). These islands, their surrounding coastal waters, and the adjacent mainland combine to form a unique and ecologically rich part of California, strikingly different than the windy high cliffs of the central coast's Big Sur, the massive embayment at San Francisco, and the rainy far north coast. Important for the resources they provided to human inhabitants, the islands are habitable, reachable, and provide a buffer against open-ocean swells for the inner coastal waters. The four tightly bunched northern Channel Islands are parallel to the coast and guard the Santa Barbara Channel, creating a bit more of a barrier than the dispersed southern islands. Such protection helped to enable local oceanic travel and deep-water fishing in relatively small watercraft, although rough and unpredictable channel waters still took the lives of many people, according to oral histories (Blackburn 1975).

The intervisibility of the islands and the mainland coast undoubtedly encouraged exploration and seasonal settlement throughout the area at very early dates, and many remarkable archaeological sites, some more than 13,000 years old, are found on the islands. A long and interesting sequence marked by subsistence and settlement shifts, new interaction networks, and technological innovations unfolded over the ensuing millennia on both the mainland and the larger islands. Good-sized villages thrived relatively unaffected on the islands even as Europeans established multiple missions on the mainland during the 1700s and 1800s. At contact, and for many centuries before, substantial permanent populations lived on all but the diminutive Anacapa and Santa Barbara islands. It appears, however, that throughout

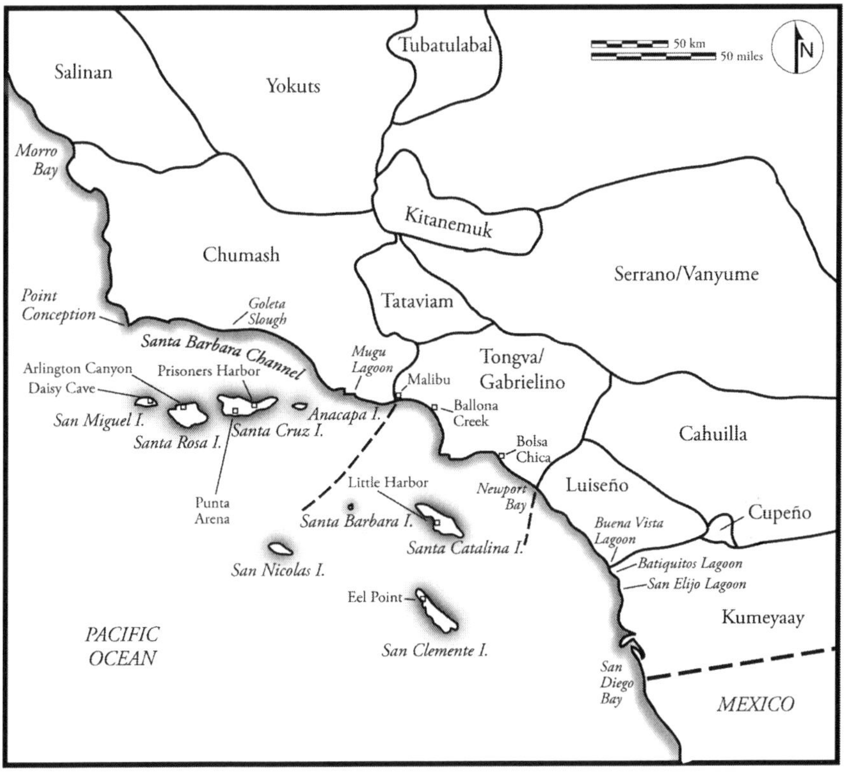

Figure 6.1. Santa Barbara and South Coast ethnographic groups and selected archaeological localities. Map by Clarus J. Backes, Jr.

prehistory, the most robust populations resided in mainland villages located wherever reliable supplies of freshwater punctuated the coast. Mainlanders of the southern California coast enjoyed a bounty of attractive resources drawn from a diverse spectrum of land mammals, marine mammals, fish, shellfish, local and migratory birds, and plant foods.

The northern half of this portion of the California coast was the domain of the Chumash, a group of eight linguistically affiliated subgroups who are, as we will see, renowned for their enduring occupation of this territory and for exhibiting, late in prehistory, what may have been the highest population density of any hunter-gatherer group in global history. Their lands extended from Morro Bay to Malibu and encompassed the four northern Channel Islands. The southern part of this region extends from the Los Angeles Basin to northern Baja California and encompasses the four southern Channel

Islands and the estuary-dotted San Diego coastline. Native groups of these territories included, from north to south, the Tongva (formerly the Gabrielino) of the Los Angeles and southern Channel Islands area, the Luiseño, and the Kumeyaay (formerly the Ipai and Tipai) near San Diego.

A Mediterranean climate prevails in the region, marked by warm temperatures and sporadic rainfall, averaging 25–40 cm (10–16") per year, concentrated in the winter months. Coastal southern California has always been vulnerable to moderate and severe droughts (Jones et al. 1999) to which populations have had to adjust. Under normal climatic conditions, groves of live oaks produce large masts of prized, calorie-rich acorns (with off-years and intermittent poor yields), and coastal sage scrub, chaparral, and grassland ecosystems produce an abundance of nutritious hard seeds. Many southern California tribes used controlled, seasonal grassland fires to stimulate new seed yields and attract foraging mammals to open areas where they could be hunted (Blackburn and Anderson 1993; Timbrook et al. 1982).

Large estuary systems to the south, such as the Bolsa Chica wetlands near Newport Beach and the Buena Vista, Batiquitos, and San Elijo lagoons and Mission Bay along the San Diego County coast, yielded shellfish and attracted various terrestrial mammals and migratory birds (Figure 6.1). Adjacent coastlines provided fish and marine mammals. Substantial native villages were located at places of unusual abundance such as these. To the north, the large estuary at Goleta was home to nearly 1,000 Barbareño Chumash distributed across several villages. For mainlanders in these productive locales, migratory fowl and larger mammals such as elk and deer, along with rabbits and other rodents, complemented a rich, marine diet dominated by fish, shellfish, and marine mammals. In contrast, islanders had no large land mammals to hunt—deer, elk, bear, even rabbits were absent on all eight islands—and thus relied heavily on marine animals such as fish, shellfish, pinnipeds (sea lions and seals), and dolphins, which were unusually abundant. Many medium-sized communities of 100 to 250 inhabitants were situated near the best freshwater sources on the northern Channel Islands during later prehistory (Arnold 1992, 2001a; Kennett 2005; McLendon and Johnson 1999; Rick 2007). Throughout the region, small villages and hamlets were positioned at the mouths of secondary streams, inland near springs, and along natural corridors for travel and exchange.

Houses in much of southern California were simple but well-designed pole-and-thatch constructions (Figure 6.2). Residents could build such

Figure 6.2. Artist's conception of a Chumash coastal village showing typical pole-and-thatch house structures. Illustration by Adan Treganza.

houses in a day or two with little assistance, drawing on locally available raw materials such as willow branches, reeds, and grasses. Villages of up to 20 households were situated in the richer coastal areas, as illustrated by the settlement plan of the Late period/early contact period site of *Shawa* (SCRI-192) on Santa Cruz Island (Figure 6.3). The modest variability we see in structure diameter within villages appears to have been unrelated to rank and status, at least on the Channel Islands (Arnold 2001a; Arnold and Graesch 2004). Recent analyses of thousands of contact-era artifacts indicate that the largest houses do not consistently yield the highest proportions of wealth and prestige objects (Graesch 2004). We attribute the absence of a firm correlation between prestige and house size to the ease of home construction and the mild climate, which provided little practical reason to invest great labor effort in houses. Chumash people of higher rank did not generally invest symbolic capital in houses to demonstrate social standing, and it would have been easy for individuals of lesser means to build a relatively large-diameter house. Rather, elites had other ways to signal their status and wealth, as we discuss shortly.

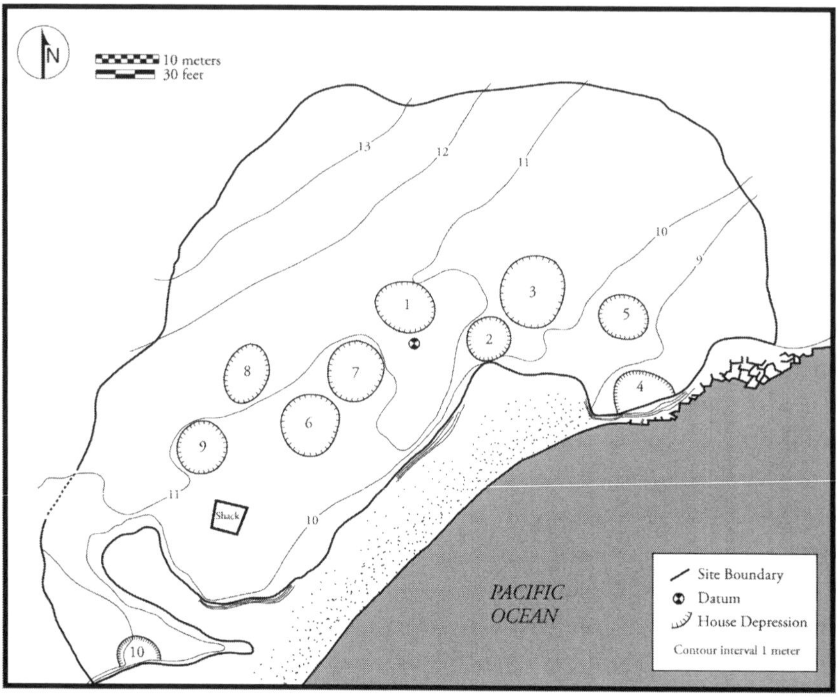

Figure 6.3. Map of a typical Late/Historic period Island Chumash village site (*Shawa*, SCRI-192 on Santa Cruz Island). Note the ten well-defined house depressions. Adapted by Clarus J. Backes, Jr. from original by Jeanne E. Arnold and Anthony P. Graesch.

Peopling: Early Settlement

Shifts in oceanic currents and rising and falling sea-surface temperatures have affected coastal California peoples through the millennia, although the details and scale of the impacts of ancient oceanic perturbations remain controversial (Arnold 2001a; Kennett and Kennett 2000). Near the close of the Pleistocene, cold ocean waters were at least 100 m (300') lower than at present, and the four northern islands were joined into a mega-island called *Santarosae*. Early human remains dating to about 13,000 years ago were recovered decades ago at Arlington Canyon on the north side of the mega-island (on what is now Santa Rosa Island). Recent redating of the bones and associated materials from the surrounding block of soil establishes the Arlington Springs skeleton as the oldest on the North American Pacific coast, and possibly the oldest in North America. A team of archaeologists and geologists has revisited the site and assessed the soil layers that yielded the bones, and the remains appear unassociated with other burials, tools, or residential debris. Researchers identified the original location of the bones within the complex stratigraphic sequence preserved in the canyon walls via two methods: (1) comparing the bones of an extinct species of mouse (*Peromyscus nesodytes*) in the excavated block and in the undisturbed strata; and (2) comparing old photos and maps with new digital plans of the canyon wall (Johnson et al. 2000).

The antiquity of these bones places people on Santarosae Island at about the same time that pygmy mammoths (*Mammuthus exilis*) were becoming extinct. Mammoths lived on this landmass for millennia, getting progressively smaller due to the island rule, or island effect. Archaeologists such as Phil Orr, who first considered this issue back in the 1950s, asserted that people probably hunted these small mammoths into extinction, but most scholars consider it much more likely that they died off due to disease or climate change before humans reached the islands. A new date for a *Mammuthus* vertebra discovered near Arlington Canyon may alter this interpretation. The date of 11,030 ± 50 RYBP (radiocarbon years), when converted to calendar years, places the mammoth within roughly 100–200 years of the age of the human bones at Arlington, potentially indicating that they coexisted for a short span (Agenbroad et al. 2005). So once again we consider the possibility that humans were partially responsible for the demise of the pygmy mammoth. It remains to be seen how these findings articulate with a new discovery of nanodiamonds in multiple glaciers and soil horizons of the northern hemisphere, suggesting that a comet exploded above northern North America at about 12,900 B.P. This event could have independently precipitated sudden climatic change with the ultimate consequence of a rapid die-off of mammoths and other continental megafauna such as camels and saber-toothed cats (Kennett et al. 2009).

Located less than 20 km to the west of Arlington Canyon, very early food and artifactual remains at Daisy Cave, a small rockshelter on San Miguel Island, challenge the long-standing argument that the first occupants of the Americas had a terrestrial dietary orientation. Daisy Cave represents the earliest known residential locus on the Channel Islands. People clearly adapted quite early to littoral and marine ecosystems, gathering resources such as shellfish and fish from nearshore and kelp-bed areas. The initial short-term (likely seasonal) occupation dates to ca. 11,600 calendar years B.P., making it the oldest shell midden in North America. From a chronological standpoint, we would certainly say these were "Paleoindian" people, but we can infer that they were using simple boats on ocean waters for island-mainland travel and likely for some of their fishing activities.

Also at the Daisy Cave site, we find more substantial Early Holocene occupation from ca. 8,500–10,000 calendar years B.P. (Rick et al. 2001). Excavations reveal substantial faunal assemblages with tens of thousands of fish bones and shellfish specimens representing nearly 40 taxa, evidence of a pronounced orientation to the sea. Inhabitants used diverse capture tactics including shore-based collecting, hook-and-line fishing, and small boats to reach kelp forests. Investigators found shell beads, stone tools, bone fishing implements (which appear to be the oldest fishhooks in North America), and woven sea grass artifacts. Sea grass cordage from the site is abundant and is the oldest such material from the entire Pacific coast. Dense midden layers dating to the Middle and Late Holocene cap the Daisy Cave site. More than 50 reliable radiocarbon dates anchor this important multi-component site firmly in time.

It is clear that people were not just infrequent visitors to the northern Channel Islands. They were residing there at least seasonally at an early date, and we now have dozens of securely dated components between about 12,000 and 7,000 calendar years to verify this (Rick et al. 2005). Without a doubt this means that some kind of watercraft was developed that could traverse roughly 20 km of channel seas. Most likely this was a tule reed raft or balsa-like boat, small and simple in design. Such boats were still in use for nearshore fishing and local travel into the historic Mission era (Arnold 2001a:14), and while they were vulnerable to rotting and cumbersome to paddle when the bundles of reeds become waterlogged, they were adequate to transport small numbers of people back and forth across the channel on days when seas were calm (Hudson et al. 1978). Archaeological evidence indicates that the large redwood-plank canoes that plied the waters of the Santa Barbara Channel and mainland-to-Catalina Island routes farther south at contact originated thousands of years later, very likely after A.D. 500 (Arnold 2007; see below). Although some authors speculate that wood canoes may have been present at much earlier dates (Fagan 2004), there is no evidence from the Chumash region to support that proposition.

Quite early sites also appear on the southern Channel Islands, including the deep, basal stratum of the Eel Point site on San Clemente Island, dating to ca. 8200 B.P. (6500–6000 cal B.C.). Human occupation at this proposed residential base on San Clemente Island (Raab et al. 1994; Rick et al. 2005) conjures up a harrowing and much longer sea journey, including two segments of at least 30 km (at the sea levels prevailing during the Early Holocene). Seafarers almost certainly first crossed from the coast to Santa Catalina Island, then from that island to distant San Clemente Island in watercraft of unknown form, perhaps made of wood (Cassidy et al. 2004). The inferred presence of boats at these early dates, whatever their type, has led some scholars to suggest that the islands may have been colonized before the mainland. In this scenario, people first reached southern California via a coastal route, arriving in boats and likely encountering the islands before the mainland. Since the Arlington Canyon human remains from Santa Rosa Island are roughly contemporaneous with Clovis sites of the interior American west, some hard evidence exists to support the postulate that peopling of the continent followed a coastal pathway, or perhaps multiple pathways (Erlandson et al. 2007). The coastal migration hypothesis certainly reverses conventional thinking, positioning the early hunters of megafauna on the Great Plains as descendants (or contemporaries) of people who traveled south from the Bering Sea, skirting the coasts of Alaska, British Columbia, and the northwestern U.S., arriving in California before 13,000 years ago. Clearly it will take considerable evidence from throughout North America to more fully tell this story.

The first signs of occupation on the mainland north of Los Angeles are sparse but include a fluted point from the western Santa Barbara Channel coast and a deep, shell-filled stratum from the Surf site (SBA-931) north of Point Conception, both dating to well before 10,000 years ago (Glassow et al. 2007:192). The earliest indicators of a more sustained presence in the mainland coastal zone are associated with the Millingstone Horizon, which began ca. 9000 B.P. and lasted at least two millennia. Some 40 sites of this age, many yielding abundant metates, manos, hammerstones, and large core tools, have been discovered, mostly in near-coastal locations. The intensively investigated Tecolote Canyon area just west of Santa Barbara has several rather ephemeral Millingstone deposits (Erlandson et al. 2008). Seeds, nuts, shellfish, and mammals, but not fish, were commonly consumed at the coastal sites of this era. Over the next two millennia, mortars and pestles and large, side-notched projectile points were added to the tool repertoires, likely signaling an expansion of the diet, and highly favorable locations near estuaries such as the Aerophysics site on the Goleta Slough (SBA-53) may have become important residential bases for local populations (Glassow et al. 2007:197). Clearly, however, largely mobile lifeways continued.

Beginning in the Late Holocene (1500 cal B.C.), mainland Santa Barbara area sites started to reflect a more balanced orientation in peoples' exploitation of terrestrial *and* marine resources, with signs of intensified fishing and marine mammal hunting as well as new technologies such as circular shell fishhooks, stone net weights, refined mortars, and new dart point types. Settlement was strongly focused in coastal locations, and increased sedentism is suggested by evidence for large clusters of houses, formal cemeteries, and high densities of artifacts and food refuse at sites in Tecolote Canyon (e.g., SBA-72) and elsewhere near Santa Barbara (Erlandson et al. 2008; Glassow et al. 2007:202). These developments along the mainland coast and the gradual population growth that accompanied them laid the foundation for increasing elaboration in ritual life, intensification of regional exchange systems, and complexity in political organization that emerged later in prehistory (Erlandson and Rick 2002).

The earliest occupation of the San Diego coastal region occurred at ca. 9000 B.P. Large estuaries attracted the San Dieguito people, who thrived on bountiful plant and animal species, including shellfish and birds. Scholars have not fully resolved whether these people arrived from the desert interior, where the drying and eventual disappearance of large Late Pleistocene lakes forced out-migrations to the better watered and resource-rich coastal zones, or whether coastal populations may have expanded into the region from other parts of the coast, such as the Santa Barbara region. Compared to more northerly coastal populations, the San Diego estuary dwellers did quite a bit less open-ocean fishing and sea mammal hunting. Evidence from cremations and ceramics points to desert influence, especially in the northern San Diego County area. Gallegos (1991) is among the majority who argue that people moved toward the coast when lakes in the Great Basin desiccated, taking Great Basin toolkits with them and thriving in the xeric, estuary-dotted coast. The San Dieguito people practiced diversified resource exploitation, a continuation of "the Western Pluvial Lakes tradition" (Gallegos 1991:41), and their culture gradually transformed into the La Jolla tradition. According to Masters and Gallegos (1997:19) and others, coastal San Diego was later significantly depopulated due to the siltation of the region's large lagoons during the Late Holocene, but Byrd and Reddy (2002) contend that most lagoons did not silt in at that time, and coastal abandonment did not occur. Byrd (1998) pointedly refutes the "coastal decline model" but acknowledges that the extensive Batiquitos Lagoon was one important locus that apparently did silt in, prompting localized abandonment.

Much of the discussion that follows regarding the later archaeology of coastal southern California centers on archaeological evidence from the Channel Islands. We have several reasons for this emphasis. Principally, more sustained and integrated problem-oriented research has been conducted there than on the mainland coast during the past few decades, and sites are far better preserved. Hundreds if not thousands of important sites along mainland shores were destroyed between the early 1900s and the 1960s as cities and highways were developed. Many mainland sites that survived construction are severely churned by gopher activity (Bocek 1986). Ongoing development-driven research by cultural resource management (CRM) archaeologists does, however, continue to generate significant new information about mainland adaptations, and several important publications have resulted (e.g., Erlandson [1994], Erlandson et al. [2008], and Glassow [1996] in the northern area; Altschul et al. [2005] in the Los Angeles Basin).

The islands have quite a different trajectory of ownership and development. After the departure of the last Chumash and Tongva people by the early 1800s, the eight islands came to be owned by large, private ranching concerns (whose owners kept their lands open for free-ranging cattle and sheep) or by the federal government. Today, several islands are now under the control of Channel Islands National Park or the Nature Conservancy, and others are owned by the U.S. military. Private development was kept at bay, paved roads are rare or absent, buildings are few (except at Avalon on Catalina Island and at the larger military complexes on San Nicolas and San Clemente islands), and vast expanses remain open wilderness areas. Consequently, there has been no parallel to the devastating obliteration of mainland sites, and most of the islands are free of gophers. While the mainland clearly once had an archaeological record every bit the equal of that on the islands, and some mainland sites still produce valuable insights into the region's past, the islands serve as an unusually rich source of current data and interpretations.

The islands have also yielded discoveries of unusual significance, some capturing the public imagination as well as scholarly attention. Roaming pygmy mammoths on the northern islands may have borne the brunt of the arrival of the continent's earliest dwellers. Daring teams of fishermen in swift redwood plank canoes captured huge swordfish on the open seas and hosted feasts at island villages. Early traders seemingly extended their webs of social networks to distant culture areas as distant as the high desert, Oregon, and the Great Basin. And hundreds of specialized bead makers in more than 20 villages on the northern islands manufactured millions of pieces of shell-bead currency.

The Southern Channel Islands and Adjacent Mainland

People arrived on the southern Channel Islands at least eight to nine millennia ago, as recently summarized by Raab et al. (2009). Aridity and a scarcity of reliable springs and streams presented challenges to human occupation, although Early Holocene conditions were wetter than those of today. Salls (1991), Raab et al. (1994, 2009), Porcasi et al. (2000), and Yatsko (2000) discuss a range of sites on San Clemente Island, including the earliest, Eel Point. Also of note is the Early Holocene-era Little Harbor site on Santa Catalina Island. It was an important residential site, and its deposits and collections were among the first from the Pacific coast to undergo intensive ecological and paleoenvironmental analyses (Meighan 1959; Raab et al. 1995). These many quite early residential sites clearly implicate a long and enduring tradition of local seafaring in both the northern and southern Channel Islands areas that culminated in the composite redwood plank boats of the Late period (the *tomol* and *ti'at*, respectively; see below). Recent speculations that Polynesians introduced plank boats to California (Jones and Klar 2005) are inconsistent with the Californian and the Hawaiian chronologies and find no support in the existing archaeological evidence (Arnold 2007 and others).

Populations on San Clemente, Santa Catalina, and San Nicolas islands consumed high proportions of shellfish, fish, and selected marine mammals, varying according to local marine conditions, and they weathered various climatic disruptions and climatic optima (Cameron 2000; Raab et al. 1994, 2009; Yatsko 2000). Porcasi and Fujita (2000) find evidence for intensive hunting of dolphins around the southern islands by 8000 B.P., using capture methods that likely did not require large boats. Faunal experts have conducted important ecological analyses of the marine fauna from hundreds of southern islands sites. It is clear that people lived in small to medium-sized villages or moved seasonally across the less bountiful landscapes in small food-gathering groups as climate and resources (including fresh water) allowed. Yatsko (2000) has documented hundreds of small encampments where shellfish processing took place near San Clemente Island's western coast. He has also documented several settlement shifts that represent adjustments to periods of drought. The southern islands have produced growing evidence for climate-induced stresses and their effects on later settlement systems. Extensive surveys on San Clemente (funded by the U.S. Navy to mitigate site impacts) have yielded up to 300 small sites per square km, among the densest concentrations of sites in North America (Raab et al. 1994).

Olivella biplicata (purple olive) shell beads of various types were common throughout California, and after about 650 B.P., virtually all of them were made on the northern Channel Islands (Arnold 1992; Arnold and Graesch 2001; Arnold and Munns 1994; Eerkens et al. 2005; Kennett 2005; see below). Much earlier, however, a rare Olivella bead type made only on the southern islands was exchanged across a wide area of the American far west. Tracing the distribution of this distinctive type, the Olivella grooved-rectangle bead, archaeologists have proposed a long-distance "southern islands interaction sphere" that may have connected the southern islands with Shoshonean speakers on the adjacent mainland and as far away as Oregon and the Great Basin at ca. 5000 B.P. (Byrd and Raab 2007; Raab 1997; Raab and Howard 2000).

Another resource of great importance on the southern islands was an extensive series of soapstone outcrops and shallow mines on Santa Catalina Island. Soft, talc-rich soapstone, easily carved, was abundant on Catalina. The Tongva exploited it to make large vessels (ollas), bowls, and comals (flat griddle-stones) for trade with neighbors during the Late and Historic periods (Howard 2000). Howard's surveys of the major soapstone-producing geological zones on the island recorded many new quarry and subsurface mining sites, and the most high-intensity quarries appear to be protohistoric in age. The production of soapstone implements was part of an interlinked regional exchange system that encompassed the southern and northern islands and the Tongva and Chumash mainland. Large soapstone ollas and other vessels were notable markers of elite status, and the Chumash highly valued these imports.

From the Lemon Tank site on the interior plateau of San Clemente Island, Raab and colleagues (1994) uncovered important evidence of sacrificial animal interments and the possible origins of the *Chiningnichich* religion, which flourished during the Historic period. At contact, the Shoshonean-speaking Tongva occupied the southern islands and adjacent mainland territories. These groups maintained strong ties to the desert interior before and after contact, as is evident by their burial practices (cremations) and trade relations. An important trade artery, the famed Mojave Trail, connects this portion of the coast to the eastern California desert and the Hohokam area of southern Arizona. Shell bracelets, baked clay anthropomorphic figurines, ceramics, and projectile points that were made in the interior desert, in the general vicinity of the Colorado River, are present at Late Holocene coastal sites such as ORA-58, the likely Historic village of *Genga* (Koerper et al. 2002; Koerper and Hedges 1996). *Genga* was one of roughly 20 early Historic-era villages situated near streams and bays such as Newport Bay.

A lively debate has emerged regarding whether Shoshoneans arrived and displaced preceding populations as late as 1500 B.P. or as early as 5000 B.P. (Sutton 2009). Within the coastal Los Angeles Basin, clear evidence for cultural connections to the desert interior can be attributed to an ancient Shoshonean migration to the coast. Projectile point types and cremations from roughly 3500 B.P. to contact indicate that Shoshonean culture-bearers lived at Ballona Creek and vicinity for more than two millennia. Throughout the Middle period (locally defined as 1000 B.C.–A.D. 1000), these people maintained closer connections to the desert than to the Chumash or groups to the south (Altschul et al. 2005). Although most scholars suggest that there were several Shoshonean incursions to the coast, some assert that a single, late migration occurred at 1500 B.P. from the east, emboldened by new bow and arrow technology. If, however, Olivella grooved-rectangle beads and other indicators of a "southern interaction sphere" in the interior, the coast, and the southern Channel Islands were produced by local Shoshoneans (rather than solely through trade *with* Shoshoneans), then the case can be made that the migrations had started by 5,000 years ago.

Political Evolution and the Chumash of the Northern Channel Islands and Nearby Mainland

A notable chronological successor to the earliest northern island sites such as Daisy Cave is the Punta Arena site, an expansive locus on Santa Cruz Island's southwestern shore, with well-defined Early period strata after ca.

6500 B.P. revealing considerable evidence for dolphin hunting and extensive shellfish exploitation (Glassow 2004). Glassow suggests that a submarine canyon near the site funneled cetaceans into shallow waters where they could be hunted from small tule reed boats. This key resource was supplemented by the capture of many species of shellfish and fish just offshore and from nearby rocky headlands and beaches. Apart from Punta Arena and a few other large sites on each of the northern islands (e.g., SCRI-333 on Santa Cruz; SRI-109, SRI-3, and SRI-41 on Santa Rosa; SMI-87, SMI-350, and SMI-481 on San Miguel), much of the documented activity on the islands during the first few millennia of the lengthy Early period (7450–2550 B.P.) occurred at small sites near the coast and at relatively small, higher elevation localities away from the coast (Glassow 1997a; Rick et al. 2005). Red abalone (*Haliotis rufescens*) was an abundant food species during this era, and Glassow (2004) has documented many small midden sites on the west half of Santa Cruz Island dominated by thick lenses of red abalone shells dating to ca. 6450–4950 B.P. Red abalone could be harvested most easily when cooler sea temperatures prevailed, since it may shift into shallower water where divers may expend less effort. At this time, island populations were modest in size and mobile, moving frequently as prime resources became available.

By the Middle period (2550–800 B.P), diet, technologies, and settlement locations were changing radically, and more robust populations of islanders established much larger communities along productive sectors of the coasts. It appears that people resided in these villages year-round. Several changes allowed them to intensify fishing and engage in more frequent maritime trade, including most significantly the adoption of new fishing gear and, in the last phases of this period, the invention of the oceangoing plank canoe (the tomol; Figure 6.4).

It is a challenge to convey in just a few words the full importance of the tomol to the coastal and Island Chumash. By the time of European contact, when it had been in use for several centuries, it was the pivotal technology for enabling intensive trade of multiple kinds of goods throughout the region. Moreover, it permitted open-ocean fishing of aggressive, large-bodied species such as swordfish and several varieties of tuna (Bernard 2004), facilitated the transport of hefty marine mammals after their capture, and enabled rapid and frequent transmittal of information and movement of people across the channel for social and ritual activities (Arnold 2007;

Figure 6.4. Artist's conception of a plank canoe (*tomol*) on the Santa Barbara Channel. Illustration by Jon Standley (from Arnold 2001b:51). Used with permission from *The Origins of a Pacific Coast Chiefdom: The Chumash of the Channel Islands*, University of Utah Press.

Arnold and Bernard 2005). The tomol was costly to make, and very few individuals had the resources to own one. Those who did were chiefs and wealthy, high-ranking persons. It was made by highly skilled craft specialists who themselves had elevated standing in the community. As Arnold (2001, ed.; 2007, 2009) and others have argued, it was crucial in the development of more complex political organization in the Chumash region. This narrative unfolds below.

A rich array of archaeological evidence from the northern Channel Islands (e.g., Arnold 1987, 2001b; Arnold and Graesch 2001; Arnold et al. 2001; Graesch 2004; Kennett 2005; Perry 2004) makes it clear that at the onset of the Transitional period (800–650 B.P.), islanders began to specialize in the manufacture of great numbers of chert microdrills and shell beads, mainly of Olivella shell (Figure 6.5, 6.6). Prior to this, shell beads had been made in modest quantities throughout the region and were used largely as personal ornamentation and to mark social status. The steep climb in production output represented a dramatic and important change in labor organization as well as shifting political and economic organization for the region. Rather abruptly, villagers on eastern Santa Cruz Island developed exclusive control over access to the series of substantial chert outcrops and quarries located along a volcanic/shale geological contact zone on the northeastern part of that island. Knapping specialists shifted their techniques to produce much greater quantities of microblades and forms that were superior to the older and less robust Middle period tools (Arnold et al. 2001).

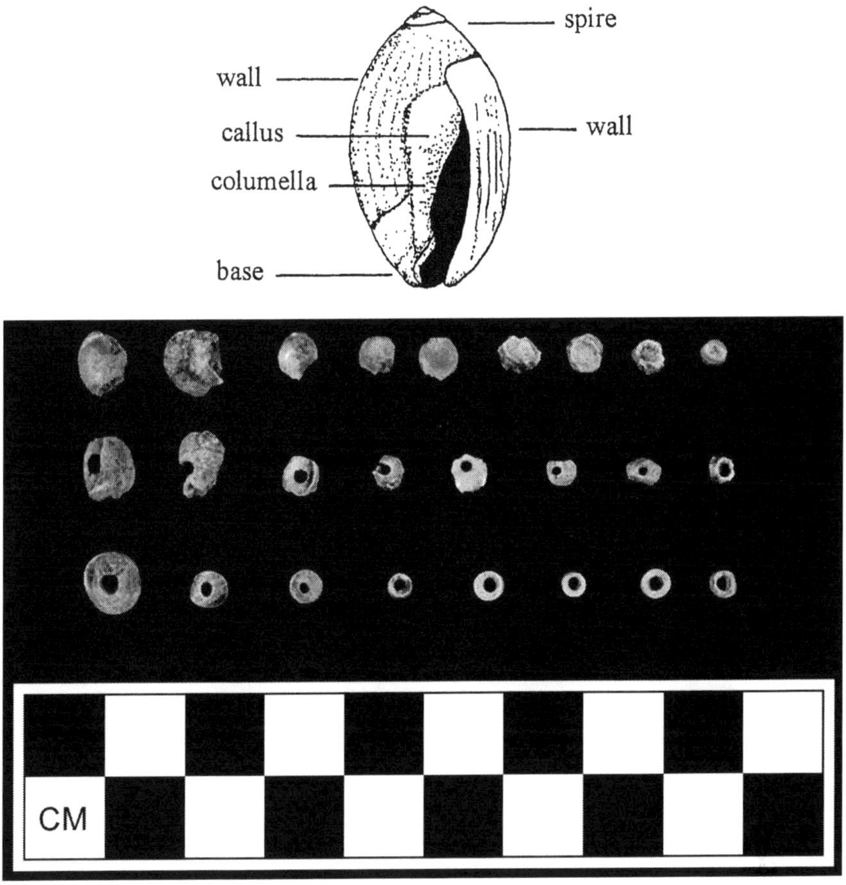

Figure 6.5. Shell bead-making industries of the Channel Islands. Upper: *Olivella biplicata* shell. Illustration by Jeanne E. Arnold. Used with permission from *The Origins of a Pacific Coast Chiefdom: The Chumash of the Channel Islands*, University of Utah Press. Lower: *Olivella* callus bead blanks, beads-in-production, and finished beads. Photo by Jeanne E. Arnold.

Other places in Chumash territory dropped out of the microblade-making activity. Villages at several locales on the Channel Islands (none on the mainland) became the exclusive end-points for microlithic tools and collectively developed a massive-scale shell-bead making industry. The vast majority of the millions of beads were made from Olivella shell, with far smaller numbers of mussel, clam, and abalone beads and several rare types. These northern Channel Islands-centered production arrangements per-

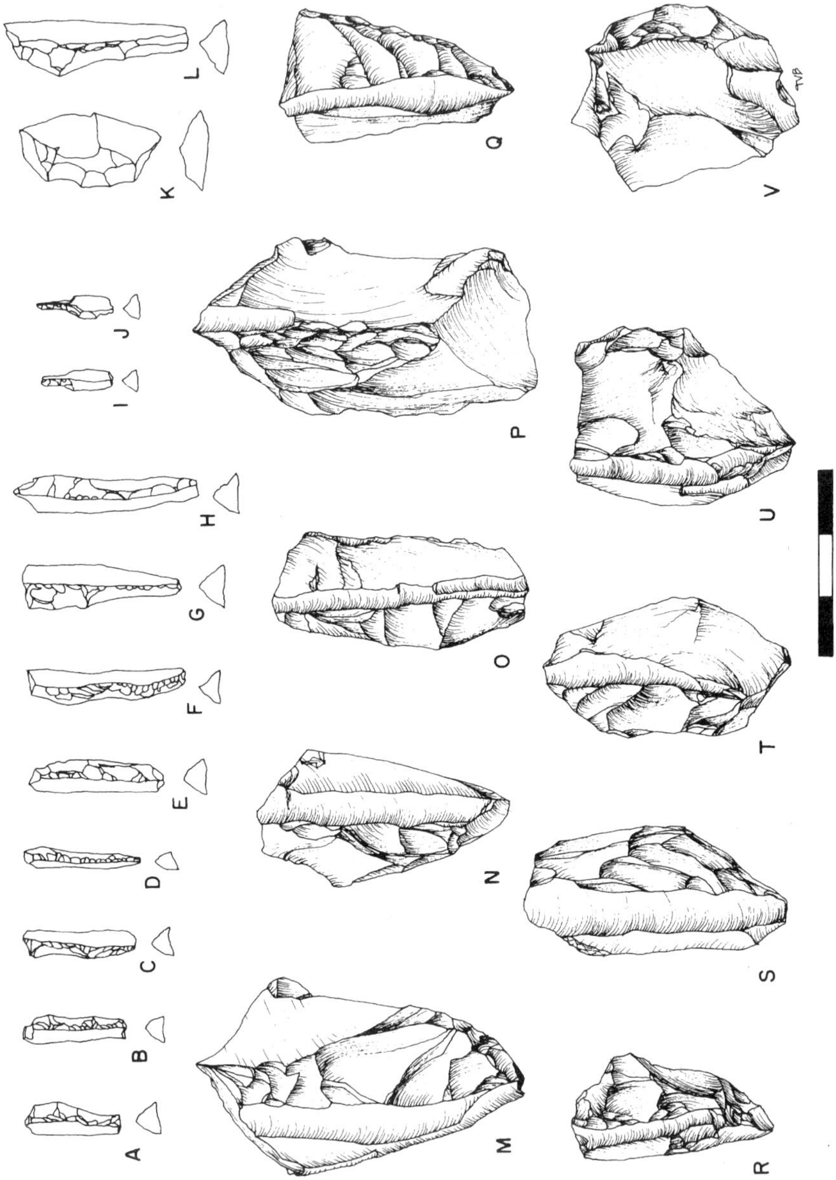
A
B
C
D
E
F
G
H
I
J
K
L
M
N
O
P
Q
R
S
T
U
V
Cm

sisted for the next seven centuries (Arnold 2001c). But why did this happen only on the islands and not on the more populous mainland coast?

These developments were possible because near the El Montañon highlands that divide the eastern tip of Santa Cruz Island from the rest of the landmass are more than a dozen large outcroppings of chert that were quarried on a small scale for millennia to make various implements. This cluster of quarries was the only major source of medium- to high-grade chert near the coastline between Point Conception and San Diego, making it a valuable and controllable resource. Scattered biface preforms and debitage at local sites show that early exploitation of the quarries focused on making large cores and bifacial tools. This trend shifted toward the end of the Middle period (ca. 1050 B.P.), when knappers began to make modest numbers of small chert drills for perforating shell disk beads. The naturally blocky characteristics of the eastern Santa Cruz Island chert made it ideal for this task. Investigations at the quarry localities show that over the course of the next couple of centuries, many thousands of cores were used for the detachment of diminutive, trapezoidal microblades (Arnold 1987; Arnold et al. 2001; Perry 2004). During this era (1050–800 B.P.), few beads were made directly at the quarry localities; most microblades were traded out or taken back to residential sites for small-scale bead drilling enterprises throughout the Santa Barbara Channel region.

Recent excavations at several Santa Cruz and Santa Rosa island sites reveal that output then rose exponentially beginning in the twelfth century, measured by shifts in both microlithic tools and shell bead-making by-products at various sites. Olivella bead-making detritus from typical late Middle period deposits includes a mean of about 8,000 fragments per m^3 (2,200 g/m^3), along with about 1,200 bead blanks and beads-in-production per m^3. In the subsequent Transitional and then Late period deposits, these figures rise to means of 102,000 fragments of detritus per m^3 (16,200 g/m^3) and about 3,800 bead blanks and beads-in-production per m^3 (Arnold and Graesch 2001:78–82; see also Arnold and Munns 1994; Kennett 2005; Rick 2007). Local and regional demand for beads accelerated significantly and

Figure 6.6 (opposite). Microblade-making industries of the Channel Islands. All specimens are of island chert. A-H: Late period microblades; J-I: Late period microdrills; K-L: rejected microblades; M-U, microblade cores; V: core. Illustration by T. Van Bueren. Used with permission from *The Origins of a Pacific Coast Chiefdom: The Chumash of the Channel Islands*, University of Utah Press.

production efficiencies rose, marking the onset of specialized craft production in the microblade-making activities near the chert sources and bead making at island coastal villages near good sources of shell.

These changes corresponded to a profound conceptual shift in how beads were used by the Chumash and their neighbors and trade partners. Whereas all beads appear to have had primarily ornamental and status-marking functions for millennia (King 1990), some became true standards of value, or currency, for the Chumash sometime prior to contact with Europeans. Archaeologists (Arnold 2001a; Arnold and Graesch 2001) contend that it was at the onset of the Transitional period that this shift occurred and a true currency was developed. Several lines of evidence support this view. First, a new pair of bead types made from the densest (callus) part of the Olivella shell—known as callus cupped and lipped beads—abruptly emerged as the predominant products throughout the region during the mid-Transitional (Figure 6.5). Second, lithic specialists transformed the configuration of the microblade/microdrill from a fairly fragile type prone to snapping (trapezoidal in cross section) to a much more sturdy type (triangular in cross section) that could perforate the hard callus portion of the Olivella (callus hardness is 5.0–5.5 on the Moh's scale; Arnold and Rachal 2002:193). Third, lithic specialists increased microlith output by a factor of more than 10 (Arnold 1987; Arnold et al. 2001). Fourth, shellworking specialists increased total bead outputs about tenfold, despite the fact that cupped and lipped beads were more laborious and challenging to make. Fifth, just one callus bead could be made from each shell, adding notable value and exclusivity to the type. In contrast, several wall beads can be made from each Olivella shell, and dozens of beads can be made from individual pieces of many other shell types that were used as bead-making material, such as mussel, clam, or abalone. So the appearance of callus beads appears to signal the emergence of costly, prized, exclusive money beads, made more efficiently and at an increased scale in just one part of the region by specialists, and these forms persisted throughout the Late period. Finally, the historic-era Chumash were repeatedly observed using strings of these callus beads for all kinds of transactions, with carefully measured lengths representing varying money values.

Tremendous quantities of microdrills and Olivella beads were manufactured on the islands on a sustained basis from the 1100s to the early1800s A.D. (by 1819, the last islanders left to join the missions). Substantial samples extracted from a number of sites across Santa Cruz and Santa Rosa islands make it clear that, all told, millions were produced at the most specialized village sites during this period. Many of the region's scholars describe the islands as the exclusive "mint" for the shell-bead money, which was used throughout southern California. Although reported cases of broken Olivella shell and a few unfinished beads on the mainland may represent minor counterfeiting episodes, these *very* rare exceptions prove the rule (see Arnold and Grasech 2001:74–75). On the other side of the channel, the Santa Cruz Island quarry zone and nearby villages, including the China Harbor and Prisoners Harbor sites, represent the most intensive, large-scale microblade industry known in the Americas. And the roughly 20 specialized bead-making villages on Santa Cruz, Santa Rosa, and San Miguel islands constituted perhaps the most extensive pre-Columbian shellworking industry north of Mexico, even surpassing the scale of the shell crafts associated with the great Mississippian cultures.

Even more important than these major changes in the material culture, the Transitional period marked the onset of a chiefdom organization on the Channel Islands, with the emergence of hereditary leaders who controlled production systems and trade routes, in part through their ownership of tomols and manipulation of the emerging currency system (Arnold 1992, 2001c, 2009). Although there is broad scholarly consensus that a simple chiefdom organization was in place well before the first explorers interacted with coastal villagers in 1542, debates persist regarding whether political centralization dates to the Transitional era (Arnold 2001a; Arnold and Green 2002; Hollimon 1990; see also Kennett 2005; Lambert 1994) or to many centuries before (Gamble et al. 2001; King 1990). The possibility has also been raised that multiple small, interacting Chumash chiefdoms may have emerged at different times in the region, rather than a single unified polity (Arnold and Green 2002). Certainly we can say that a great preponderance of data from dozens of well-preserved residential sites and cemeteries on the Channel Islands points to an emerging Transitional-era chiefdom political structure there, one that continued into the Late and early Historic periods. The disturbed cemeteries of the mainland (Malibu) coast are, taken on their own, far from an ideal source of data from which to ascertain when a mainland chiefdom-level polity (if indeed separate from an island polity) may have emerged (Gamble et al. 2001). Convincing evidence for political centralization in the region before the Transitional period has not yet materialized.

During the Late period, coastal Chumash people on both sides of the channel lived in villages with their houses situated on dense, thick midden accumulations. Villagers could sample the ocean waters for dozens of species of marine mammals (from seals to dolphins), hundreds of fish species (from rockfish to large tunas and swordfish), many shellfish (dominated by mussel, abalone, and clam), and two primary seabirds (cormorant, pelican), augmented on the mainland by land mammals such as deer, bear, and rabbit. Some of the densest fish bone deposits found anywhere on the globe have been recovered from Island Chumash sites, as many as 500,000 specimens/m^3 (Arnold 2001b).

Beyond the wealth of production data, household data, and mortuary data from the later periods on the Channel Islands (see especially Arnold 2001, 2004, ed.; Kennett 2005; Rick 2007), paleoclimatologists and archaeologists have uncovered intriguing evidence that groups were also responding to notable climatic fluctuations before and during the Transitional period. Coastal southern California's climatic record indicates that this era was punctuated by severe droughts and unsettled sea-surface temperature conditions that generated stresses for people living in large communities (Arnold 2001a; Arnold and Tissot 1993; Jones et al. 1999; Kennett 2005; Kennett and Kennett 2000). Many villages on Santa Cruz Island were abandoned for a discernable period after 800 B.P., likely due to diminishing freshwater supplies. Populations aggregated at just a few well-watered coastal communities (Arnold 2001b). Such stresses may have contributed notably to stimulating new ways of organizing household labor, making intensive, interlinked occupational specialization advantageous. Arnold (2001c) summarizes the evidence that the emergent leaders of that time were those few individuals who could assume the costs of ownership of expensive, rare plank canoes, and who could, seizing the opportunity to orchestrate a wide spectrum of labor, prompt people to devote considerable time to specialized bead production. They could then begin to redirect and expand the existing cross-channel trade systems, which further enhanced the importance of the tomol. Staple wild plant foods were among the goods traded widely around the region as drought cut into acorn and seed supplies on the less plant-rich islands (Arnold 2001c).

The complex hunter-gatherer-fishers of the Channel Islands thrived through the Late period and into the early Historic era. Meticulous analysis of undisturbed assemblages recovered from numerous distinct houses at six contact-era bead-making and microlith-making villages on the islands reveals subtle distinctions within these communities in status, access to exotic goods and prized foods, and intensity of participation in making craft goods of various classes (Arnold 2001b; Arnold and Graesch 2004; Dietler 2003; Graesch 2004; Noah 2005). Such distinctions shed light on social and political differentiation in Chumash communities. Roughly 25 named villages existed on the three largest islands in the 1780s (Johnson 2001), and most that have been tested indicate sustained occupation through the preceding Late period. All told, archaeologists have recorded more than 2,200 sites on the islands and estimate that island population density was about 6 persons per km^2. Mainland Barbareño Chumash population density was 6–10 persons per km^2, and people in the coastal zones lived in year-round, permanent villages at places such as Malibu, Mugu Lagoon, Ventura, Goleta Slough, Carpinteria, and Santa Barbara.

We have good reason to believe that the outline of the story of later political evolution on the mainland is similar in many respects, although we currently have little direct evidence for specialists, and we do not know that specific developments were necessarily contemporaneous with those on the islands. If there were mainland occupational specialists, Arnold (2001c) and others have suggested that they may have focused on plant processing for export and making the large sandstone grinding tools that would permit overproduction of ground acorn meal or seeds. There were also undoubtedly plank-canoe making specialists living near the pure asphaltum seeps at the Carpinteria bluffs (the name derives from the canoe-making Chumash carpenters observed by the Spanish) east of Santa Barbara, and it is almost certain there were tomol-making counterparts on the islands (see Arnold and Bernard 2005). Large, important villages thrived on the mainland into the early contact era (Gamble 2008).

Indeed, the mainland Santa Barbara Channel coast was one of the most densely settled areas of North America, and its deep shell middens complete with houses, sweat lodges (temescals), dance floors, and cemeteries attracted the interest of several early archaeologists (principally David Banks Rogers and Ronald Olson) who excavated local sites at a feverish pace during the first one-third of the 1900s. At the same time the brilliant ethnographer John Peabody Harrington began a five-decades-long chronicle working with living Chumash descendants and compiling several hundred thousand pages of notes (now in the archives of the Smithsonian Institution) about their vanishing language, technologies, and customs (Blackburn 1975). Much of what we know about the details of Chumash life has emerged from Harrington's records and from the burial assemblages and dense middens of large, Late period village sites in the vicinity of the Santa Barbara Channel coast. Rich assemblages of beads, ornaments, flaked stone tools, cores, flakes, weapons, milling gear, cooking implements, fine bone awls and hairpins, fishhooks, bone fish barbs, whistles, flutes, charmstones, effigies, tarring pebbles, asphaltum, and water bottle/cordage remnants are characteristic of the whole coastal region in the later phases, including the early Mission period (post–1782). Moreover, physical anthropologist Phillip Walker and colleagues (Hollimon 1990; Lambert 1994) have learned a great deal about health, stature, diet, trauma, genetics, and patterns of violence among Chumash populations through the study of skeletal remains exhumed long ago by Rogers, Olson, and others.

We cannot close without mention of another important domain of potentially sacred or ritual activity in the region: the spectacular rock art found in the mountains of mainland Chumash territory (Figure 6.7). The back country is pocketed with large sandstone outcrops that served as the canvas for polychrome pictographs. The Chumash employed a complex array of elements and motifs primarily in red, black, and white pigments (more rarely, orange, yellow, and blue-green). Circular (some interpreted as suns or stars), linear, ladder, triangle, and grid forms competed for space on crowded panels with anthropomorphic and zoomorphic motifs. Human hands, figures with headdresses, and lizard-salamander, bear, snake, and condor forms are well represented.

William Hyder's (1989) analysis identifies at least 15 rock art sites in a single mountain pass near the coast at Santa Barbara, although far more sites occur in remote inland locales, and the area's most extensive and richly polychromatic panels are more than 100 km inland in Emigdiano Chumash territory (Grant 1965). Whereas most scholars attribute the Chumash pictographs more or less exclusively to secret, ritual, and/or shamanistic activity, including perhaps astronomical observations such as the marking of summer and winter solstices, Hyder argues that the placement of certain images in easily viewable locations near frequented camps and gathering areas in the mountains indicates that some panels had public, communicative functions.

Figure 6.7 (opposite). Mainland Chumash rock art panel. Illustration by Campbell Grant. Used with the permission of the UCLA Rock Art Archive.

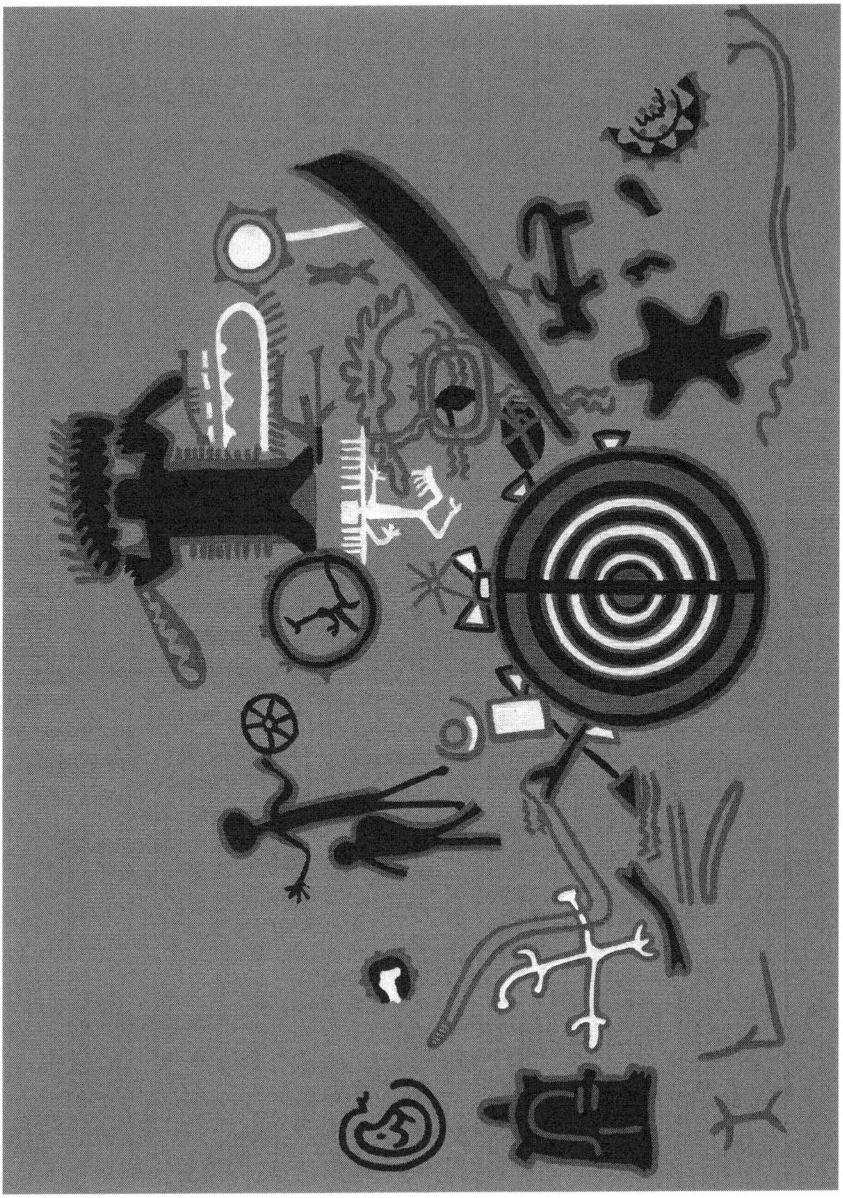

He suggests that public displays included motifs that promoted social order, marked ownership or social boundaries, maintained the natural order, and/or served as public shrines (Hyder 1989:35). However, both Hyder and David Whitley (2000a), who has examined rock art in several southern California regions, agree that some of the art was not public and likely reflects shamanic activity and personal quests for power.

Coastal southern California embodies many contrasts: sparkling ocean waters, endless beaches, and rich estuaries lie adjacent to arid foothills and marginally productive mountain zones. Much of the land is dotted with chaparral and oaks but limited in crucial freshwater supplies. Some of the earliest people in the Americas quickly acclimated to lives in this region, but they and many generations of descendants were sporadically challenged to adapt to dramatic shifts in precipitation, oceanic currents, and ocean temperatures. Their ultimate survival and cultural success are measured by at least two important yardsticks. First, they had the technological skill to reach and then settle on the northern and southern Channel Islands at very early dates. Within the northern part of the region, the people we know historically as the Chumash apparently endured for some thirteen millennia on the islands and mainland without being supplanted by other peoples. Second, by the time of European contact, the tribes of coastal southern California were among the world's most populous and densely settled hunter-gatherer populations, living in large, permanent villages and exhibiting considerable economic, ritual, and technological complexity throughout the region.

7

Hunters and Artists of the High Desert

All of the deserts of California are formidable places, with oppressive, deadly heat in the summers and freezing nights during the winter. The aptly named Death Valley in the Mojave Desert frequently has the highest daily temperatures in North America. Even given climatic fluctuations over the last few millennia, the deserts were, by the standards of the rest of California, *always* forbidding. Hardy plant life is scrubby, thorny, and largely inedible. Water is scarce, widely dispersed, seasonal, and unpredictable. Animals are wary, quick, and small. Yet several resilient groups managed to wrest at least a partial living from these harsh deserts for many centuries. They did this primarily through adoption of a highly mobile lifestyle that focused on maximizing the seasonal yields of small but productive patches of resources found near springs on the desert floor and from groves of nut-bearing trees that dot the surrounding foothills.

These groups ranged far and wide during the course of the year, perhaps farther than any other California natives over an annual round. Although this may not have been true throughout prehistory, as we discuss shortly, at contact the deserts tended to serve as seasonal destinations for people largely based close to the eastern Sierra Nevada piedmont (the Owens Valley Paiute), the foothill regions of the Tehachapi Mountains (Kawaiisu), the Panamint Mountains (Panamint Shoshone), or the San Bernardino Mountains (Cahuilla; see Figure 1.2). In some cases, groups such as the Vanyume in the western Mojave Desert maintained ties with those who *did* have regular access to the foothills and higher elevations, such as the Serrano of the San Gabriel Mountains (Bean and Smith 1978:570).

Desert peoples' lives thus depended fundamentally on the foothills, at least as we have come to understand their lifeways through oral histories, ethnography, and archaeological investigations. The greater elevations in these places provided some relief from the heat and a more robust set of resources than the desert floors could yield. For example, among the Cahuilla of the Colorado Desert, at least 60 percent of their territory consists of true desert, while the remainder is within or above the Piñon-Juniper zone that begins at about 1067 m elevation (3500 feet). As much as three-quarters of their annual diet—plant foods and game—was obtained in the higher elevation zones (Bean 1978:576). In the northern Mojave Desert the Kawaiisu claimed vast tracts of the desert floor (Underwood 2006) but maintained their core area in the acorn- and piñon-rich Tehachapi Mountains to the west (Zigmond 1986:398). In all cases, the foothills surrounding the deserts additionally provided greater opportunities for hunting large game, particularly deer and bighorn sheep. Only in the exceptionally well-watered Owens Valley, technically within the Great Basin province, did appreciable villages persist into the historic era on the desert floor, where small seeds and tubers still provided a reliable and substantial part of the diet. Even so, foothill piñon nut harvests, though annually variable in their yields, provided a very substantial source of storable surplus for the Owens Valley Paiute (Liljeblad and Fowler 1986:416; Steward 1933:241).

This is not to suggest that the desert floors were insignificant to most desert cultures. Fully one quarter of the Cahuilla diet derived from lower elevations within the desert, far too large a percentage to dismiss as somehow nonessential to survival. Moreover, many desert resources were available during the spring and summer months, including agave root, yucca shoots, mesquite and screwbean pods, as well as a variety of seasonal roots, greens, edible cacti, and small grass seeds (Bean 1978:576). The nut-bearing trees of the highlands were productive mainly in the fall. In the northern Mojave and the Owens Valley, highly organized rabbit drives on the desert floor yielded important windfalls of protein and hides and provided significant social occasions for alliance formation and maintenance, information exchange, and general revelry (Steward 1938:82–83). In all cases, the deserts provided critical raw materials for tool manufacture, especially obsidian and chert from untold numbers of sources.

Drawing territorial borders for the ethnographic peoples of the deserts is a difficult task (Underwood 2006), and some would call it a fool's errand. As Zigmond (1986:398) reminds us for the Kawaiisu, "The concept of territory was weakly developed, and the idea of boundary was probably nonexistent." It is almost certainly the case that territorial boundaries hold more interest for anthropologists than they did for California's desert hunter-gatherers. This is simply because extensive desert hinterlands were impossible to defend in any effective way, so concern over distant borders was futile. Resource patches on the desert floor, such as springs with small stands of mesquite (and their nutritious bean pods), patches of rice and rye grasses, and concentrations of game animals, were so widely scattered that they were risky destinations. Not only was patch productivity difficult to predict, but also such places were liable to have been picked clean by rival hunter-gatherers, perhaps complete strangers; a day late may have been tantamount to a seasonal shortfall. The prehistoric record suggests that the deserts supported small bands of highly mobile foragers for millennia. However, with the growth of populations in certain parts of the desert regions, these mobile foragers became increasingly circumscribed in their movements, with some settling into larger communities.

To illustrate a number of exciting discoveries from the California desert areas, in this chapter we turn our attention primarily to a region of the far-northern Mojave Desert (and at the southwestern margin of the Great Basin) that has captured the attention of several generations of archaeologists. This region is the Coso Mountain Range, which is located just north of the China Lake area (see Figure 2.1). The region does not appear to have been a primary destination for sustenance per se, but nevertheless was the focus of throngs of prehistoric hunter-gatherers over several centuries at least. No fewer than three cultural groups claimed the region in the ethnographic present: the Owens Valley Paiute (Liljeblad and Fowler 1986:413; Steward 1938: his Figure 7), the Panamint (Western) Shoshone (Thomas et al. 1986:264), and the Kawaiisu (Zigmond 1986:399).

The Coso Mountain Region

The Coso Mountain Range (Figure 7.1) rises humbly above the eastern California desert where the Great Basin and California culture areas intersect. For most people today, it is a desolate place to traverse, but a closer examination reveals a stark desert beauty appreciated by many archaeologists, geologists, and photographers. And for prehistoric hunter-gatherers, the Coso region was nothing less than enchanted, the focus of a creative efflorescence that left arroyo walls, lava flows, and pyroclastic boulders festooned with pecked rock art images.

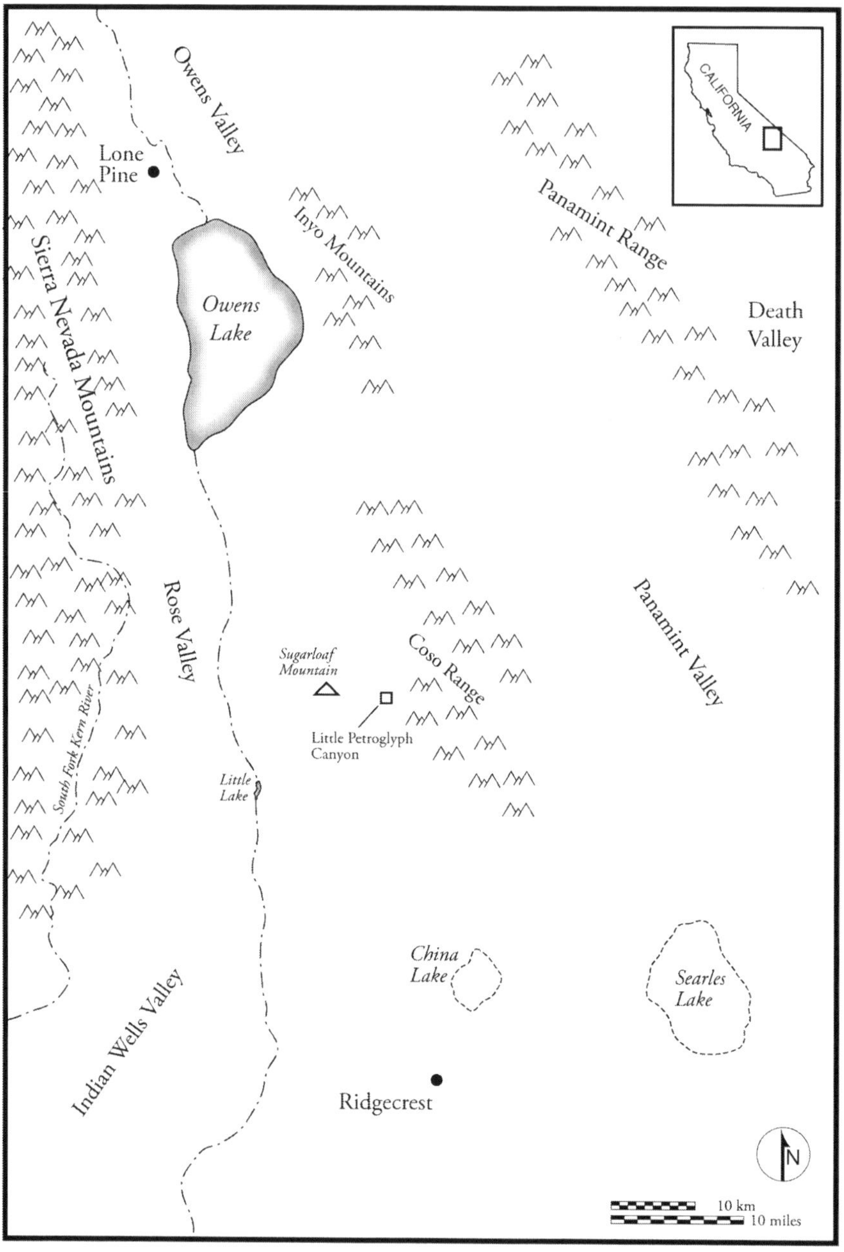

Figure 7.1. Coso Mountain Range/China Lake area, at the junction of the northwestern Mojave Desert and southwestern Great Basin. Corresponds to the territories of the Panamint Shoshone, Owens Valley Paiute, and Kawaiisu at contact. Map by Clarus J. Backes, Jr.

A conservative estimate puts the numbers of individual rock art elements in the Coso region at more than 100,000, all within an area just 150 km^2 (Garfinkel 2006:230; Gilreath 1998; Hildebrandt and McGuire 2002:245). This figure seems to grow year by year, and so far no archaeologist has scoffed that the estimate is too *high*. Images appear in the thousands within a one-mile stretch of Little Petroglyph Canyon alone (Figure 7.1). Pecked images include a wide array of geometric and other abstract forms, anthropomorphic figures, and a variety of zoomorphic representations. But our primary concern here is the most common rock art element found in the Coso Range, a highly conventionalized representation of the bighorn sheep (Figure 7.2).

Bighorn sheep images alone account for over half of the rock art elements recorded for the Coso region (Gilreath and Hildebrandt 2008:1). This conventional image is found throughout the Great Basin and the American Southwest, yet the number of bighorn images in this small portion of the Cosos is thought to exceed that for the remainder of western North America *combined* (Grant 1968:34; Hildebrandt and McGuire 2002:245). These are staggering statistics, particularly for a poorly watered region that saw only transient habitation in all of prehistory, for *either* humans or bighorn sheep. Bighorn images occur singly on isolated rock faces and by the dozens on sheer arroyo walls. Often, bighorns are portrayed as part of a tableau with anthropomorphic hunters, or neatly in rows, as if on a tally sheet. Nobody really knows why these images were pecked or why they were pecked in such great numbers. Furthermore, it is not easy to explain why this particular region was selected for the display. But archaeologists have developed a few competing ideas, and the two most popular are more or less mutually exclusive, leading to a fascinating and turbulent debate between rival camps.

One camp suggests that sheep represent mythical spirit helpers for artists concerned with weather control, as a means to increase productivity of wild plant foods (Keyser and Whitley 2006). An alternative model suggests that prestige-seeking hunters were letting the world know about their prowess in taking ever-dwindling numbers of bighorn sheep (Hildebrandt and McGuire 2002). Thus, the fundamental disagreement between the two camps is over *why* the rock art was created. It turns out, as we shall see, that the answer to this question depends on *when* the rock art was made. Efforts to establish chronological control over rock art images are notoriously controversial, and so the debate is not only lively but unlikely to be resolved

Figure 7.2. Petroglyph of Coso-style bighorn sheep, Little Lake. Photo by Clarus J. Backes, Jr.

anytime soon, and certainly not to everyone's satisfaction. Nonetheless, as one of the most striking archaeological localities of the American west, the Coso rock art panels deserve close examination.

The Coso Range is famed for another reason, so we must raise a second important issue. Volcanic flows that provided the backdrop for petroglyph panels also oozed glass: more than 150 distinct obsidian quarry sites are present in the Coso Range (Gilreath and Hildebrandt 1997:7). Source localities for obsidian include immense seams that emerge from steep rhyolitic domes, as well as extensive secondary sources of pyroclastic and alluvial debris. These secondary, or "lag," deposits range from a few scattered cobbles to fields with literally tons of obsidian nodules spread over 10 hectares or more. Primary seam deposits of high-quality obsidian, such as those on Sugarloaf Mountain (Figure 7.1), were subject to formal quarrying. A thriving industry of biface production based at these quarries appears to have well exceeded local needs for the greater part of the Late Holocene (Gilreath and Hildebrandt 1997:174). Roughed-out biface blanks were exchanged throughout much of southern and central California, an industry that appears to have been finally disrupted by population upheavals associated with the Medieval Climatic Anomaly (discussed below). Secondary obsidian deposits are of variable quality and may represent a more informal collection strategy, one that was embedded in other tasks (Eerkens et al. 2007; Walsh and Clewlow 2004). We should not downplay the significance of these "secondary" deposits, however. It is practically an axiom among archaeologists who work in the Coso region that every secondary source of obsidian in the area, no matter how small, reveals at least one chipping station, a place where obsidian was assayed. Thus the Coso region was clearly well traveled, and not just by those making rock art. However, obsidian sources and the core area of rock art production are largely separate (Hildebrandt and McGuire 2002:246). It is unlikely that obsidian sources are directly connected to rock art production per se, and neither competing model makes such a claim. Still, the obsidian sources may be peripherally related to rock art production, if the resultant high traffic for the region maximized visibility of the art. Neither model is ill served by this observation.

One thing that archaeologists agree on is that the greater part of the rock art—and all of the rock art that is the focus of the competing models—is of fairly recent vintage, well within the Late Holocene (Garfinkel et al. 2010). Most of the rock art is attributed to the later end of the prehistoric spectrum based on several lines of evidence. One of these is simple spatial association with late-dated archaeological sites (Gilreath and Hildebrandt 2008). A second form of dating derives from content of the images themselves. Although images interpreted as atlatls are common elements on Coso rock art panels, where anthropomorphic figures are armed, only 4 percent wield what are interpreted as atlatls, while the rest hold the bow and arrow (Grant 1968:120–121). In at least one instance, a single rock art panel shows *both* atlatl- and bow-wielding anthropomorphic figures (Figure 7.3), suggesting a time frame that coincides with the earliest introduction of the bow. The bow and arrow appeared in this portion of the desert no earlier than 1750 B.P. and probably not until roughly 1350 B.P. (Sutton et al. 2007:241–242; Yohe 2000). In a few cases, defined projectile point types are identifiable in the art, all of which are known to postdate 1350 B.P. (Garfinkel 2006:227). Finally, direct dating of the rock art images has been attempted, notably

Figure 7.3. Petroglyph of Coso-style bighorn sheep, abstract elements, archer (lower right), and hunter with atlatl (upper right), Little Lake. Photo by Clarus J. Backes, Jr.

through cation-ratio dating of accumulated rock varnish, or through careful inspection (and essentially counting) of micro-laminations in rock varnish (Dorn 1998, 2004; Whitley and Dorn 2010). These are experimental procedures with great promise but are as yet coarse grained and difficult to verify through cross-dating. Still, these procedures *tend* to show that much of the Coso rock art is late. Unfortunately, the critical test for either model is not precisely whether the rock art is late, but rather, *how* late.

Early and Middle Holocene (10,000–3500 B.P.)

We first provide a brief chronological framework for the Coso region in order to set the context for the disputed models. Although the Coso region closely tracks general chronological trends found throughout the desert west, the Late Holocene in this portion of eastern California carries its own peculiar designations for time periods. Our focus here is primarily on the Late Holocene, not just because it is presumed that most of the Coso rock art is of a Late Holocene origin, but because earlier time frames are not well represented in the local archaeological record.

The terminal Pleistocene for most of California's desert regions is informed by isolated fluted points and scattered surface deposits that are typically found near the shorelines of ancient playa lakes (Basgall 2000a, 2000b, 2005; Scott 2004:29–31). Among these ancient lakes is China Lake, immediately south of Coso (Figure 7.1). However, the Coso Range itself has yet to reveal sites of terminal Pleistocene age despite the discovery of fluted points found elsewhere that were made from obsidian derived from Coso sources (Dillon 2002:113–114; Warren and Phagan 1988:122). Terminal Pleistocene activities are thus clearly indicated for Coso, but it is possible that very ancient acquisition of obsidian has been obscured by subsequent quarry activities. In any case, the earliest known sites in the Coso Range derive from the Early Holocene, known locally as the Lake Mojave Period (10,000–7000 B.P.). Although Lake Mojave-era sites are common in many portions of the Mojave Desert to the south and to the east, they appear to be relatively uncommon in and directly around the Coso region, and are limited almost exclusively to obsidian assay and crude core production at secondary lag deposits (Gilreath and Hildebrandt 1997:89). Very low population densities and high mobility characterized the surrounding lowlands during the Lake Mojave Period (Eerkens et al. 2007).

Middle Holocene sites (7000–3500 B.P.), locally known as the Little Lake Period and elsewhere as the Pinto Period, are somewhat more common both in the Cosos and in surrounding lowland locations. Little Lake Period sites are marked by a wide variety of raw materials used to make stone tools, suggesting a vast and nonrepetitive annual round encompassing much of the surrounding desert and foothill regions (Bettinger 1999:46). Tool kits are largely expedient and quite uniform from site to site, suggesting a highly mobile, unspecialized foraging strategy (Delacorte et al. 1995:323). The lack of resource specialization or intensification is linked to low regional population density and little territorial competition (Bettinger 1999:47). That was to change with the onset of the Late Holocene.

Newberry Period (also, Middle Archaic or Gypsum Period) 3500–1350 B.P.

Following the Middle Holocene drought, Late Holocene "Newberry Period" populations grew rapidly. One consequence of this was increased competition for, and constriction of, resource-use territories (Bettinger 1999:47). Within these restricted territories, people exploited resource patches more intensively and with more specialized tool kits. Encounter strategies, sufficient to maintain earlier population levels, gave way to systematized, repetitive seasonal rounds. Functionally distinct site types feature "site furniture," particularly cached milling stones. These are found in lowland locations where populations are presumed to have targeted grass seeds. Separate, specialized hunting camps targeted large mammal species—such as bighorn sheep—at some distance from gathering localities (Stevens 2005). This dichotomy in site types suggests an effort to simultaneously exploit differing resources when periods of availability overlapped (Bettinger 1999:48). Although extended-stay winter villages appeared during the Newberry Period, residential mobility remained high for the remainder of the year, in a busy but well-orchestrated seasonal round designed to maximize resource returns within diminishing territories.

Faunal profiles document the importance of bighorn sheep in the Newberry-era diet (Garfinkel 2006:229; Hildebrandt and McGuire 2002:238; McGuire et al. 2007:360). Bighorn appears to have accounted for nearly 65 percent of animal foods, the remainder made up of small mammal species and other artiodactyls. This level of bighorn exploitation exceeds that for any time frame before or after.

Haiwee Period (Late Archaic, Rose Spring Period, Saratoga Period) 1350–650 B.P.

In the Haiwee Period, trends in population growth and territorial constriction continued unabated. By the end of the Haiwee, social groups "operated within annual ranges so small they were made sedentary virtually by default" (Bettinger 1999:49). Winter villages became permanent settlements, located in the valley lowlands, and territories were essentially confined to narrow east-west trending bands running from the Sierra Nevada foothills to the west, through a narrow strip of valley floor, and on to sundry ranges to the east (including the Cosos). This provided a "vertical" aspect to territorial variability and the seasonal round (see Bettinger 1999:46, his Figure 5.2), one that would have profound effects on the Haiwee lifestyle. Although lowland territories continued to be an important source of grass seeds and other edible plant foods, the foothill regions began to be exploited for tree crops, particularly piñon nuts. The highly nutritious but labor-intensive piñon nuts were gathered annually and in massive amounts in locations that were once the sole domain of the hunter.

Bighorn sheep accounted for about 50 percent of the faunal diet at the beginning of the Haiwee, but by period's end the proportion of bighorn in the diet fell below 5 percent. Much of this shortfall was counteracted by intensified exploitation of plant foods, especially piñon nuts, which were actively sought for storable surplus (Bettinger 1999:50). It is this basic subsistence and territorial pattern, first visible at the end of the Haiwee Period, that was also documented by Steward (1933, 1938) during the ethnographic present in much of the southwestern Great Basin.

Logistically organized, labor-intensive forays for storable surplus during the end stages of the Haiwee Period is thought to be a hallmark of the expansion of Numic-speaking peoples—linguistic forbears to the Great Basin Shoshone, Ute, and Paiute (Madsen and Rhode 1994). According to the "Numic Expansion" model, the presumed greater efficiency of the logistically organized Numa permitted them to out compete other mobile foragers, either driving them off or assimilating them wholesale. The impetus for the Numic expansion may have been the Medieval Climatic Anomaly (MCA), in which drought-related environmental deterioration resulted in increased territorial requirements and essentially hostile expansion (Sutton 1986; Sutton and Rhode 1994). The model was generated through linguistic analysis (Golla 2007:74; Grayson 1994), so the timing of the Numic expansion—if it happened at all—is debatable (Thomas 1994). However, archaeologists tend to accept the model because a distinctive form of social and subsistence organization—especially logistical organization centered on permanent villages—appeared rather suddenly and spread like wildfire. The Numic expansion may have begun as early as the mid-Haiwee Period, perhaps about 700–1000 B.P.

Marana Period (Late Prehistoric or Shoshone Period) 650 B.P.–Historic

The ensuing Marana Period witnessed a continuation of cultural developments established during late Haiwee times. Most archaeologists agree that all of the known ethnographic peoples—Numic speakers—were fully ensconced during the Marana. Intensification and new kinds of settlement systems are suggested by an increased variety of tool forms, new technological emphases (especially the use of ceramic vessels), more extensive storage facilities, and increased specialization in the locations of residential sites. Specifically, satellite villages arose to accommodate extended stays at prime plant food-gathering localities (Bettinger 1999:51). Organizational changes are suggested by greater numbers of bedrock milling stations near piñon-gathering locales as well as by increased numbers of smaller, lighter, portable milling tools, particularly metates. These changes strongly imply increased on-site food processing at remote resource patches, presumably to facilitate transport of storable surpluses to the home village. Perhaps because people were settling into semi-permanent villages, extra-regional trade increased dramatically during the Marana Period (Eerkens et al. 2008:677, 679). Ethnographers recorded satellite village locations that varied by season, and regular visits to a permanent "home" village were mandated by the ceremonial calendar (Steward 1938).

Bighorn sheep hunting provided a negligible contribution to the diet throughout the Marana Period and into the ethnographic present (Garfinkel 2006:229). It is unclear whether this fall-off was a consequence of overexploitation of the bighorn during the Haiwee or the result of privations exerted on bighorn populations by the MCA. But the fall-off in bighorn exploitation is central to disagreements over the competing explanations for Coso rock art. We now turn to these models.

Models for Coso Rock Art

Two models dominate current thinking, but we must first introduce a historically influential third. This is the "Hunting Magic" model, first proposed in the early 1960s and designed to characterize the entire Great Basin (Heizer and Baumhoff 1962; see also Grant 1968). The model derived from the recurrence of game animal images—particularly bighorn sheep—in locations considered suitable for hunting. Heizer and Baumhoff proposed an obvious and clearly reasonable explanation for the art: images of prized game animals were made in prime hunting localities in order to ensure success in the hunt. Not everyone was happy with the model (Garfinkel 2006:209), but it held sway well into the 1980s, if only for a lack of suitable alternatives. Among its failings were (1) abundant bighorn sheep images in places unsuited to hunting; (2) many "suitable hunting locations" that feature rock art but no independent archaeological evidence that hunting actually took place there; (3) clear hunting sites without rock art; (4) no ethnographic evidence directly connecting rock art with hunting magic; and (5) very few bones from bighorn sheep in local sites, at least at the end of the prehistoric period. The latter two observations, it turns out, are at the heart of the debate over current models describing Coso rock art.

The Shamanistic Model

Bighorn sheep played only a negligible role in the diet during the latter Haiwee and Marana periods. Given the improbability that a profusion of rock art would have as its focus a game animal that simply was not there, the ethnographic record was scoured for an alternative explanation for the abundance of bighorn petroglyphs. Thus was born the Shamanistic Model (Keyser and Whitley 2006; Whitley 1992, 1994a, 1994b, 1998a; Whitley and Dorn 2010; Whitley et al. 1999). The model draws an ethnographic connection between rain shamanism and bighorn sheep "spirit helpers" among the historic Numic-speakers of the Coso region (Panamint Shoshone and Owens Valley Paiute). The model is "shamanistic," rather than "shamanic," because the practice need not have been limited to full-time ritual specialists, i.e., true shamans (Keyser and Whitley 2006:25, fn. 1). Numic men are said to have entered into dream states, including drug-induced trances, during rain-making rituals. The mental impressions gained during these dream states are thought to be transcribed through the medium of rock art (Whitley 1998a:150–156). Abstract curvilinear and geometric forms that are frequent components of rock art panels are attributed to specific, sequenced stages of the hallucinatory experience, committed to stone (Figure 7.3). This latter suggestion has the additional benefit of explaining the superposition of certain rock art styles. Where rock art images are superimposed over one another, there is a general tendency to follow a sequence from abstract (earliest), to rectilinear, to representational (latest) images (Gilreath 2007:284). This sequence of mental imagery is thought to follow the "three stages of trance," a predictable neuropsychological sequence during altered states of consciousness (Whitley 1998a:150–154). The final transformation of Numic men into their bighorn spirit helpers is suggested by occasional images that conflate attributes of humans and bighorns (Keyser and Whitley 2006:19).

The general Shamanistic Model is not precisely time dependent, and its proponents recognize that some Coso rock art is demonstrably quite ancient (Whitley et al. 1999:24). But the ethnographic underpinnings of the model are best served if the rock art is quite late, that is, if the phenomenon post-dates the Numic expansion. Not only does this preserve continuity with ethnographic Numic speakers, but also it serves to focus on the paramount importance of plant foods during the last few hundred years. The centrality of plants presumably placed a premium on weather-control ritual for ensuring bountiful harvests. In concert with a spirit helper—the bighorn sheep—these rituals were carried out "by the hunter, for the gatherer" (Whitley 1994a:356). In a nutshell, the model suggests that weather control provided men with a critical responsibility within a subsistence economy that was almost entirely driven by women.

Although often elegantly and painstakingly argued (e.g., Whitley 2000b, 2000c), the Shamanistic Model's ethnographic foundations have been critiqued (Gilreath and Hildebrandt 2008:7; Hildebrandt and McGuire 2002:245; Quinlan 2000a, 2000b; Quinlan and Woody 2003:377–378). No *direct* ethnographic link has yet been established between a local Native American group and pecked images of bighorn sheep for rain making or any other reason. The Shamanistic Model cobbles together various local (and some not so local) ethnographic sources that associate (1) shamanism with the Coso region; (2) weather control as a shamanic duty; (3) rain-shamans with bighorn sheep spirit helpers; and (4) rock art with shamans and supernatural forces in general (Whitley 2000b, 2000c). But no single ethnographic source connects this entire web of ideas. For some critics, funneling a patchwork of ethnographic sources into a coherent model requires multiple leaps of inference, each more perilous than the last.

A second objection concerns certain controversial neuropsychological aspects of the model (Helvenston and Bahn 2005:80–110; cf. Whitley 1998a:150–156). The model suggests that there are three progressive mental stages of a hallucinatory experience, each with distinctive imagery that is sequentially recorded in rock art (Whitley 1998a:150–154). In the first stage, abstract geometric and curvilinear "entoptic" images are formed, of essentially the sort seen if the eyes are closed and massaged. In the second, certain of these images are construed to represent meaningful images, a "hard-wired" human imperative to make sense of even fantastic apparitions. "Sense" in this case is culturally conditioned: whether a particular shape is construed by the trancer as a fish or a bighorn sheep is determined by cultural experience. Surely, the trancer seeking a bighorn spirit helper will interpret forms as the latter. These images are committed to stone, often with exaggerated features or improbable postures. Finally, the third stage of a trance sees the images of the first two combined and converted into recognizable representations or, more specifically, representations that are recognizable to others without benefit of a trance state. The trance sequence should therefore combine geometric and curvilinear abstractions, somewhat more representational images, and finally, representational images with geometric design features. Whitley is careful to emphasize that the "three stages of trance" model does not permit us to interpret the *meanings* of images (Whitley 1998a:154). Rather, the visible sequence of rock art images permits us only to establish that rock art was indeed created during a state of altered consciousness.

However, Helvenston and Bahn argue that the sequence of abstract imagery cited for certain superimposed clusters of Coso rock art can derive from only three known hallucinogens, and none of these three was available in prehistoric North America (Helvenston and Bahn 2005:58). This criticism of one small aspect of the Shamanistic Model is not a mere exercise in nit-picking because the "three stages of trance" sequence proposed by the model seeks to explain the variety of certain rock art images as part and parcel of a single, staged vision quest. In other words, it suggests that rock art elements of quite differing appearance may have been systematically created in a matter of hours. However, others have maintained that shifting rock art styles—abstract and curvilinear to representational—reflect change on a far broader chronological scale, with some utility as a local method for relative dating (Gilreath 1999, 2007:284; Grant et al. 1968; Heizer and Baumhoff 1962; Ritter 1994). Because both the "three stages" sequence and the proposed chronological change sequence are virtually identical, occasional cases of directly superimposed stylistic elements appear to support either interpretation. Subjective consideration of repatination of the differing stylistic forms *tends* to support the notion that some considerable time intervened within the geometrical-abstract-representational sequence. But to truly clarify this issue it will be necessary to date specific rock art elements through independent means.

The final criticism of the Shamanistic Model concerns the proposed dates for the rock art. In order for the Shamanistic Model to maintain its explanatory power, it is necessary to link it with ethnographic sources. Some believe that most Coso rock art, and in particular the bighorn sheep motif, was created *prior to* 1000 B.P., that is, during pre-Numic times. If this is so, the very bedrock of the Shamanistic Model is shaken. More significantly, the earlier time frame for the images puts actual hunting of bighorn sheep back into the equation. This brings us to the Costly Signaling Model.

The Costly Signaling Model

The Costly Signaling Model (CSM) arose in part because there is no proven direct link between Coso bighorn petroglyphs and the local ethnographic record (Hildebrandt and McGuire 2002:245). The model places primary explanatory emphasis on archaeological data alone and, more particularly, on archaeological data recovered in direct spatial association with bighorn art (Garfinkel 2006; Gilreath 2007:284; Gilreath and Hildebrandt 2008; McGuire and Hildebrandt 2005). Based on independent dates derived for archaeological sites in direct proximity to bighorn images, proponents of the model suggest that the classic bighorn motif predates ca. 1000 B.P. That is, the bighorn images largely derive from the mid-Haiwee Period *and earlier*. Recall that prior to the mid-Haiwee, bighorn sheep held considerable significance for the hunters of the Coso region, accounting for over 50 percent of the faunal component of the diet. The proponents of the CSM thus see literal bighorn sheep, rather than metaphoric spirits, in the region's rock art images. Significantly, 1000 B.P. also signals the general time frame for the Numic expansion, which serves to account for the missing ethnographic memory of pecked bighorn images: the model proposes that the images were pecked by pre-Numic sheep hunters.

The model differs from the original Hunting Magic Model in the sense that it does not use rock art as a clue to hunting localities per se. It explains the profusion of rock art not in "magical" terms but in specific behavioral terms within a specific time frame. Rock art assemblages are viewed as complex sets of data that support a broader model regarding shifting hunting practices and evolving societal relationships rather than the phenomena to be explained. The CSM suggests that something of a "sheep cult" arose during the Newberry Period (3500–1350 B.P.), and the prestige gained by hunters through successful bighorn acquisition well exceeded the simple calculation of calories (Garfinkel 2006; Gilreath and Hildebrandt 2008:17). According to the model, "show-off hunting" of bighorn sheep conferred status to the hunter that was converted, ultimately, into marriage opportunities and reproductive success (Hildebrandt and McGuire 2002:235). The practice of signaling hunting success through the medium of rock art is not considered to have been precisely magical. Instead, rock art may have been a means to advertise hunting prowess, perhaps for the purpose of forming alliance networks among elite men or as an announcement directed at marriage-eligible women (or their families). Alternatively, rock art may have conveyed the presence of an esteemed hunter, perhaps as a warning to competing males or to trespassing social groups (McGuire and Hildebrandt 2005:707). In any case, the ubiquity of the bighorn images suggests a whole population of boastful hunters accruing power (Garfinkel 2006; Hildebrandt and McGuire 2002:246). This takes the rock art out of the hands of only a few ritual specialists. Note that the Shamanistic Model does essentially the same thing. *Any* model has to account for the apparently very large number of artists. However, the CSM suggests that the representational images are to be taken at face value; literally, as bighorn sheep.

The CSM suggests that prestige-motivated hunting pressure on bighorns depleted their numbers drastically, particularly following the introduction of the bow and arrow at the onset of the Haiwee Period, ca. 1350 B.P. Here is where the signaling proposed in the model turned quite costly. Prestige hunting was in this case maladaptive, violating the tenets of Optimal Foraging Theory (McGuire and Hildebrandt 2005:708). That is, increased costs associated with declining prey populations did *not* result in substitution of less costly, alternative prey species. Rather, prestige-seeking hunters merely redoubled their efforts to take bighorn, encouraged by steadily increasing returns in prestige gained by taking an increasingly elusive prey species (Garfinkel et al. 2010:50). This is in part suggested by increased intensity of rock art signaling during the Haiwee Period. It is of interest that, some 100 km to the south of Coso, Allen (2010) finds evidence for unabated bighorn hunting in the post–1350 B.P. era. That portion of the Mojave is rich in rock art but is notably poor in "Coso style" art, suggesting that the geographic distribution of bighorn extirpation closely corresponds to the profusion Coso-style sheep—and *only* Coso-style sheep. In the Coso region at least, the social and representational significance of bighorn sheep rose as their actual numbers fell. The intensity of rock art production thus does not reflect productivity, but rather, it tracks the prestige attached to the animals by hunters (Hildebrandt and McGuire 2002:245).

An unintended and quite significant cost of this cultural tradition may have been social collapse. Prestige hunting, at the expense of hunting efficiency, is a particularly dangerous tactic if external forces cause the playing field to change (McGuire and Hildebrandt 2005:708). In this case, it appears to have changed radically at ca. 1000 B.P. through the continuing escalation of drought conditions (the MCA) and the territorial circumscription and social conflict that accompanied the arrival of Numic-speaking immigrants (Jones et al. 1999; McGuire and Hildebrandt 2005:708). According to the model, expanding Numic populations encountered a population that was on the verge of systemic collapse, brought on in part by too much time and energy diverted to social display, particularly during a climatic regime that was unforgiving of inefficient, even wasteful, resource acquisition strategies. The more efficient Numa and their descendants had little interest in hunting the depleted bighorn sheep, and they apparently had still less interest in committing their images to stone.

The CSM has been criticized on several fronts. Some complain that the model cannot be said to apply to the Great Basin at large (Hockett 2005). But in fact the CSM makes no claim beyond the Coso region, and the observation that the demise of bighorn closely tracks the spatial blossoming of Coso-style rock art actually *strengthens* the tenets of the CSM as a localized cultural phenomenon. A second critique suggests that the dramatic increase in bighorn in the diet, evident at Newberry and early Haiwee archaeological sites, may not reflect prey selection driven by social dictates but simply elevated populations of bighorn sheep, thanks to the salubrious climate that defined much of the pre-MCA Late Holocene (Broughton and Bayham 2003). Thus, Newberry and Haiwee populations may have, in fact, been foraging optimally after all. However, while this suggestion may salvage some of the cherished tenets of Optimal Foraging Theory, it does not precisely invalidate the "sheep cult" aspects of the CSM, not least because we still have a lot of contemporaneous rock art to explain. Creating this art carried an enormous additional cost to the hunter in terms of time and effort expended in the signaling of prowess (Hildebrandt and McGuire 2003:792). One way or another, bighorn hunting was made costly, and all of these costs should be accounted for when we measure optimal behavior. A third critique suggests that the CSM has lost sight of the fact that, whether used to signal hunting prowess or not, bighorn hunting did indeed provide a wind-fall in calories. It may not be possible to distinguish simple success at provisioning from showing off, particularly since either may confer reproductive success (Cannon 2009; Codding and Jones 2007). How do we distinguish between a good provider and a show off? According to the CSM, it is at the point when either the energy expended in hunting the preferred species exceeds its potential energy return or the potential energy return of alternative prey species that went ignored (McGuire et al. 2007:361).

The CSM has also been challenged because some Coso rock art is demonstrably *not* attributable to the Newberry and mid-Haiwee periods (ca. 2000–1000 B.P.). Critics cite pecked images that are obviously of historic derivation, such as men on horseback (Whitley and Dorn 2010). Moreover, direct dating of rock art images through cation-ratio analysis has found certain bighorn images dated to 350–700 B.P. (Whitley 1994a:360–361, 1998b:58–59; Whitley and Dorn 2010; Whitley et al. 1999:7–9). Even with significant standard error rates (100 years or more), this places at least *some* sheep images well within the Marana—or Numic—era. Still, most sheep images appear to be earlier. The Shamanistic Model is roughly supported by these late dates, but they do not precisely diminish the CSM.

Finally, the CSM has been criticized for its simplistic interpretation of rock art images. Keyser and Whitley (2006:22) suggest that literal interpretation of rock art elements—such as the assumption that a bighorn sheep image represents an animal, rather than a spirit helper—is nothing less than Eurocentric arrogance. However, the implication that the meaning of rock art is ceaselessly metaphorical and always arcane is unsupported. Most archaeologists seem inclined to acknowledge that there are multiple possible meanings that may attach to certain rock art elements. One such meaning is its literal interpretation. There is no evidence that rock art elements are *invariably* more than what they appear to be.

Summary: Impacts of the Rock Art Controversies

Rock art is a salient feature of the eastern California deserts, and uncovering its contexts and significance for its makers is an important step in understanding desert adaptations. In the case of the extensive Coso rock art assemblage, both models considered here recognize rock art as a means to test far-reaching, comprehensive behavioral propositions of interest to anthropological archaeology. Each transcends an interest in rock art as purely *art*. The Shamanistic Model seeks to explain the images in terms of ritual designed to increase rain and the productivity of plant foods during the Marana and historic periods, 650 B.P. and later. The Costly Signaling Model seeks to explain the very same images in terms of hunters motivated largely by prestige accrual during the Newberry and early Haiwee periods of 2000–1000 B.P. At least one of these models is wrong. But the controversy sparked by these competing models has resulted in a tremendous intellectual effort directed at a relatively small plot of land. As a by-product of the debate, we are forced to confront issues of equifinality in the archaeological record because the regional culture history supports parts of both models, yet they cannot both be right. We are further forced to address the broad issue of ethnographic analogy, more especially the application and limitation of a record generated long ago. Issues explored by ethnographers are not necessarily the same issues of interest to modern archaeologists, and some creative interpretation is often demanded of us. Finally, at the heart of the dispute is the age of the rock art itself, and these images are at this time intractable to uncontested dating methods. But the intense interest in the Coso rock art has focused experimental efforts to date individual images, and this should eventually benefit archaeologists worldwide.

Related Research Issues in the Deserts

The controversy over these models has enjoyed a relatively high profile. This should by no means be construed to mean that this is the only important work in progress in the California deserts. Indeed, it should not be viewed as the only important ongoing research in the immediate vicinity of the Coso Range and the Owens Valley. In addition to significant strides in reconstructing Coso/Owens prehistoric settlement patterns over time, reflected in part by our thumbnail sketch of culture history presented above, archaeologists have made critical advances in our understanding of arid-land adaptations. In particular, scholars have begun to elucidate a suite of technological and sociocultural responses to changing climate, population fluctuations in "marginal environments," and shifting resource bases and collection strategies. In the course of these studies, the archaeological record has presented several serious challenges to the singular authority of the region's superb ethnographic record (Clemmer 2009; Clemmer et al.1999). This has been facilitated by relatively shallow site deposits with excellent preservation and pristine site conditions (especially on military bases), clearly visible surface components, a rich selection of available dating methods (radiometric, obsidian hydration, and a superb point typology), and relatively low population levels, which coalesce to create an ancient landscape that is fruitful and amenable to regional analysis.

Strides have been made in elucidating an Owens Valley sequence of less residential mobility (increased sedentism), increased reliance on communal storage, and intensified resource gathering strategies (Eerkens 2003a; Eerkens et al. 2004; Hildebrandt and Ruby 2006). Haiwee period sedentism (ca. 1350–650 B.P.) appears to anticipate heightened reliance on storage and resource intensification by many generations (Eerkens 2003a:302). This contrasts with the usual expectation that the three phenomena occur virtually simultaneously, as a single, massive organizational response to increased population pressure and reduced carrying capacity. At present, it is difficult to pinpoint the combination of factors that contributed to this sequence for the Owens Valley, although prime candidates include the roughly contemporary appearance of the bow and arrow, the unusually rich environment, and the possibility of incipient horticulture (Lawton et al. 1993), any or all of which may have fostered year-round resource-gathering opportunities in an increasingly crowded human landscape.

Finally, patterns of pottery manufacture and distribution in the Owens Valley and the northern Mojave Desert have been summoned for inferences regarding prehistoric social organization, sedentism, and the development of notions of personal property (Eerkens 2001, 2003b, 2003c, 2004; Eerkens et al. 2002). In short, a suite of systemic organizational change swept through the Coso/Owens Valley region in relatively short order, some following standard expectations for arid lands adaptations and some not. There remains a rich store of archaeological information that should keep archaeologists busy for years to come, and we anticipate more surprises.

We cannot ignore the likelihood that an influx of Numic peoples may be at the heart of many of the systemic and technological changes observed in the Coso/Owens region. It has been suggested that the Numa may have their roots in the general vicinity of the southern Sierra Nevada, the Owens Valley, and the western Mojave Desert (Madsen and Rhode 1994; Sutton et al. 2007:243). If this is so, the deserts of eastern California formed the first frontier for Numic expansion and may thus prove critical to further testing and elucidation of this complex, far-reaching model. In addition to the search for sociocultural changes and linguistic studies suggestive of an in influx of Numic immigrants, innovative studies of mitochondrial DNA among modern Numic populations are beginning to explore when, under what conditions—and even *whether*—the Numic expansion took place (Cabana et al. 2008; Kaestle and Smith 2001).

Elsewhere in the Mojave Desert studies of prehistoric patterns of mobility and exchange have been greatly facilitated by reference to obsidian derived from Coso sources (Eerkens and Rosenthal 2004; Eerkens et al. 2008; Ericson and Glascock 2004). For the greater Mojave Desert, scholars have begun to explore the social implications of climate change (Gardner 2006), gender relations (Walsh 2000), and inter-community strife and interpersonal violence (Allen 1998; Walsh 2010). All of these research avenues are worthy of further pursuit.

In the Colorado Desert, scholars have made use of petrographic analyses to determine the origin and distribution of selected pottery wares (Hildebrand et al. 2002; Schaefer and Laylander 2007:252–253). Additionally, considerable attention has been paid to subsistence and annual settlement patterns in the Colorado Desert, particularly with reference to the now-extinct (Late Holocene) Lake Cahuilla (Arnold et al. 2004:46–47; Schaefer and Laylander 2007:250–251). Furthermore, archaeologists are attempting to establish the antiquity and the spatial distribution of agricultural practices in the Colorado Desert (Laylander 1995; Schaefer et al. 2002). While the ethnographic record suggests that small-scale planting of tobacco, gourds, and wild grasses occurred in parts of the Colorado Desert, and the cultivation of beans and maize was likely in prehispanic times right along the Colorado River (Bean and Lawton 1993), evidence from the prehistoric era is generally spotty and ambiguous. Caches of edible seeds—including corn and squash—have been recovered, but it is difficult to distinguish home-grown seeds from those obtained through trade (Schaefer and Laylander 2007:254; Wilke et al. 1977:57–58). In other words, it is difficult to distinguish between food stores and caches of seeds meant for planting. In this regard it is well worth noting that trade between the southernmost deserts of California and the greater American Southwest was vibrant during the late prehistoric era (Schaefer 1994; Schaefer and Laylander 2007:254–255), and the Colorado Desert peoples were undoubtedly well aware that their neighbors to the east planted as well as ate those seeds.

Research into rock art, ritual behavior, and ethnohistory is hardly confined to the Coso Range, of course (Christensen and Dickey 2004). Rock art style and imagery is seen as central to reconstructing patterns of contact between eastern California and the greater American Southwest (Connick 2000; Smith and Lee 2004). New photographic techniques enhance the resolution of painted rock art for the purpose of discerning faded images as well as establishing element superposition (Backes 2004). Such means for establishing superposition may provide clues to social succession, a particularly important facet of the Numic Expansion model. Other researchers have explored the ritual aspects of rock cairns, geoglyphs (intaglios), and other rock features that cluster in various locations in the California desert (McDonald and McCarthy 2006; Reed 2006; Walsh and Clewlow 2006). Moreover, advances have been made toward improving the association between ethnohistorically known populations in the western Mojave Desert and specific prehistoric landscapes (Earle 2004; Underwood 2006). Much of the current research into the deserts of eastern California is facilitated by cultural resources inventories conducted at several major military preserves whose access to the general public is severely restricted. Despite weapons-testing programs and field maneuvers ("war games"), these regions provide among the most pristine and fruitful archaeological landscapes for problem-oriented research in mainland California.

8

The Future of California Archaeology

Much remains to be written about the fascinating prehistory and early colonial history of California's tribes. What unfolds during the next few decades will depend on our ability to ask good questions and amass reliable data. Even more so, the future of the field may depend on a range of new analytical techniques, collaborations, and alliances.

Protoagriculture: Were They All Hunter-Gatherers?

Parts of California as we know it today have much in common with three distinctive, adjacent cultural regions: the Pacific Northwest, the Great Basin, and the Southwest. The nature of shared traits and contacts with each of these culture areas is worthy of further study, but perhaps nowhere is this more the case than in the investigation of incipient agriculture in interior southern California. While it is clear that agriculture was practiced directly along the Colorado River, this small subregion was by all measures part of the American Southwest culture area. But it is possible that pre-contact agriculture existed farther west, in the desert interior of California. Archaeologists would like to definitively verify or refute this possibility for periods preceding the eighteenth century.

Direct archaeological evidence for use of domesticated plants is scanty and generally takes the form of fortuitous finds of small, carbonized seed caches or rare grains of maize pollen adhering to interiors of pots (Bayman et al. 1996:143; Hildebrand and Hagstrum 1995:92; Laylander 1995; Schaefer and Laylander 2007:254; Schaefer et al. 2002; Wilke and Fain 1974; Wilke et al. 1977:57–58). It is difficult to suggest from these finds the actual practice of *growing* crops. Spanish chroniclers in the interior Colorado Desert failed to mention farming or domesticated plants. But the ethnographic record for the Desert Cahuilla provides tantalizing clues that agricultural activities may have been entrenched among the Cahuilla before the arrival of Europeans.

The historic-era Desert Cahuilla grew species introduced by Spanish missionaries and American settlers, but their primary crops were the *native* species of corn, beans, and squash (Barrows 1900:71–73). Although the Spanish missionaries urged them to plant in neat, well-spaced rows, the Cahuilla grew their native crops in patches that precisely mirror practices found among Southwestern agriculturists. Furthermore, the missionaries introduced the use of the hoe for planting and weeding, yet the Cahuilla continued to use the traditional digging stick (Drucker 1937b:11). Moreover, corn, beans, and squash have native Cahuilla names (Bean and Saubel 1972:17–18). It seems unlikely that the Cahuilla would have adopted European agriculture from scratch without also adopting its techniques, tools, and vocabulary. Finally, plant domesticates—especially corn—are incorporated into Cahuilla creation stories (Lando and Modesto 1977:Table 3; Lawton 1974:72). In contrast, a survey of some 200 creation stories derived from missionized natives failed to find a single agricultural motif or mention of crop plants of any sort (Bean and Lawton 1993:35). Based on this evidence, some scholars are prepared to argue that Cahuillan agricultural practices stem from the pre-contact period. Perhaps future archaeological finds will reveal a more complete picture as we apply the paleobotanical and palynological methods that have enhanced investigations elsewhere in California.

California Indians also practiced intensive manipulations of the natural environment. Lightfoot and Parrish (2009:124–140) summarize various forms of landscape management practiced by certain tribes, including purposeful burning of vegetation to stimulate edible new growth (and to draw in game animals attracted to the wild plants), as well as pruning, weeding, and transplanting on a small scale in some areas. In their view, such practices were significant but quite distinct from what farmers do and should not be characterized as incipient or "proto-" agricultural practices. Other authors believe these activities are seriously underappreciated today, and they prefer to draw attention to their importance by using the term "protoagriculture" (Anderson 2005; Bendix 2002; Blackburn and Anderson 1993; Parker 2002; Weigel 1993). Whatever term we choose, it is noteworthy that most of California's oak species and several other major tree and shrub species are well adapted to surviving fires (Pavlik et al. 1991), leaving little or no downside to brush fires in California until the modern era.

Another case deemed protoagricultural by some proponents comes from the Owens Valley, where the growth of wild plants was encouraged by selective irrigation of plots among the ethnographic Owens Valley Paiute (Lawton et al. 1993). Purposeful burning (Parker 2002) and rudimentary irrigation can leave subtle archaeological signatures that are difficult to decipher, but these ethnographic practices were so firmly entrenched that it is a virtual certainty that they originated in the prehistoric era. These topics will provide fruitful study for the next generation of scholars.

Frontiers in Dating

Given the great importance of rock art throughout California, efforts to develop and refine current means for the direct dating of petroglyphs are warranted. Among the more promising are: (1) cation-ratio dating of rock varnish accumulated since pecked surfaces were created, and (2) counting microscopic lamina accrued since the rock was pecked (Dorn 1998, 2004).These are painstaking procedures, and are at least minimally destructive. Both require independent dating for verification of results, which of course defines the problem in the first place. But the rewards of direct dating of petroglyphs will be immense.

We point also to advances being made to enhance the accuracy of obsidian hydration dating. Archaeologists are continuing to test a technique that assesses molecular water content for single pieces of obsidian. In this procedure, each piece of obsidian is provided with its own unique hydration rate, which replaces the necessity to rely on a source-wide average (Friedman et al. 1997; Stevenson et al. 1993, 1998, 2000). The procedure requires critical but surmountable assumptions about ambient temperature and local humidity (Stevenson et al. 2000:230) and is further complicated by the context of discovery—especially the depth of the retrieved obsidian—and by changing climate throughout the Holocene. But the technique may be particularly valuable where source identification is impossible, or where source-wide hydration averages are undependable.

California's archaeologists have made good use of advances in radiocarbon dating, particularly in the sphere of AMS dating. Not only does AMS permit scholars to date very small amounts of carbon derived from sparse cultural deposits—as has been done with samples from Daisy Cave and Tule Lake—or to date rare or culturally sensitive finds, such as bones from Arlington Canyon (Johnson et al. 2000), but AMS also permits dating of inherently small *objects*, including shell beads and fishhooks (Fitzgerald et al. 2005; Koerper et al. 1995; Vellanoweth 2001). Because both beads and fishhooks have intrinsic potential as typological time-markers, absolute dates from selected type specimens have far-reaching benefits. California archaeologists have helped pioneer these kinds of studies, which have been furthered by advances in the calibration of the "reservoir effect," which impacts the reliability of radiocarbon dates derived from marine shell (Ingram 1998; Ingram and Southon 1996).

DNA and Geochemical Advances

A particularly prickly issue is the potential associated with the chemical analysis of human bone. Isotopic analyses of bone have proven immensely useful in reconstructing prehistoric diet (Bartelink 2009; Newsome et al. 2004). There is the possibility that DNA profiles extracted from ancient bones will provide insights into other important anthropological questions, including major population movements in California (Eshleman and Smith 2007). Ancient DNA might also yield significant information about relationships among neighboring polities, as among the San Francisco Bay mound villages or the mainland and island populations of the Santa Barbara region. Because of the sensitivity that must attend the treatment of human remains, progress in these areas will depend critically on the relationships between Native Americans and members of the archaeological community.

Of clear future importance will be the expanded use of geochemical sourcing of animal bone (e.g., trace element analysis searching for correspondence between regional soil chemistry and trace elements in bone) and ancient DNA analysis of animal remains from California's archaeological sites (Beck 2009). These methods can shed light on the natural history of various species—including invaluable information regarding the specific home ranges of captured individuals—and can be used to trace changing relationships between human populations and important game species across the millennia. Although the use of these techniques is growing among researchers in the far west who are studying salmon, mammoth, dog, otter, deer, and other fauna, such approaches are currently underutilized in California.

An Embarrassment of Riches: California's Colonial-Era Archaeology

This book is about pre-contact California, but the reader should be aware that the region has a fascinating and informative set of stories to tell from the era of early European colonization, more than enough for a separate volume. We count at least four main categories of post-contact archaeology, each with its own substantial literature. First we have the archaeology of California's tribes after Europeans arrived. Individuals of many groups continued to live in indigenous villages for generations into the "historic" era, and for some their lives paralleled the ways they had lived traditionally, although with modifications (such as adjustments to epidemics and intrusive technologies) to be sure. To note a few examples, archaeologists and ethnohistorians are documenting the households and communities of the Chumash and Wintu people, respectively, in the decades just after contact (e.g., Gamble 2008; Graesch 2004; Hildebrandt and Darcangelo 2008). Second, many tribal peoples were coerced or enticed to live directly in the shadows of European institutions, primarily under duress as laborer/neophytes at the 21 Franciscan missions from San Diego to San Francisco Bay. Archaeologists have documented significant impacts on native social organization, dietary practices, and technologies at these locations (e.g., Milliken 2008). Another major nexus of direct contact was at Colony Ross on the mid-northern coast, where Russian fur traders built Fort Ross in 1812. Over the ensuing several decades, they and the native Alaskan otter hunters they forced to join them co-resided with, and intermarried, local Pomo peoples. The intersections of foodways, technologies, and daily practices of the three cultures at Ross are fascinating (Lightfoot 2005).

Two other domains of historic archaeology focus more on colonial experiences. After the 1830s or so, many disparate activities led to diverse local histories (and differing impacts on native peoples). New developments included the deeding of large tracts of land (ranchos) up and down the state to wealthy men of Hispanic descent, and at many of these ranches, Indian labor fueled economic success (Silliman 2004). The famed California Gold Rush in 1848–49 brought thousands of Euroamericans into the western Sierra and in direct contact with interior tribes, with grave environmental and demographic results. A shameful and tragic era of genocide ensued. Archaeologists have documented many Gold Rush towns, mines, and other transformations of the landscape. And finally, nineteenth-century urban locales have attracted the interest of scholars seeking to document the emergence of unique ethnic sectors such as the large Chinatowns of San Francisco and Los Angeles.

Native American Heritage

Upon first meeting Ishi, Alfred Kroeber was aware that given names are a sacred thing to many Native Americans, not lightly spoken by others nor ever volunteered to strangers. Kroeber called him "Ishi," Yana for "man," a gracious act that Ishi recognized immediately and returned with lasting affection for Kroeber (Kroeber 1969:128). From that point on relationships with anthropologists—and especially archaeologists—went largely downhill. Strained if not hostile relationships ensued in some circles, but today, Native Californians are routinely incorporated into field operations and, in some cases, lab settings, not just to ensure that archaeological materials are properly handled, but also to provide insights and interpretations possibly not otherwise available to archaeologists.

An energetic set of Native American communities exists today in California and appears to be strengthening as elders are encouraging youngsters to learn native languages and lore, reinvigorating pride in ancestry and curiosity about tribal histories. As tribes are revitalized, Native American concerns and priorities play a growing role in research and salvage archaeology in the state. Many constituents of both sides recognize the potential gains to be had through collaboration, and tribal wealth from legalized gambling operations allows greater self determination and much more robust investment in heritage research. Despite a more alliance-oriented association of native and scientific interests overall, strong disputes that are difficult to resolve still arise over NAGPRA claims and the retention of human remains by institutions throughout the state. These ongoing problems are not unique to California.

Lessons Regarding Our Global Past and Future

Archaeology periodically has to burnish its image to stay relevant to a public sector increasingly absorbed in challenging global economic and environmental problems. California has a large and thriving Cultural Resources Management (CRM) industry that articulates far more frequently with governmental agencies and the business world than do most academic archaeologists. CRM generates a vast but not very accessible literature brimming with important, primary data essential to any good discussion of the region's archaeological record. Most practicing archaeologists in the state have experience in this domain (including the authors), and fully two-thirds of the contributors to a recent edited volume on California prehistory (Jones and

Klar 2007) are employed in the CRM sector. As landscape development intensifies, CRM will continue to be a large part of the public face of California archaeology and will play a crucial role in future heritage management. Continued watchful collaboration among academics, CRM leaders, tribal representatives, and the public will be required to preserve what remains of California's amazing archaeological heritage. Untold numbers of sites that remain are threatened by looting, erosion, shoreline loss due to sea-level rise, development, and a host of other processes. Fortunately, most federal and state agencies require project directors to be on the Register of Professional Archaeologists, which upholds important standards. We must all remember that the archaeological record is owned by all of us, and it is a non-renewable resource. The public must embrace the cause of preservation in order to save the past for the future.

Finally, serious concerns about the ramifications of earth's atmospheric warming have precipitated scientific and public interest in lessons we might learn from paleoclimatic data and past human experiences with climate change. California archaeologists are among scholars at the leading edge in studies of ancient environmental impacts wrought by human populations (Rick and Erlandson 2008, 2009). The systematic exploration of such ecological processes over the long term has been dubbed "historical ecology." Collections from exceptionally well-preserved sites in California are yielding archaeological data with great relevance in informing us about both ancient ecology and contemporary environmental problems.

* * *

Every part of North America has important archaeological resources. California's past encompasses some of North America's oldest sites, possibly yielding intriguing hints of evidence for a new and more complicated story about the peopling of the Americas. It also harbors perhaps the most striking cultural variability within any one of the continent's regions, reflecting the state's great ecological complexity. And it was home to several of the world's most populous and politically complex hunter-gatherer cultures, as well as those who ingeniously survived in some of the harshest deserts on the planet. Many living descendants of these people and all scholars and readers who treasure the past can celebrate their enduring legacy.

References

Agenbroad, Larry D., John R. Johnson, Don Morris, and Thomas W. Stafford, Jr.

2005 Mammoths and Humans as Late Pleistocene Contemporaries on Santa Rosa Island. In *Proceedings of the Sixth California Islands Conference*, edited by D. K. Garcelon and C. A. Schwemm, pp. 3–7. National Park Service Technical Publications CH15-05-01, Institute for Wildlife Studies, Arcata, California.

Allen, Mark W.

1998 Fort Irwin Archaeology: A Preserved Past for the Mojave Desert. *San Bernardino County Museum Association Quarterly* 45:124–142.

2010 Three Archaeological Landscapes of the Mojave B Range, China Lake Naval Air Weapons Center: Pilot Knob, Indian Spring, and North Eagle Crags. *Pacific Coast Archaeological Quarterly Special Publication* 43(1–2):26–41.

Altschul, Jeffrey H., Richard Ciolek-Torrello, Donn Grenda, Jeffrey A. Homberg, Su Benaron, and Anne Q. Stoll

2005 Ballona Archaeology: A Decade of Multidisciplinary Research. *Proceedings of the Society for California Archaeology* 18:283–301.

Ames, Kenneth M., and Herbert D. Maschner

1999 *Peoples of the Northwest Coast: Their Archaeology and Prehistory.* Thames and Hudson, London.

Anderson, M. Kat

2005 *Tending the Wild: Native American Knowledge and the Management of California's Natural Resources.* University of California Press, Berkeley.

Arnold, Jeanne E.

1987 *Craft Specialization in the Prehistoric Channel Islands, California.* University of California Press, Berkeley.

1992 Complex Hunter-Gatherer-Fishers of Prehistoric California: Chiefs, Specialists, and Maritime Adaptations of the Channel Islands. *American Antiquity* 57:60–84.

2001a The Chumash in World and Regional Perspectives. In *The Origins of a Pacific Coast Chiefdom: The Chumash of the Channel Islands*, edited by Jeanne E. Arnold, pp. 1–19. University of Utah Press, Salt Lake City.

2001b The Channel Islands Project: History, Objectives, and Methods. In *The Origins of a Pacific Coast Chiefdom: The Chumash of the Channel Islands*, edited by Jeanne E. Arnold, pp. 21–52. University of Utah Press, Salt Lake City.

2001c Social Evolution and the Political Economy in the Northern Channel Islands. In *The Origins of a Pacific Coast Chiefdom: The Chumash of the Channel Islands*, edited by Jeanne E. Arnold, pp. 287–296. University of Utah Press, Salt Lake City.

2007 Credit Where Credit is Due: The History of the Chumash Oceangoing Plank Canoe. *American Antiquity* 72:196–209.

2009 The Role of Politically Charged Property in the Appearance of Institutionalized Leadership: A View from the North American Pacific Coast. In *The Evolution of Leadership: Transitions in Decision Making from Small-Scale to Middle-Range Societies*, edited by Kevin J. Vaughn, Jelmer W. Eerkens, and John Kantner, pp. 121-146. School of Advanced Research Press, Santa Fe, New Mexico.

Arnold, Jeanne E. (editor)

2001 *The Origins of a Pacific Coast Chiefdom: The Chumash of the Channel Islands*. University of Utah Press, Salt Lake City.

2004 *Foundations of Chumash Complexity*. Cotsen Institute of Archaeology, University of California, Los Angeles.

Arnold, Jeanne E., and Julienne Bernard

2005 Negotiating the Coasts: Status and the Evolution of Boat Technology in California. *World Archaeology* 37:109–131.

Arnold, Jeanne E., and Anthony P. Graesch

2001 The Evolution of Specialized Shellworking among the Island Chumash. In *The Origins of a Pacific Coast Chiefdom: The Chumash of the Channel Islands*, edited by Jeanne E. Arnold, pp. 71–112. University of Utah Press, Salt Lake City.

2004 The Later Evolution of the Island Chumash. In *Foundations of Chumash Complexity*, edited by Jeanne E. Arnold, pp.1–16. Cotsen Institute of Archaeology, University of California, Los Angeles.

Arnold, Jeanne E., and Terisa M. Green

2002 Mortuary Ambiguity: The Ventureño Chumash Case. *American Antiquity* 67:760–771.

Arnold, Jeanne E., and Ann Munns

1994 Independent or Attached Specialization: The Organization of Shell Bead Production in California. *Journal of Field Archaeology* 21:473–489.

Arnold, Jeanne E., Aimee M. Preziosi, and Paul Shattuck

2001 Flaked Stone Craft Production and Exchange in Island Chumash Territory. In *The Origins of a Pacific Coast Chiefdom: The Chumash of the Channel Islands*, edited by Jeanne E. Arnold, pp. 113–131. University of Utah Press, Salt Lake City.

Arnold, Jeanne E., and Diana Rachal

2002 The Value of Pismo Clam Tube Beads in California: Experiments in Drilling. *North American Archaeologist* 23(3):187–207.

Arnold, Jeanne E., and Brian Tissot

1993 Measurement of Significant Marine Paleotemperature Variation Using Black Abalone Shells from Prehistoric Middens. *Quaternary Research* 39:390–394.

Arnold, Jeanne E., Michael R. Walsh, and Sandra E. Holliman

2004 The Archaeology of California. *Journal of Archaeological Research* 12:1–73.

Atwater, Brian F., Edward J. Helley, and Charles W. Hedel
1977 Late Quaternary Depositional History, Holocene Sea Level Changes, and Vertical Crustal Movement, Southern San Francisco Bay, California. *United States Geological Survey Professional Papers* 1014:1–15.
Atwater, Brian F., Susan G. Conard, James N. Dowden, Charles W. Hedel, Roderick L. MacDonald, and Wayne Savage
1979 History, Landforms, and Vegetation of the Estuary's Tidal Marshes. In *San Francisco Bay: The Urbanized Estuary*, edited by T. J. Conomos, pp. 347–381. American Association for the Advancement of Science, Pacific Division, San Francisco.
Backes, Clarus J., Jr.
2004 More Than Meets the Eye: Fluorescence Photography for Enhanced Analysis of Pictographs. *Journal of California and Great Basin Anthropology* 24:193–206.
Barrett, Samuel A.
1908 The Ethnography of the Pomo and Neighboring Indians. *University of California Publications in American Archaeology and Ethnology* 6:1–332. Berkeley.
Barrows, David Prescott
1900 *The Ethno-Botany of the Coahuilla Indians of Southern California.* University of Chicago Press, Chicago. Reprinted by Malki Museum Press, Banning, California, 1977.
Bartelink, Eric J.
2009 Late Holocene Dietary Change in the San Francisco Bay Area: Stable Isotope Evidence for an Expansion in Diet Breadth. *California Archaeology* 1:227-251.
Basgall, Mark E.
1987 Resource Intensification among Hunter-Gatherers: Acorn Economies in Prehistoric California. *Research in Economic Anthropology* 9:21–52.
1993 Early Holocene Prehistory of the North-Central Mojave Desert. Unpublished Ph.D. dissertation, Department of Anthropology, University of California, Davis.
2000a The Structure of Archaeological Landscapes in the North-Central Mojave Desert. In *Archaeological Passages: A Volume in Honor of Claude Nelson Warren*, edited by Joan S. Schneider, Robert M. Yohe II, and Jill K. Gardner, pp. 123–138. Western Center for Archaeology and Paleontology Publications in Archaeology, No. 1, Hemet, California.
2000b Patterns of Tool Use in Late Pleistocene/Early-Holocene Assemblages of the Mojave Desert. *Current Research in the Pleistocene* 17:4–6.
2005 *Another Look at the Ancient Californians: Resurvey of the Emma Lou Davis Stake Areas and Reassessment of Collections, Naval Air Weapons Station, China Lake, Kern County, California.* Report submitted to the Naval Air Weapons Station, Environmental Area, China Lake, California.
Basgall, Mark E., and Michael G. Delacorte
2003 *Phase II Evaluations at Nine Archaeological Sites Near Independence, Inyo County, California.* Archaeological Research Center Technical Report 02-59. Department of Anthropology, California State University, Sacramento.

Bayman, James N., Richard H. Hevly, Roma Johnson, Karl J. Reinhard, and Richard Ryan
1996 Analytical Perspectives on a Protohistoric Cache of Ceramic Jars from the Lower Colorado Desert. *Journal of California and Great Basin Anthropology* 18:131–154.

Bean, Lowell J.
1978 Cahuilla. In *California,* edited by Robert F. Heizer, pp. 575–587. Handbook of North American Indians, vol. 8, William C. Sturtevant, general editor. Smithsonian Institution, Washington, D.C.

Bean, Lowell J., and Harry Lawton
1993 Some Explanations for the Rise of Cultural Complexity in Native California with Comments on Proto-Agriculture and Agriculture. In *Before the Wilderness: Environmental Management by Native Californians,* edited by Thomas C. Blackburn and Kat Anderson, pp. 27–54. Ballena Press, Menlo Park, California.

Bean, Lowell J., and Katherine S. Saubel
1972 *Tamalpakh: Cahuilla Indian Knowledge and Usage of Plants.* Malki Press, Banning, California.

Bean, Lowell J., and Charles R. Smith
1978 Serrano. In *California,* edited by Robert F. Heizer, pp. 570–574. Handbook of North American Indians, vol. 8, William C. Sturtevant, general editor. Smithsonian Institution, Washington, D.C.

Bean, Lowell J., and Dorothea Theodoratus
1978 Western Pomo and Northeastern Pomo. In *California*, edited by Robert F. Heizer, pp. 289–305. Handbook of North American Indians, vol. 8, William C. Sturtevant, general editor. Smithsonian Institution, Washington, D.C.

Beaton, John M.
1991a Paleoindian Occupation Greater than 11,000 Years BP at Tule Lake, Northern California. *Current Research in the Pleistocene* 8:5–7.
1991b Extensification and Intensification in Central California Prehistory. *Antiquity* 65:947–951.

Beck, R. Kelly
2009 The Molecular Genetics of Prey Choice: Using Ancient DNA to Infer Prehistoric Population Histories. *California Archaeology* 1:253–268.

Beck, Charlotte, and George T. Jones
1997 The Terminal Pleistocene/Early Holocene Archaeology of the Great Basin. *Journal of World Prehistory* 11:161–236.

Bellifemine, Viviana
1997 Mortuary Variability in Prehistoric Central California: A Statistical Study of the Yukisma Site, CA-SCL-38. Unpublished Master's thesis, Department of Interdisciplinary Studies, San Jose State University, California.

Bendix, Jacob
2002 Pre-European Fire in California Chaparral. In *Fire, Native Peoples, and the Natural Landscape,* edited by Thomas R. Vale, pp. 269–293. Island Press, Washington, D.C.

Bennyhoff, James A.
1950 California Fish Spears and Harpoons. *University of California Anthropological Records* 9(4). Berkeley.

1994a Variation within the Meganos Culture. In *Toward a New Taxonomic Framework for Central California Archaeology*, edited by Richard E. Hughes, pp. 15–24. Contributions of the University of California Archaeological Research Facility, No. 52, Berkeley.

1994b A Delta Intrusion to the Bay in the Late Middle Period in Central California. In *Toward a New Taxonomic Framework for California Archaeology: Essays by James A. Bennyhoff and David A. Fredrickson*, edited by Richard E. Hughes, pp. 7–13. Contributions of the University of California Archaeological Research Facility, No. 52, Berkeley.

Bennyhoff, James A., and David A. Fredrickson

1994 A Proposed Integrative Taxonomic System for Central California Archaeology. In *Toward a New Taxonomic Framework for California Archaeology: Essays by James A. Bennyhoff and David A. Fredrickson*, edited by Richard E. Hughes, pp. 15–24. Contributions of the University of California Archaeological Research Facility, No. 52, Berkeley.

Bennyhoff, James A., and Richard E. Hughes

1987 Shell Bead and Ornament Exchange Networks between California and the Western Great Basin. *Anthropological Papers of the American Museum of Natural History* 64:79–175.

Benson, L. V.

2004 Western Lakes. In *The Quaternary Period of the United States*, edited by A. Gillespie, S. Porter, and B. F. Atwater, pp. 185–204. Elsevier, Amsterdam.

Berger, Rainer, and Reiner Protsch

1989 UCLA Radiocarbon Dates XI. *Radiocarbon* 31:55–67.

Bernard, Julienne

2004 Status and the Swordfish: The Origins of Large-Species Fishing among the Chumash. In *Foundations of Chumash Complexity*, edited by Jeanne E. Arnold, pp.25–51. Cotsen Institute of Archaeology, University of California, Los Angeles.

Bettinger, Robert L.

1999 From Traveler to Processor: Regional Trajectories of Hunter-Gatherer Sedentism in the Inyo-Mono Region, California. In *Settlement Pattern Studies in the Americas: Fifty Years since Viru*, edited by Brian R. Billman and Gary F. Feinman, pp. 39–55. Smithsonian Institution, Washington, D.C.

Bettinger, Robert L., Bruce Winterhalder, and Richard McElreath

2006 A Simple Model of Technological Intensification. *Journal of Archaeological Science* 33:538–545.

Bickel, Polly McW.

1978 Changing Sea Levels along the California Coast: Anthropological Implications. *Journal of California Anthropology* 5:6–20.

1981 *San Francisco Bay Archaeology: Sites Ala-328, Ala-13, and Ala-12.* Contributions of the University of California Archaeological Research Facility, No. 43, Berkeley.

Bieling, David. J., Roger M. La Jeunesse, and John H. Pryor

1996 Skyrocket, a Central Sierran Paleoindian Archaic Transition Site. *Current Research in the Pleistocene* 13:4–6.

Blackburn, Thomas C. (editor)
1975 *December's Child: A Book of Chumash Oral Narratives*. University of California Press, Berkeley.
Blackburn, Thomas C., and Kat Anderson (editors)
1993 *Before the Wilderness: Environmental Management by Native Californians*. Ballena Press, Menlo Park, California.
Bocek, Barbara
1986 Rodent Ecology and Burrowing Behavior: Predicted Effects on Archaeological Site Formation. *American Antiquity* 51:589–603.
Braje, Todd J., Douglas J. Kennett, Jon M. Erlandson, and Brendan J. Culleton
2007 Human Impacts on Nearshore Shellfish Taxa: A 7,000 Year Record from Santa Rosa Island, California. *American Antiquity* 72:735–756.
Breschini, Gary S., and Trudy Haversat
2004 *The Esselen Indians of the Big Sur Country: The Land and the People*. Coyote Press, Salinas, California.
Broughton, Jack M.
1994a Declines in Mammalian Foraging Efficiency during the Late Holocene, San Francisco Bay, California. *Journal of Anthropological Archaeology* 13:371–401.
1994b Late Holocene Resource Intensification in the Sacramento Valley, California: The Vertebrate Evidence. *Journal of Archaeological Science* 21:501–514.
1997 Widening Diet Breadth, Declining Foraging Efficiency, and Prehistoric Harvest Pressure: Ichthyofaunal Evidence from the Emeryville Shellmound, California. *Antiquity* 71:845–862.
1999 *Resource Depression and Intensification During the Late Holocene, San Francisco Bay: Evidence from the Emeryville Shellmound Vertebrate Fauna*. University of California Anthropological Records, No. 32, Berkeley.
2001 Resource Intensification and Late Holocene Human Impacts on Pacific Coast Bird Populations: Evidence from the Emeryville Shellmound Avifauna.In *Posing Questions for a Scientific Archaeology*, edited by Terry L. Hunt, Carl P. Lippo, and Sarah L. Sterling, pp. 251–278. Bergin and Garvey, Westport, Connecticut.
Broughton, Jack M. (editor)
1996 *Excavation of the Emeryville Shellmound, 1906: Nels C. Nelson's Final Report*. Contributions of the University of California Archaeological Research Facility, No. 54, Berkeley.
Broughton, Jack M., and Frank E. Bayham
2003 Showing Off, Foraging Models, and the Ascendance of Large-Game Hunting in the California Middle Archaic. *American Antiquity* 68:783–789.
Broughton, Jack M., Daniel Mullins, and Tamara Ekker
2007 Avian Resource Depression or Intertaxonomic Variation in Bone Density? A Test with San Francisco Bay Avifaunas. *Journal of Archaeological Science* 34:374–391.
Burk, Jack H.
1995 Sonoran Desert Vegetation. In *Terrestrial Vegetation of California,* edited by Michael G. Barbour and Jack Major, pp. 869–889. California Native Plant Society Special Publication, No. 9, Sacramento.

Byrd, Brian F.
1998 Harvesting the Littoral Landscape during the Late Holocene: New Perspectives from Northern San Diego County. *Journal of California and Great Basin Anthropology* 20:195–218.

Byrd, Brian F., and L. Mark Raab
2007 Prehistory of the Southern Bight: Models for a New Millennium. In *California Prehistory: Colonization, Culture, and Complexity*, edited by Terry L. Jones and Kathryn A. Klar, pp. 215–227. AltaMira Press, Lanham, Maryland.

Byrd, Brian F., and Seetha N. Reddy
2002 Late Holocene Adaptations along the Northern San Diego Coast: New Perspectives on Old Paradigms. In *Catalysts to Complexity: Late Holocene Societies of the California Coast*, edited by Jon M. Erlandson and Terry L. Jones, pp. 41–62. Cotsen Institute of Archaeology, University of California, Los Angeles.

Cabana, Graciela S., Keith Hunley, and Frederika A. Kaestle
2008 Population Continuity or Replacement? A Novel Computer Simulation Approach and its Application to the Numic Expansion (Western Great Basin, USA). *American Journal of Physical Anthropology* 135:438–447.

Cameron, Constance (editor)
2000 The Archaeology of San Clemente Island, Part 1 and 2 (special issue). *Pacific Coast Archaeological Society Quarterly* 36(1&2).

Cannon, Michael D.
2009 When Should We Expect to See Hunting as Mating Effort? *California Archaeology* 1:79–92.

Cassidy, Jim, L. Mark Raab, and Nina A. Kononenko
2004 Boats, Bones, and Biface Bias: The Early Holocene Mariners of Eel Point, San Clemente Island, California. *American Antiquity* 69:109–130.

Chartkoff, Joseph L.
1990 Cracking and Grinding, Chipping and Swapping: Summers on Skunk Creek. *Proceedings of the Society for California Archaeology* 5:21–34.

Chartkoff, Joseph L., and Kerry Kona Chartkoff
1984 *The Archaeology of California.* Stanford University Press, Palo Alto, California.

Chase-Dunn, Christopher, and Kelly M. Mann
1998 *The Wintu and their Neighbors: A Very Small World-System in Northern California.* University of Arizona, Tucson.

Christensen, Don D., and Jerry Dickey
2004 An Overview of Rock Art Research in the East Mojave Desert. In *The Human Journey and Ancient Life in California's Deserts: Proceedings from the 2001 Millennium Conference*, edited by Mark W. Allen and Judyth Reed, pp. 25–38. Maturango Museum Publication No. 15. Ridgecrest, California.

Clemmer, Richard O.
2009 Pristine Aborigines or Victims of Progress? The Western Shoshone in the Anthropological Imagination. *Current Anthropology* 50:849–881.

Clemmer, Richard O., L. Daniel Myers, and Mary Elizabeth Rudden (editors)
1999 *Julian Steward and the Great Basin: The Making of an Anthropologist.* University of Utah Press, Salt Lake City.

Codding, Brian F., and Terry L. Jones
2007 Man the Showoff? Or the Ascendance of a Just-So-Story: A Comment on Recent Applications of Costly Signaling Theory in American Archaeology. *American Antiquity* 72:349–357.
Colten, Roger H., and Jeanne E. Arnold
1998 Prehistoric Marine Mammal Hunting on California's Northern Channel Islands. *American Antiquity* 63:679–701.
Connick, Francis
2002 Some Kachina Masks among Petroglyph Images in the Mojave Desert and in the Coso Range. In *Rock Art Papers Vol. 15*, edited by Ken Hedges, pp. 55–64. San Diego Museum Papers, No. 39. San Diego.
Cook, Sherburne F.
1978 Historical Demography. In *California,* edited by Robert F. Heizer, pp. 91–98. Handbook of North American Indians, Vol. 8, William C. Sturtevant, general editor, Smithsonian Institution, Washington, D.C.
Davis, James T.
1960 The Archaeology of the Fernandez Site, a San Francisco Bay Region Shellmound. *University of California Archaeological Survey Reports* 49:11–53. Berkeley.
Davis, James T., and Aden E. Treganza
1959 The Patterson Mound: A Comparative Analysis of the Archaeology of Site Ala-328. *University of California Archaeological Survey Reports* 47:1–92. Berkeley.
Davis, Owen K.
1999 Pollen Analysis of Tulare Lake, California: Great Basin-Like Vegetation in Central California During the Full-Glacial and Early Holocene. *Review of Palaeobotany and Palynology* 107:249–257.
Delacorte, Michael G., Matthew C. Hall, and Mark E. Basgall
1995 *Final Report on the Evaluation of Twelve Archaeological Sites in the Southern Owens Valley, Inyo County, California.* Submitted to California Department of Transportation, District 9, Bishop, California.
Dietler, John E.
2003 The Specialist Next Door: Microblade Production and Status in Island Chumash Households. Unpublished Masters thesis, Department of Anthropology, University of California, Los Angeles.
Dillon, Brian D.
2002 California Paleoindians: Lack of Evidence or Evidence of Lack? In *Essays in California Archaeology: A Memorial to Franklin Fenenga*, edited by William J. Wallace and Francis A. Riddell, pp. 110–128. Contributions of the University of California Archaeological Research Facility, No. 60, Berkeley.
Donald, Leland
1997 *Aboriginal Slavery on the Northwest Coast of North America.* University of California Press, Berkeley.
Dorn, Ronald I.
1998 Age Determination of the Coso Rock Art. In *Coso Rock Art: A New Perspective*, edited by Elva Younkin, pp. 69–96. Maturango Museum. Ridgecrest, California.

2004 Experimental Approaches to Dating Petroglyphs and Geoglyphs with Rock Varnish in the California Deserts: Current Status and Future Directions. In *The Human Journey and Ancient Life in California's Deserts: Proceedings from the 2001 Millennium Conference*, edited by Mark W. Allen and Judyth Reed, pp. 211–224. Maturango Museum Publication, No. 15, Ridgecrest, California.

Douglas, Charles L., Dennis L. Jenkins, and Claude N. Warren

1988 Spatial and Temporal Variability in Faunal Remains from Four Lake Mojave-Pinto Period Sites in the Mojave Desert. In *Early Human Occupation in Far Western North America: The Clovis-Archaic Interface*, edited by Judith A. Willig, C. Melvin Aikens, and John L. Fagan, pp. 131–144. Nevada State Museum Anthropological Papers, No. 21, Carson City.

Dowdall, Katherine M.

2002 Late Holocene Cultural Diversity on the Sonoma Coast. In *Catalysts to Complexity: Late Holocene Societies of the California Coast*, edited by Jon M. Erlandson and Terry L. Jones, pp. 282–302. Cotsen Institute of Archaeology, University of California, Los Angeles.

Drucker, Philip

1937a The Tolowa and their Southwest Oregon Kin. *University of California Publications in American Archaeology and Ethnology* 36(4):221–300. Berkeley.

1937b Culture Element Distributions: Southern California. *University of California Anthropological Records* 1:1–52. Berkeley.

Earle, David D.

2004 Native Population and Settlement in the Western Mojave Desert in the 18th and 19th Centuries. In *The Human Journey and Ancient Life in California's Deserts: Proceedings from the 2001 Millennium Conference*, edited by Mark W. Allen and Judyth Reed, pp. 173–186. Maturango Museum Publication, No. 15, Ridgecrest, California.

Eerkens, Jelmer W.

2001 The Origins of Pottery among Late Prehistoric Hunter-Gatherers in California and the Western Great Basin. Unpublished Ph.D. dissertation, Department of Anthropology, University of California, Santa Barbara.

2003a Sedentism, Storage, and the Intensification of Small Seeds: Prehistoric Developments in Owens Valley, California. *North American Archaeologist* 24:281–309.

2003b Towards a Chronology of Brownware Pottery in the Western Great Basin: A Case Study from Owens Valley. *North American Archaeologist* 24:1–27.

2003c Residential Mobility and Pottery Use in the Western Great Basin. *Current Anthropology* 44:728–738.

2004 Privatization, Small-Seed Intensification, and the Origins of Pottery in the Western Great Basin. *American Antiquity* 69:653–670.

Eerkens, Jelmer W., Gregory S. Herbert, Jeffrey S. Rosenthal, and Howard J. Spero

2005 Provenance Analysis of *Olivella biplicata* Shell Beads from the California and Oregon Coast by Stable Isotope Fingerprinting. *Journal of Archaeological Science* 32:1501–1514.

Eerkens, Jelmer W., Jay King, and Eric Wohlgemuth

2004 The Prehistoric Development of Intensive Green-Cone Piñon Processing in Eastern California. *Journal of Field Archaeology* 29:17–27.

Eerkens, Jelmer W., Hector Neff, and Michael D. Glasscock
2002 Ceramic Production among Small-Scale and Mobile Hunters and Gatherers: A Case Study from the Southwestern Great Basin. *Journal of Anthropological Archaeology* 21:200–229.
Eerkens, Jelmer W., and Jeffrey S. Rosenthal
2004 Are Obsidian Subsources Meaningful Units of Analysis? Temporal and Spatial Patterning of Subsources in the Coso Volcanic Field, Southeastern California. *Journal of Archaeological Science* 31:21–29.
Eerkens, Jelmer W., Jeffrey Rosenthal, D. Craig Young, and Jay King
2007 Early Holocene Landscape Archaeology in the Coso Basin, Northwestern Mojave Desert, California. *North American Archaeologist* 28:87–112.
Eerkens, Jelmer W., and Amy M. Spurling
2008 Obsidian Acquisition and Exchange Networks: A Diachronic Perspective on Households in the Owens Valley. *Journal of California and Great Basin Anthropology* 28:111–126.
Eerkens, Jelmer W., Amy M. Spurling, and Michelle A. Gras
2008 Measuring Prehistoric Mobility Strategies Based on Obsidian Geochemical and Technological Signatures in the Owens Valley, California. *Journal of Archaeological Science* 35:668–680.
Elsasser, Albert B., and Robert F. Heizer
1964 Archaeology of HUM-67, the Gunther Island Site in Humboldt Bay, California. *University of California Archaeological Survey Reports* 65:5–122. Berkeley.
1966 Excavation of Two Northwestern California Coastal Sites. *University of California Archaeological Survey Reports* 67:1–149. Berkeley.
Ericson, Jonathon E., and Michael D. Glascock
2004 Subsource Characterization: Obsidian Utilization of Subsources of the Coso Volcanic Field, Coso Junction, California, USA. *Geoarchaeology* 19:779–805.
Erlandson, Jon M.
1993 Evidence for a Terminal Pleistocene Human Occupation of Daisy Cave, San Miguel Island, California. *Current Research in the Pleistocene* 10:17–21.
1994 *Early Hunter-Gatherers of the California Coast*. Plenum, New York.
1997 The Middle Holocene on the Western Santa Barbara Coast. In *Archaeology of the California Coast during the Middle Holocene*, edited by Jon M. Erlandson and Michael A. Glassow, pp. 91–109. Cotsen Institute of Archaeology, University of California, Los Angeles.
2002 Anatomically Modern Humans, Maritime Voyaging, and the Pleistocene Colonization of the Americas. In *The First Americans: The Pleistocene Colonization of the New World*, edited by Nina G. Jablonski, pp. 59–92. Memoirs of the California Academy of Sciences, No. 27. San Francisco.
Erlandson, Jon M., and Todd J. Braje
2008a A Chipped Stone Crescent from CA-SMI-681, San Miguel Island, California. *Journal of California and Great Basin Anthropology* 28:184–188.
2008b Five Crescents from Cardwell: Context and Chronology of Chipped Stone Crescents from CA-SMI-679. *Pacific Coast Archaeological Society Quarterly* 40:35–45.

Erlandson, Jon M., and Roger H. Colten
1991 An Archaeological Context for Early Holocene Studies on the California Coast. In *Hunter-Gatherers of Early Holocene Coastal California,* edited by Jon M. Erlandson and Roger H. Colten, pp. 1–10. Institute of Archaeology, University of California, Los Angeles.

Erlandson, Jon M., and Terry L. Jones (editors)
2002 *Catalysts to Complexity: Late Holocene Societies of the California Coast.* Cotsen Institute of Archaeology, University of California, Los Angeles.

Erlandson, Jon M., Douglas J. Kennett, B. Lynn Ingram, Daniel A. Guthrie, Don P. Morris, Mark A. Tveskov, G. James West, and Phillip L. Walker
1996 An Archaeological and Paleontological Chronology for Daisy Cave (CA-SMI-261), San Miguel Island, California. *Radiocarbon* 38:355–373.

Erlandson, Jon M., and Torben C. Rick
2002 Late Holocene Cultural Developments along the Santa Barbara Coast. In *Catalysts to Complexity: Late Holocene Societies of the California Coast,* edited by Jon M. Erlandson and Terry L. Jones, pp. 166–182. Cotsen Institute of Archaeology, University of California, Los Angeles.

Erlandson, Jon M., Torben C. Rick, and Melissa R. Batterson
2004 Busted Balls Shell Midden (CA-SMI-606): An Early Coastal Site on San Miguel Island, California. *North American Archaeologist* 25:251–272.

Erlandson, Jon M., Torben C. Rick, Todd J. Braje, Alexis Steinberg, and René L. Vellanoweth
2008 Human Impacts on Ancient Shellfish: A 10,000 Year Record from San Miguel Island, California. *Journal of Archaeological Science* 35:2144–2152.

Erlandson, Jon M., Torben C. Rick, Terry L. Jones, and Judith F. Porcasi
2007 One If by Land, Two If by Sea: Who Were the First Californians? In *California Prehistory: Colonization, Culture, and Complexity,* edited by Terry L. Jones and Kathryn A. Klar, pp. 53–62. AltaMira Press, Lanham, Maryland.

Erlandson, Jon M., Torben C. Rick, and René L. Vellanoweth
2008 *A Canyon through Time: The Archaeology, History, and Ecology of the Tecolote Canyon Area, Santa Barbara County, California.* University of Utah Press, Salt Lake City.

Eshleman, Jason A., and David Glenn Smith
2007 Prehistoric Mitochondrial DNA and Population Movements. In *California Prehistory: Colonization, Culture, and Complexity,* edited by Terry L. Jones and Kathryn A. Klar, pp. 291–298. AltaMira Press, Lanham, Maryland.

Fagan, Brian
2004 The House of the Sea: An Essay on the Antiquity of Planked Canoes in Southern California. *American Antiquity* 69:7–16.

Fenenga, Gerrit L.
1991 A Preliminary Examination of Faunal Remains from Early Sites in the Tulare Lake Basin. In *Contributions to Tulare Lake Archaeology I: Background to a Study of Tulare Lake's Archaeological Past,* edited by William J. Wallace and Francis A. Riddell, pp. 11–22. Tulare Lake Archaeological Research Group, Coyote Press, Salinas, California.

1992 Regional Variability in the Early Prehistory of the American Far West. Unpublished Ph.D. dissertation, Department of Anthropology, University of California, Berkeley.

Fitzgerald, Richard T., Jr.

1993 *Archaic Milling Cultures of the Southern San Francisco Bay Region.* Coyote Press Archives of California Prehistory 35. Salinas, California.

Fitzgerald, Richard T., and William R. Hildebrandt

2002 Early Holocene Adaptations of the North Coast Ranges: New Perspectives on Old Ideas. *Proceedings of the Society for California Archaeology* 15:1–7.

Fitzgerald, Richard T., and Terry L. Jones

1999 The Milling Stone Horizon Revisited: New Perspectives from Northern and Central California. *Journal of California and Great Basin Anthropology* 21:65–93.

Fitzgerald, Richard T., Terry L. Jones, and Adella Schroth

2005 Ancient Long-Distance Trade in Western North America: New AMS Radiocarbon Dates in Southern California. *Journal of Archaeological Science* 32:423–434.

Fredrickson, David A.

1973 Early Cultures of the North Coast Ranges, California. Unpublished Ph.D. dissertation, Department of Anthropology, University of California, Davis.

1994 Changes in Prehistoric Exchange Systems in the Alamo Locality, Contra Costa County, California. In *Toward a New Taxonomic Framework for Central California Archaeology: Essays by James A. Bennyhoff and David A. Fredrickson*, edited by Richard E. Hughes, pp. 57–64. Contributions of the University of California Archaeological Research Facility, No. 52, Berkeley.

1996 Obsidian Studies, Social Boundaries, Theoretical Models, and the Development of Tribelet Structure in Central California. *Proceedings of the Society for California Archaeology* 9:25–29.

1997 Review. *Journal of California and Great Basin Anthropology* 19:294–297.

Fredrickson, David A., and Joel W. Grossman

1977 A San Dieguito Component at Buena Vista Lake, California. *Journal of California Anthropology* 4:173–190.

Fredrickson, David A., and Thomas M. Origer

2002 Obsidian Hydration in the Borax Lake Basin, Lake County, California. In, *Essays in California Archaeology: A Memorial to Franklin Fenenga,* edited by William J. Wallace, and Francis A. Riddell, pp. 148–165. Contributions of the University of California Archaeological Research Facility No. 60, Berkeley.

Friedman, Irving, Fred W. Trembour, and Richard E. Hughes

1997 Obsidian Hydration Dating. In *Chronometric Dating in Archaeology*, edited by R. E. Taylor and Martin J. Aitken, pp. 297–321. Plenum Press Advances in Archaeological and Museum Studies, vol. 2, New York.

Gallegos, Dennis R.

1991 Antiquity and Adaptation at Agua Hedionda, Carlsbad, California. In *Hunter-Gatherers of Early Holocene Coastal California*, edited by Jon M. Erlandson and Roger H. Colten, pp. 19–41. Institute of Archaeology, University of California, Los Angeles.

Gamble, Lynn
2008 *The Chumash World at European Contact: Power, Trade, and Feasting among Complex Hunter-Gatherers.* University of California Press, Berkeley.
Gamble, Lynn, and Chester King
1997 Middle Holocene Adaptations in the Santa Monica Mountains. In *Archaeology of the California Coast during the Middle Holocene,* edited by Jon M. Erlandson and Michael A. Glassow, pp. 61–72. Cotsen Institute of Archaeology, University of California, Los Angeles.
Gamble, Lynn, Phillip L. Walker, and Glenn Russell
2001 An Integrative Approach to Mortuary Analysis: Social and Symbolic Dimensions of Chumash Burial Practices. *American Antiquity* 66:185–212.
Gardner, Jill K.
2002 *Testing a Regional Model of Changing Settlement and Subsistence Patterns in the Western Mojave Desert: Results from the Coffee Break Site.* Coyote Press Archives of Great Basin Prehistory, No. 6, Salinas, California.
2006 The Potential Impact of the Medieval Climatic Anomaly on Human Populations in the Western Mojave Desert. Unpublished Ph.D. dissertation, Department of Anthropology, University of Nevada, Las Vegas.
Garfinkel, Alan P.
2006 Paradigm Shifts, Rock Art Studies, and the "Coso Sheep Cult" of Eastern California. *North American Archaeologist* 27:244–206.
Garfinkel, Alan P., David A. Young, and Robert M. Yohe II
2010 Bighorn Hunting, Resource Depression, and Rock Art in the Coso Range, Eastern California: A Computer Simulation Model. *Journal of Archaeological Science* 37:42–51.
Gerow, Bert A. with Roland W. Force
1968 *An Analysis of the University Village Complex with a Reappraisal of Central California Archaeology.* Stanford University Press, Palo Alto, California.
Giambastiani, Mark A., and Thomas Bullard
2010 Terminal Pleistocene-Early Holocene Occupations on the Eastern Shoreline of China Lake, California. *Pacific Coast Archaeological Society Special Publication* 43(1–2):50–70.
Gifford, E. W.
1926 Clear Lake Pomo Society. *University of California Publications in American Archaeology and Ethnography* 18(2):287–390. Berkeley.
1940 Californian Bone Artifacts. *University of California Anthropological Records* 3:153-237. Berkeley.
Gilreath, Amy J.
1998 *National Register of Historic Places: Registration for the Coso Rock Art District.* Submitted to Naval Air Weapons Station, China Lake, California. Copies available at Naval Air Weapons Station, China Lake, California.
1999 The Archaeology and Petroglyphs of the Coso Rock Art Landmark. *American Indian Rock Art* 25:33–44.
2007 Rock Art in the Golden State: Pictographs and Petroglyphs, Portable and Panoramic. In *California Prehistory: Colonization, Culture, and Complexity,* edited

by Terry L. Jones and Kathryn A. Klar, pp. 273–290. AltaMira Press, Lanham, Maryland.

Gilreath, Amy J., and William R. Hildebrandt

1997 *Prehistoric Use of the Coso Volcanic Field.* Contributions of the University of California Archaeological Research Facility, No. 56, University of California, Berkeley.

2008 Coso Rock Art Within Its Archaeological Context. *Journal of California and Great Basin Anthropology* 28:1–22.

Glassow, Michael A.

1996 *Purisimeño Chumash Prehistory: Maritime Adaptations along the Southern California Coast.* Harcourt Brace, Fort Worth, Texas.

1997a Middle Holocene Cultural Development in the Central Santa Barbara Channel Region. In *Archaeology of the California Coast during the Middle Holocene,* edited by Jon M. Erlandson and Michael A. Glassow, pp. 73–90. Cotsen Institute of Archaeology, University of California, Los Angeles.

1997b Research Issues of Importance to Coastal California Archaeology of the Middle Holocene. In *Archaeology of the California Coast during the Middle Holocene,* edited by Jon M. Erlandson and Michael A. Glassow, pp. 151–161. Cotsen Institute of Archaeology, University of California, Los Angeles.

2004 Identifying Complexity during the Early Prehistory of Santa Cruz Island, California. In *Foundations of Chumash Complexity,* edited by Jeanne E. Arnold, pp. 17–24. Cotsen Institute of Archaeology, University of California, Los Angeles.

Glassow, Michael A., Lynn H. Gamble, Jennifer E. Perry, and Glenn S. Russell

2007 Prehistory of the Northern California Bight and the adjacent Transverse Ranges. In *California Prehistory: Colonization, Culture, and Complexity,* edited by Terry L. Jones and Kathryn A. Klar, pp. 191–213. AltaMira Press, Lanham, Maryland.

Glassow, Michael A., Larry R. Wilcoxon, and Jon Ericson

1988 Cultural and Environmental Change During the Early Period of Santa Barbara Channel Prehistory. In *The Archaeology of Prehistoric Coastlines,* edited by Geoff Bailey and John Parkington, pp. 64–77. Cambridge University Press, Cambridge.

Golla, Victor

2007 Linguistic Prehistory. In *California Prehistory: Colonization, Culture, and Complexity,* edited by Terry L. Jones and Kathryn A. Klar, pp. 71–82. AltaMira Press, Lanham, Maryland.

Gould, Richard A.

1964 Exploitive Economics and Culture Change in Central California. *University of California Archaeological Survey Reports* 62:123–163. Berkeley.

1966a Archaeology of the Point St. George Site and Tolowa Prehistory. *University of California Publications in Anthropology* 4. Berkeley.

1966b The Wealth Quest among the Tolowa Indians of Northwestern California. *Proceedings of the American Philosophical Society* 110(1): 67–89. Philadelphia.

1978 Tolowa. In *California,* edited by Robert F. Heizer, pp. 128–136. Handbook of North American Indians, vol. 8, William C. Sturtevant, general editor. Smithsonian Institution, Washington, D.C.

Grady, Diane L., Kate A. Latham, and Valerie A. Andrushko
2001 *Human Skeletal Biology of CA-SCL-674, the Rubino Site, City of San Jose, Santa Clara County, California, Volume 2: Human Skeletal Biology.* Coyote Press Archives of California Prehistory, No. 50, Salinas, California.

Graesch, Anthony P.
2004 Specialized Bead Making among Island Chumash Households: Community Labor Organization during the Historic Period. In *Foundations of Chumash Complexity,* edited by Jeanne E. Arnold, pp. 133–171. Cotsen Institute of Archaeology, University of California, Los Angeles.

Grant, Campbell
1965 *The Rock Paintings of the Chumash.* University of California Press, Berkeley.

Grant, Campbell, James W. Baird, and J. Kenneth Pringle
1968 *Rock Drawings of the Coso Range.* Maturango Museum, Ridgecrest, California.

Graumlich, L. J.
1993 A 1000-Year Record of Temperature and Precipitation in the Sierra Nevada. *Quaternary Research* 39:249–255.

Grayson, Donald K.
1994 Chronology, Glottochronology, and Numic Expansion. In *Across the West: Human Population Movement and the Expansion of the Numa,* edited by David B. Madsen, and David Rhode, pp. 20–23. University of Utah Press, Salt Lake City.

Hartzell, Leslie L.
1992 Hunter-Gatherer Adaptive Strategies and Lacustrine Environments in the Buena Vista Lake Basin, Kern County, California. Unpublished Ph.D. dissertation, Department of Anthropology, University of California, Davis.

Heizer, Robert F.
1978 Introduction. In *California,* edited by Robert F. Heizer, pp. 1–5. Handbook of North American Indians, vol. 8, William C. Sturtevant, general editor. Smithsonian Institution, Washington, D.C.

Heizer, Robert F., and Martin A. Baumhoff
1962 *Prehistoric Rock Art of Nevada and Eastern California.* University of California Press, Berkeley.

Heizer, Robert F., and Theodora Kroeber (editors)
1979 *Ishi the Last Yahi: A Documentary History.* University of California Press, Berkeley.

Helvenston, Patricia A., and Paul G. Bahn
2005 *Walking the Trance Fixed.* Wasteland Press, Louisville, Kentucky.

Hildebrand, John G., G. Timothy Gross, Jerry Schaefer, and Hector Neff
2002 Patayan Ceramic Variability: Using Trace Elements and Petrographic Analysis to Study Brown and Buff Wares in Southern California. In *Ceramic Production and Circulation in the Greater Southwest: Source Determination by INNA and Complementary Mineralogical Investigations,* edited by Donna M. Glowacki and Hector Neff, pp. 121–139. Cotsen Institute of Archaeology, University of California, Los Angeles.

Hildebrand, John A., and Melissa B. Hagstrum
1995 Observing Subsistence Change in Native Southern California: The Late Prehistoric Kumeyaay. *Research in Economic Anthropology* 16:85–127.

Hildebrandt, William R.
2007 Northwest California: Ancient Lifeways among Forested Mountains, Flowing Rivers, and Rocky Ocean Floors. In *California Prehistory: Colonization, Culture, and Complexity*, edited by Terry L. Jones and Kathryn. A. Klar, pp. 83–97. AltaMira Press, Lanham, Maryland.
Hildebrandt, William R., and Michael J. Darcangelo
2008 *Life on the River: The Archaeology of an Ancient Native American Culture.* Heyday Press, Berkeley, California.
Hildebrandt, William R., and John F. Hayes
1993 Settlement Pattern Change in the Mountains of Northwest California: A View from Pilot Ridge. In *There Grows a Green Tree: Papers in Honor of David A. Fredrickson*, edited by Greg White, Pat Mikkelsen, William R. Hildebrandt, and Mark E. Basgall, pp. 107–120. Center for Archaeological Research at Davis, No. 11, University of California, Davis.
Hildebrandt, William R., and Terry L. Jones
1992 Evolution of Marine Mammal Hunting: A View from the California and Oregon Coasts. *Journal of Anthropological Archaeology* 11:360–401.
Hildebrandt, William R., and Valerie A. Levulett
1997 Middle Holocene Adaptations on the Northern California Coast: Terrestrial Resource Productivity and its Influence on the Use of Marine Foods. In *Archaeology of the California Coast during the Middle Holocene*, edited by Jon M. Erlandson and Michael A. Glassow, pp. 143–150. Institute of Archaeology, University of California, Los Angeles.
2002 Late Holocene Emergence of Marine-focused Economies in Northwest California. In *Catalysts to Complexity: Late Holocene Societies of the California Coast*, edited by Jon M. Erlandson and Terry L. Jones, pp. 303–319. Cotsen Institute of Archaeology, University of California, Los Angeles.
Hildebrandt, William R., and Kelly R. McGuire
2002 The Ascendance of Hunting During the California Middle Archaic: An Evolutionary Perspective. *American Antiquity* 67:231–256.
2003 Large-Game Hunting, Gender-Differentiated Work Organization, and the Role of Evolutionary Ecology in California and the Great Basin: A Reply To Broughton and Bayham. *American Antiquity* 68:790–792.
Hildebrandt, William R., and Allika Ruby
2006 Prehistoric Pinyon Exploitation in the Southwestern Great Basin: A View from the Coso Range. *Journal of California and Great Basin Anthropology* 26:11–31.
Hockett, Bryan
2005 Middle and Late Holocene Hunting in the Great Basin: A Critical Review of the Debate and Future Prospects. *American Antiquity* 70:713–731.
Hollimon, Sandra E.
1990 Division of Labor and Gender Roles in Santa Barbara Channel Area Prehistory. Unpublished Ph.D. dissertation, Department of Anthropology, University of California, Santa Barbara.

Hopkins, Jerry
1991 Tulare Lake Fluted Points. In *Background to a Study of Tulare Lake's Archaeological Past*, edited by William J. Wallace and Francis A. Riddell, pp. 41–52. Coyote Press, Salinas, California.
Howard, Virginia
2000 Santa Catalina's Soapstone Vessels: Production Dynamics. In *Proceedings of the Fifth California Islands Symposium*, edited by David R. Brown, Kathryn L. Mitchell, and Henry W. Chaney, pp. 598–606. U. S. Department of the Interior, Washington, D.C.
Hudson, Travis, Jan Timbrook, and Melissa Rempe (editors)
1978 *Tomol: Chumash Watercraft as Described in the Ethnographic Notes of John P. Harrington*. Anthropological Papers, No. 9, Ballena Press, Socorro, New Mexico.
Hughes, Richard E.
1978 Aspects of Prehistoric Wiyot Exchange and Social Ranking. *Journal of California Anthropology* 5:53–66.
Hughes, Richard E., and Randall Milliken
2007 Prehistoric Material Conveyance. In *California Prehistory: Colonization, Culture, and Complexity*, edited by Terry L. Jones and Kathryn A. Klar, pp. 259–271. AltaMira Press, Lanham, Maryland.
Hull, Kathleen L.
2002 Culture Contact in Context: A Multiscalar View of Catastrophic Depopulation and Culture Change in Yosemite Valley, California. Unpublished Ph.D. dissertation, Department of Anthropology, University of California, Berkeley.
2005 Process, Perception, and Practice: Time Perspectivism in Yosemite Native Demography. *Journal of Anthropological Archaeology* 24:354–377.
2007 The Sierra Nevada: Archaeology in the Range of Light. In *California Prehistory: Colonization, Culture, and Complexity*, edited by Terry L. Jones and Kathryn A. Klar, pp. 177–189. AltaMira Press, Lanham, Maryland.
Hull, Kathleen L., and Michael J. Moratto
1999 *Archaeological Synthesis and Research Design, Yosemite National Park, California.* Yosemite Research Center Publications in Anthropology No. 21. USDI, Yosemite National Park, California.
Hyder, William D.
1989 *Rock Art and Archaeology in Santa Barbara County, California*, San Luis Obispo County Archaeological Society Occasional Paper, No. 13, San Luis Obispo, California.
Hylkema, Mark G.
2002 Tidal Marsh, Oak Woodlands, and Cultural Florescence in the Southern San Francisco Bay Region. In *Catalysts to Complexity: Late Holocene Societies of the California Coast*, edited by Jon M. Erlandson and Terry L. Jones, pp. 233–262. Cotsen Institute of Archaeology, University of California, Los Angeles.
Ingram, B. Lynn
1998 Differences in Radiocarbon Age between Shell and Charcoal from a Holocene Shellmound in Northern California. *Quaternary Research* 49:102–110.

Ingram, B. Lynn, and John R. Southon
1996 Reservoir Ages in Eastern Pacific Coastal and Estuarine Waters. *Radiocarbon* 38:573–582.

Jackson, Thomas L.
1991 Pounding Acorn: Women's Production as Social and Economic Focus. In *Engendering Archaeology*, edited by Joan M. Gero and Margaret W. Conkey, pp. 301–328. Blackwell, Cambridge.

Johnson, Jerald J.
1990 Cosumnes Brownware: A Pottery Type Centered on the Lower Cosumnes and Adjacent Sacramento Rivers in Central California. *Nevada State Museum Anthropological Papers* 23:145–158. Carson City.

Johnson, John R.
2001 Ethnohistoric Reflections of Cruzeño Chumash Society. In *The Origins of a Pacific Coast Chiefdom: The Chumash of the Channel Islands*, edited by Jeanne E. Arnold, pp. 53–70. University of Utah Press, Salt Lake City.

Johnson, John R., Thomas W. Stafford, Jr., Henry O. Ajie, and Don P. Morris
2000 Arlington Springs Revisited. In *Proceedings of the Fifth California Islands Symposium*, edited by David R. Brown, Kathryn L. Mitchell, and Henry W. Chaney, pp. 541–545. U. S. Department of the Interior, Washington, D.C.

Jones, Terry L.
1992 Settlement Trends Along the California Coast. In *Essays on the Prehistory of Maritime California*, edited by Terry L. Jones, pp. 1–37. Center for Archaeological Research at Davis, No. 10, University of California, Davis.
2002 Late Holocene Cultural Complexity on the California Coast. In *Catalysts to Complexity: Late Holocene Societies of the California Coast*, edited by Jon M. Erlandson and Terry L. Jones, pp. 1–12. Cotsen Institute of Archaeology, University of California, Los Angeles.

Jones, Terry L., and Jennifer A. Ferneau
2002 Deintensification Along the Central Coast. In *Catalysts to Complexity: Late Holocene Societies of the California Coast*, edited by Jon M. Erlandson and Terry L. Jones, pp. 205–232. Cotsen Institute of Archaeology, University of California, Los Angeles.

Jones, Terry L., and Douglas J. Kennett
1999 Late Holocene Climate Change and Cultural Ecology of the Central California Coast. *Quaternary Research* 51:74–82.

Jones, Terry L., and Kathryn A. Klar
2005 Diffusionism Reconsidered: Linguistic and Archaeological Evidence for Prehistoric Polynesian Contact with Southern California. *American Antiquity* 70:457–484.
2007 Colonization, Culture, and Complexity. In *California Prehistory: Colonization, Culture, and Complexity*, edited by Terry L. Jones and Kathryn A. Klar, pp. 299–315. AltaMira Press, Lanham, Maryland.

Jones, Terry L., and Kathryn A. Klar (editors)
2007 *California Prehistory: Colonization, Culture, and Complexity.* AltaMira Press, Lanham, Maryland.

Jones, Terry L., Gary M. Brown, L. Mark Raab, Janet L. McVickar, W. Geoffrey Spaulding, Douglas J. Kennett, Andrew York, and Phillip L. Walker

1999 Environmental Imperatives Reconsidered: Demographic Crises in Western North America During the Medieval Climatic Anomaly. *Current Anthropology* 40:137–170.

Jones, Terry L., Douglas J. Kennett, James P. Kennett, and Brian F. Codding

2008 Seasonal Stability in Late Holocene Shellfish Harvesting on the Central California Coast. *Journal of Archaeological Science* 35:2286–2294.

Jones, Terry L., Nathan E. Stevens, Deborah A. Jones, Richard T. Fitzgerald, and Mark G. Hylkema

2007 The Central Coast. In *California Prehistory: Colonization, Culture, and Complexity*, edited by Terry L. Jones and Kathryn A. Klar, pp. 125–146. AltaMira Press, Lanham, Maryland.

Justice, Noel D.

2002 *Stone Age Spear and Arrow Points of California and the Great Basin.* Indiana University Press, Bloomington.

Kaldenberg, Russell L.

2005 Possible Proboscidean Petroglyph Found at China Lake Naval Air Weapons Station. *Current Research in the Pleistocene* 22:51–53.

Kaestle, Frederika A., and David Glenn Smith

2001 Ancient Mitochondrial DNA Evidence for Prehistoric Population Movement: The Numic Expansion. *American Journal of Physical Anthropology* 115:1–12.

Keeley, Lawrence H.

1996 *War Before Civilization.* Oxford University Press, New York.

Kelly, Robert L.

1995 *The Foraging Spectrum: Diversity in Hunter-Gatherer Lifeways.* Smithsonian Institution, Washington, D.C.

Kennedy, Michael A.

2005 An Investigation of Hunter-Gatherer Shellfish Foraging Practices: Archaeological and Geochemical Evidence form Bodega Bay, California. Unpublished Ph.D. dissertation, Department of Anthropology, University of California, Davis.

Kennett, Douglas J.

1998 Behavioral Ecology and the Evolution of Hunter-Gatherer Societies on the Northern Channel Islands, California. Unpublished Ph.D. dissertation, Department of Anthropology, University of California, Santa Barbara.

2005 *The Island Chumash: Behavioral Ecology of a Maritime Society.* University of California Press, Berkeley.

Kennett, Douglas J., and James P. Kennett

2000 Competitive and Cooperative Responses to Climate Instability in Coastal Southern California. *American Antiquity* 65:379–395.

Kennett, D. J., J. P. Kennett, J. West, C. Mercer, S. S. Que Hee, L. Bement, T. E. Bunch, M. Sellers, and W. S. Wolbach

2009 Nanodiamonds in the Younger Dryas Boundary Sediment Layer. *Science* 323:94.

Keyser, James D., and David S. Whitley
2006 Sympathetic Magic in Western North American Rock Art. *American Antiquity* 71:3–26.
King, Chester D.
1990 *Evolution of Chumash Society: A Comparative Study of Artifacts Used for Social System Maintenance in the Santa Barbara Channel Region before A.D. 1804.* Garland, New York.
King, Thomas F.
1978 Don't That Beat the Band? Nonegalitarian Political Organization in Prehistoric California. In *Social Archeology: Beyond Subsistence and Dating,* edited by Charles L. Redman, Mary Jane Berman, Edward V. Curtin, William T. Langhorne, Jr., Nina M. Versaggi, and Jeffry C. Wanser, pp. 225–248. Academic Press, New York.
Koehler, Peter A., R. Scott Anderson, and W. Geoffrey Spaulding
2005 Development of Vegetation in the Central Mojave Desert of California During the Late Quaternary. *Paleogeography, Paleoclimatology, Paleoecology* 215:297–311.
Koerper, Henry C., and Ken Hedges
1996 Patayan Anthropomorphic Figurines from an Orange County Site. *Journal of California and Great Basin Anthropology* 18:204–220.
Koerper, Henry C., Roger D. Mason, and Mark L. Peterson
2002 Complexity, Demography, and Change in Late Holocene Orange County. In *Catalysts to Complexity: Late Holocene Societies of the California Coast*, edited by Jon M. Erlandson and Terry L. Jones, pp. 63–81. Cotsen Institute of Archaeology, University of California, Los Angeles.
Koerper, Henry C., Christine Prior, R. E. Taylor, and Robert O. Gibson
1995 Additional Accelerator Mass Spectrometer (AMS) Radiocarbon Assays on *Haliotis* Fishhooks from CA-ORA-378. *Journal of California and Great Basin Anthropology* 17:273–279.
Kowta, Makoto
2000 Arbitrary is as Arbitrary Does: The Genesis of the Metric Level and the Max Uhle-to-Nels C. Nelson Connection. In *Archaeological Passages: A Volume in Honor of Claude N. Warren*, edited by Joan S. Schneider, Robert M. Yohe, II, and Jill K. Gardner, pp. 235–241. Western Center for Archaeology and Paleontology, Publications in Archaeology 1, Hemet, California.
Kroeber, Alfred L.
1925 *Handbook of the Indians of California.* Bureau of American Ethnology Bulletin 78. Smithsonian Institution, Washington, D.C.
1962 The Nature of Land-Holding Groups in Aboriginal California. *University of Archaeological California Survey Reports* 56:19–58.
Kroeber, Theodora
1969 *Ishi in Two Worlds: A Biography of the Last Wild Indian in North America.* University of California Press, Berkeley.
La Jeunesse, Roger Marks, and John Howard Pryor
1998 Romer's Rule and the Paleoindian/Archaic Transition. *Current Research in the Pleistocene* 15: 29–32.

Lambert, Patricia M.
1994 War and Peace on the Western Front: A Study of Violent Conflict and its Correlates in Prehistoric Hunter-Gatherer Societies of Coastal Southern California. Unpublished Ph.D. dissertation, Department of Anthropology, University of California, Santa Barbara.
1997 Patterns of Violence in Prehistoric Hunter-Gatherer Societies of Coastal Southern California. In *Troubled Times: Violence and Warfare in the Past*, edited by D. L. Martin and D. W. Frayer, pp. 77–109. War and Society, vol. 6, Gordon and Breach, Amsterdam.
2002 The Archaeology of War: A North American Perspective. *Journal of Archaeological Research* 10:207–241.

Lando, Richard, and Ruby E. Modesto
1977 *Temal Wakhish*: A Desert Cahuilla Village. *Journal of California Anthropology* 4:95–112.

Latta, Frank F.
1977 *Handbook of Yokuts Indians.* Bear State Books, Santa Cruz, California

Lawton, Harry W.
1974 Agricultural Motifs in Southern California Indian Mythology. *Journal of California Anthropology* 1:55–79.

Lawton, Harry W., Philip J. Wilke, Mary DeDecker, and William M. Mason
1993 Agriculture among the Paiute of Owens Valley. In *Before the Wilderness: Environmental Management by Native Californians*, edited by Thomas C. Blackburn and Kat Anderson, pp. 329–377. Ballena Press, Menlo Park, California.

Laylander, Don
1995 The Question of Prehistoric Agriculture among the Western Yumans. *Estudios Fronterizos* 35–36:187–203.

Levy, Richard
1978 Eastern Miwok. In *California,* edited by Robert F. Heizer, pp. 398–413. Handbook of North American Indians, vol. 8, William C. Sturtevant, general editor. Smithsonian Institution, Washington, D.C.

Lightfoot, Kent G.
1997 Cultural Construction of Coastal Landscapes: A Middle Holocene Perspective from San Francisco Bay. In *Archaeology of the California Coast during the Middle Holocene*, edited by Jon M. Erlandson and Michael Glassow, pp. 263–281. Cotsen Institute of Archaeology, University of California, Los Angeles.
2005 *Indians, Missionaries, and Merchants: The Legacy of Colonial Encounters on the California Frontiers.* University of California Press, Berkeley.

Lightfoot, Kent G., Robert Kalin, and James Moore
1987 *Prehistoric Hunter-Gatherers of Shelter Island, New York: An Archaeological Study of the Mashomack Preserve.* Contributions of the University of California Archaeological Research Facility, No. 46, Berkeley.

Lightfoot, Kent G., and Edward M. Luby
2002 Late Holocene in the San Francisco Bay Area: Temporal Trends in the Use and Abandonment of Shell Mounds in the East Bay. In *Catalysts to Complexity: Late Holocene Societies of the California Coast*, edited by Jon M. Erlandson and Terry L.

Jones, pp. 263–281. Cotsen Institute of Archaeology, University of California, Los Angeles.
Lightfoot, Kent G., and Antoinette Martinez
1995 Frontiers and Boundaries in Archaeological Perspective. *Annual Review of Anthropology* 24:471–492.
Lightfoot, Kent G., and Otis Parrish
2009 *California Indians and Their Environment: An Introduction.* University of California Press, Berkeley.
Liljeblad, Sven, and Catherine S. Fowler
1986 Owens Valley Paiute. In *Great Basin,* edited by Warren L. D'Azevedo, pp. 412–434. Handbook of North American Indians, vol. 11, William C. Sturtevant, general editor. Smithsonian Institution, Washington, D.C.
Loeb, E. M.
1926 Pomo Folkways. *University of California Publications in American Archaeology and Ethnography* 19(2):140–405. Berkeley.
Loud, L. L.
1924 The Stege Mounds at Richmond, California. *University of California Publications in American Archaeology and Ethnology* 17(6):366–372. Berkeley.
Luby, Edward M.
1992 Social Organization and Symbolism at the Patterson Mound, Ala–328, Alameda County, California. *California Anthropologist* 18:45–52.
2004 Shell Mounds and Mortuary Behavior in the San Francisco Bay Area. *North American Archaeologist* 25:1–33.
Luby, Edward M., Clayton D. Drescher, and Kent G. Lightfoot
2006 Shell Mounds and Mounded Landscapes in the San Francisco Bay Area: An Integrated Approach. *Journal of Island and Coastal Archaeology* 1:191–214.
Luby, Edward M., and Mark F. Gruber
1999 The Dead Must Be Fed: Symbolic Meanings of the Shellmounds of the San Francisco Bay Area. *Cambridge Archaeological Journal* 9:95–108.
Lyman, R. Lee
1995 On the Evolution of Marine Mammal Hunting on the West Coast of North America. *Journal of Anthropological Archaeology* 14:45–77.
McDonald, Meg, and Daniel F. McCarthy
2006 Rock Features, Quarrying, Rock Art, and Other Prehistoric Activities at the Pisgah Crater Lava Flow in the Mojave Desert. In *A Festschrift Honoring the Contributions of California Archaeologist Jay von Werlhof,* edited by Russell L. Kaldenberg, pp. 127–144. Maturango Museum Publication, No. 20, Ridgecrest, California.
McGuire, Kelly R.
2007 Models of Glass: A Prehistory of Northeast California. In *California Prehistory: Colonization, Culture, and Complexity*, edited by T. L. Jones and K. A. Klar, pp. 165–176. AltaMira Press, Lanham, Maryland.
McGuire, Kelly R., and William R. Hildebrandt
1994 The Possibilities of Women and Men: Gender and the California Millingstone Horizon. *Journal of California and Great Basin Anthropology* 16:41–59.

2005 Re-Thinking Great Basin Foragers: Prestige Hunting and Costly Signaling during the Middle Archaic Period. *American Antiquity* 70:693–710.

McGuire, Kelly R., William R. Hildebrandt, and Kimberly Carpenter
2007 Costly Signaling and the Ascendance of No-Can-Do Archaeology: A Reply to Codding and Jones. *American Antiquity* 72:358–365.

McLendon, Sally, and John R. Johnson
1999 *Cultural Affiliation and Lineal Descent of Chumash Peoples in the Channel Islands and the Santa Monica Mountains*, Vol. 1 and 2. Santa Barbara Museum of Natural History, Santa Barbara, California.

Madsen, David B., and David Rhode (editors)
1994 *Across the West: Human Population Movement and the Expansion of the Numa.* University of Utah Press, Salt Lake City.

McKern, W. C.
1922 Functional Families of the Patwin. *University of California Publications in American Archaeology and Ethnography* 13(7):235–258. Berkeley.

Marquardt, William H.
2004 Calusa. In *Southeast*, edited by R. D. Fogelson, pp. 204–212. Handbook of North American Indians, vol. 14, William C. Sturtevant, general editor. Smithsonian Institution, Washington, D.C.

Masters, Patricia M., and Ivano W. Aiello
2007 Postglacial Evolution of Coastal Environments. In *California Prehistory: Colonization, Culture, and Complexity*, edited by Terry L. Jones and Kathryn A. Klar, pp. 35–51. AltaMira Press, Lanham, Maryland.

Masters, Patricia M., and Dennis R. Gallegos
1997 Environmental Change and Coastal Adaptations in San Diego County During the Middle Holocene. In *Archaeology of the California Coast During the Middle Holocene*, edited by Jon M. Erlandson and Michael A. Glassow, pp. 11–21. Cotsen Institute of Archaeology, University of California, Los Angeles.

Matson, R. G., and Gary Coupland
1995 *The Prehistory of the Northwest Coast.* Academic Press, New York.

Meighan, Clement W.
1959 The Little Harbor Site, Catalina Island: An Example of Ecological Interpretation in Archaeology. *American Antiquity* 24:383–405.

Milliken, Randall T.
1995 *A Time of Little Choice: The Disintegration of Tribal Culture in the San Francisco Bay Area, 1769–1810.* Ballena Press, Menlo Park, California.
2008 *Native Americans at Mission San Jose.* Malki-Ballena Press, Banning, California.

Milliken, Randall T., and James A. Bennyhoff
1993 Temporal Changes in Beads as Prehistoric California Grave Goods. In *There Grows a Green Tree: Papers in Honor of David A. Fredrickson*, edited by Gregory White, Pat Mikkelsen, William R. Hildebrandt, and Mark E. Basgall, pp. 381–395. Center for Archaeological Research at Davis, No. 11, University of California, Davis.

Milliken, Randall, Richard T. Fitzgerald, Mark G. Hylkema, Randy Groza, Tom Origer, David G. Bieling, Alan Leventhal, Randy S. Wiberg, Andrew Gottsfield, Donna Gillette, Viviana Bellifemine, Eric Strother, Robert Cartier, and David A. Fredrickson

2007 Punctuated Culture Change in the San Francisco Bay Area. In *California Prehistory: Colonization, Culture, and Complexity*, edited by Terry L. Jones and Kathryn A. Klar, pp. 99–123. AltaMira Press, Lanham, Maryland.

Minor, Rick, and Wendy C. Grant.

1996 Earthquake-Induced Subsidence and Burial of Late Holocene Archaeological Sites, Northern Oregon Coast. *American Antiquity* 61: 772–781.

Moratto, Michael J.

1972 A Study of Prehistory in the Southern Sierra Nevada Foothills, California. Unpublished Ph.D. dissertation, Department of Anthropology, University of Oregon.

1984 *California Archaeology*. Academic Press, New York.

2002 Culture History of the New Melones Reservoir Area, Calaveras and Tuolumne Counties, California. In *Essays in California Archaeology: A Memorial to Franklin Fenenga*, edited by William J. Wallace, and Francis A. Riddell, pp. 25–54. Contributions of the University of California Archaeological Research Facility, No. 60, Berkeley.

Munns, Ann M., and Jeanne E. Arnold

2002 Late Holocene Santa Cruz Island: Patterns of Continuity and Change. In *Catalysts to Complexity: Late Holocene Societies of the California Coast*, edited by Jon M. Erlandson and Terry L. Jones, pp. 127–146. Cotsen Institute of Archaeology, University of California, Los Angeles.

Nelson, Nels C.

1909 Shellmounds in the San Francisco Bay Area. *University of California Publications in American Archaeology and Ethnology* 7:309–356. Berkeley.

1910 The Ellis Landing Shellmound. *University of California Publications in American Archaeology and Ethnology* 7:357–426. Berkeley.

Newsome, Seth, Donald L. Phillips, Brendan J. Culleton, Tom P. Guilderson, and Paul L. Koch

2004 Dietary Reconstruction of an Early to Middle Holocene Human Population from the Central California Coast: Insights and Advanced Stable Isotope Mixing Models. *Journal of Archaeological Science* 31:1101–1115.

Noah, Anna C.

2005 Household Economies: The Role of Animals in a Historic Period Chiefdom on the California Coast. Unpublished Ph.D. dissertation, Department of Anthropology, University of California, Los Angeles.

Orr, Phil C.

1962 The Arlington Springs Site, Santa Rosa Island, California. *American Antiquity* 27:417–419.

Ortiz, Bev

1991 *It Will Live Forever: Traditional Yosemite Indian Acorn Preparation*. Heyday Books, Berkeley.

Parker, Albert J.
2002 Fire in Sierra Nevada Forests: Evaluating the Ecological Impact of Burning by Native Americans. In *Fire, Native Peoples, and the Natural Landscape*, edited by Thomas R. Vale, pp. 233–267. Island Press, Washington, D.C.
Pavlik, Bruce M., Pamela C. Muick, Sharon G. Johnson, and Maurice Popper
1991 *Oaks of California*. Cachuma Press, Los Olivos, California.
Perry, Jennifer E.
2004 Quarries and Microblades: Trends in Prehistoric Land and Resource Use on Eastern Santa Cruz Island. In *Foundations of Chumash Complexity*, edited by Jeanne E. Arnold, pp. 113–131. Cotsen Institute of Archaeology, University of California, Los Angeles.
Pilling, A. R.
1978 Yurok. In *California*, edited by Robert F. Heizer, pp. 137–154. Handbook of North American Indians, vol. 8, William C. Sturtevant, general editor. Smithsonian Institution, Washington, D.C.
Pope, Kevin. O., Owen K. Davis, Manuel R. Palacios-Fest, and Brian F. Byrd
2004 Paleoenvironmental History of the Northern San Diego County Coast. In *Results of NSF-Funded Archaeological and Paleontological Investigations at San Elijo Lagoon, San Diego County, California*, edited by Brian F. Byrd, Kevin O. Pope, and Seetha N. Reddy, pp. 15–71. ASM Affiliates, Carlsbad, California.
Porcasi, Judith F., and Harumi Fujita
2000 The Dolphin Hunters: A Specialized Prehistoric Maritime Adaptation in the Southern California Channel Islands and Baja California. *American Antiquity* 65:543–566.
Porcasi, Judith F., Terry L. Jones, and L. Mark Raab
2000 Trans-Holocene Marine Mammal Exploitation on San Clemente Island: A Tragedy of the Commons Revisited. *Journal of Anthropological Archaeology* 19:200–220.
Powers, Stephen
1976 [1874] *Tribes of California*. University of California Press, Berkeley.
Preziosi, Aimee M.
2001 Standardization and Specialization: The Island Chumash Microdrill Industry. In *The Origins of a Pacific Coast Chiefdom: The Chumash of The Channel Islands*, edited by Jeanne E. Arnold, pp. 151–164. University of Utah Press, Salt Lake City.
Quinlan, Angus R.
2000a The Ventriloquist's Dummy: A Critical Review of Shamanism and Rock Art in Far Western North America. *Journal of California and Great Basin Anthropology* 22:92–108.
2000b Reply to Whitley. *Journal of California and Great Basin Anthropology* 22:129–132.
Quinlan, Angus R., and Alanah Woody
2003 Marks of Distinction: Rock Art and Ethnic Identification in the Great Basin. *American Antiquity* 68:372–390.

Raab, L. Mark
1997 The Southern Channel Islands during the Middle Holocene: Trends in Maritime Cultural Evolution. In *Archaeology of the California Coast during the Middle Holocene*, edited by Jon M. Erlandson and Michael A. Glassow, pp. 23–34. Institute of Archaeology, University of California, Los Angeles.
Raab, L. Mark, Kathryn Bradford, Judith F. Porcasi, and William J. Howard
1995 Return to Little Harbor, Santa Catalina Island, California: A Critique of the Marine Paleotemperature Model. *American Antiquity* 60:287–308.
Raab, L. Mark, Kathryn Bradford, and Andrew Yatsko
1994 Advances in Southern Channel Islands Archaeology:1983–1993. *Journal of California and Great Basin Anthropology* 16:243–270.
Raab, L. Mark, Jim Cassidy, Andrew Yatsko, and William J. Howard
2009 *California Maritime Archaeology: A San Clemente Island Perspective.* AltaMira, Lanham, Maryland.
Raab, L. Mark, and William J. Howard
2000 Modeling Cultural Connections between the Southern Channel Islands and Western United States: The Middle Holocene Distribution of *Olivella* Grooved Rectangle Beads. In *Proceedings of the Fifth California Islands Symposium*, edited by David R. Browne, Kathryn L. Mitchell, and Henry W. Chaney, pp. 590–597. U.S. Department of the Interior, Washington, D.C.
Ragir, Sonia
1972 *The Early Horizon in Central California Prehistory.* Contributions of the University of California Archaeological Research Facility, No. 15, Berkeley.
Reed, Judyth
2006 Late Pleistocene/Early Holocene Archaeology of the Southwest Searles Lake Basin, Kern County, California. In *A Festschrift Honoring the Contributions of California Archaeologist Jay von Werlhof*, edited by Russell L. Kaldenberg, pp. 159–168. Maturango Museum Publication, No. 20, Ridgecrest, California.
Rick, Torben C.
2007 *The Archaeology and Historical Ecology of Late Holocene San Miguel Island.* Cotsen Institute of Archaeology, University of California, Los Angeles.
Rick, Torben C., and Jon M. Erlandson
2009 Coastal Exploitation. *Science* 325:953–954.
Rick, Torben C., and Jon M. Erlandson (editors)
2008 *Human Impacts on Ancient Marine Ecosystems: A Global Perspective.* University of California Press, Berkeley.
Rick, Torben C., Jon M. Erlandson, and René L. Vellanoweth
2001 Paleocoastal Marine Fishing on the Pacific Coast of the Americas: Perspectives from Daisy Cave, California. *American Antiquity* 66:595–613.
Rick, Torben C., Jon M. Erlandson, René L. Vellanoweth, and Todd J. Braje
2005 From Pleistocene Mariners to Complex Hunter-Gatherers: The Archaeology of the California Channel Islands. *Journal of World Prehistory* 19:169–228.
Riddell, Francis A.
1993 Intersite Spatial Considerations: Native Californian Villages. In *There Grows a Green Tree: Papers in Honor of David A. Fredrickson,* edited by Gregory White, Patri-

cia Mikkelsen, William R. Hildebrandt, and Mark E. Basgall, pp. 91–105. Center for Archaeological Research at Davis, No. 11, University of California, Davis.

Ritter, Eric W.

1994 Scratched Rock Art Complexes in the Desert West: Symbols for Socio-Religious Communication. In *New Light on Old Art: Recent Advances in Hunter-Gatherer Rock Art Research*, edited by David S. Whitley and Lawrence L. Loendorf, pp. 51–66. Institute of Archaeology, University of California, Los Angeles.

Rondeau, Michael F.

2009 Fluted Points of the Far West. *Proceedings of the Society for California Archaeology* 21:265–274.

Rondeau, Michael F., Jim Cassidy, and Terry L. Jones

2007 Colonization Technologies: Fluted Projectile Points and the San Clemente Island Woodworking/Microblade Complex. In *California Prehistory: Colonization, Culture, and Complexity*, edited by Terry L. Jones and Kathryn A. Klar, pp. 63–70. AltaMira Press, Lanham, Maryland.

Rosenthal, Jeffrey S., and Jack Meyer

2004 *Landscape Evolution and the Archaeological Record: A Geoarchaeological Study of the Southern Santa Clara Valley and Surrounding Region.* Center for Archaeological Research at Davis, No. 14, University of California, Davis.

Rosenthal, Jeffrey S., Gregory G. White, and Mark Q. Sutton

2007 The Central Valley: A View from the Catbird's Seat. In *California Prehistory: Colonization, Culture, and Complexity*, edited by Terry L. Jones and Kathryn A. Klar, pp. 147–163. AltaMira Press, Lanham, Maryland.

Salls, Roy A.

1991 Early Holocene Maritime Adaptation at Eel Point, San Clemente Island. In *Hunter-Gatherers of Early Holocene Coastal California*, edited by Jon M. Erlandson and Roger H. Colten, pp. 63–80. Institute of Archaeology, University of California, Los Angeles.

Sassaman, Kenneth E.

2004 Complex Hunter-Gatherers in Evolution and History: A North American Perspective. *Journal of Archaeological Research* 12:227–280.

Sassaman, Kenneth E., and David G. Anderson

2004 Late Holocene Period, 3750 to 650 BC. In *Southeast*, edited by R. D. Fogelson, pp. 101–114. Handbook of North American Indians, vol. 14, William C. Sturtevant, general editor. Smithsonian Institution, Washington, D.C.

Schaefer, Jerry

1994 The Challenge of Archaeological Research in the Colorado Desert: Recent Approaches and Discoveries. *Journal of California and Great Basin Anthropology* 16:60–80.

Schaefer, Jerry, Deborah Huntley, and Drew Pallette

2002 *Archaeological Investigations at the Cahuilla Village of Rincon, Agua Caliente Indian Reservation, Palm Springs, California.* Prepared by ASM Affiliates for the Agua Caliente Band of Cahuilla Indians, Palm Springs, California.

Schaefer, Jerry, and Don Laylander
2007 The Colorado Desert: Ancient Adaptations to Wetlands and Wastelands. In *California Prehistory: Colonization, Culture, and Complexity*, edited by Terry L. Jones and Kathryn A. Klar, pp. 247–257. AltaMira Press, Lanham, Maryland.
Schalk, Randall F.
1977 The Structure of an Anadromous Fish Resource. In *For Theory Building in Archaeology: Essays on Faunal Remains, Aquatic Resources, Spatial Analysis, and Systemic Modeling*, edited by Lewis R. Binford, pp. 207–249. Academic Press, New York.
Schenck, W. Egbert
1926 The Emeryville Shellmound Final Report. *University of California Publications in American Archaeology and Ethnology* 23:147–282. Berkeley.
Schimmelmann, A., C. B. Lange, and B. J. Meggers
2003 Paleoclimate and Archaeological Evidence for a 200-Year Recurrence of Floods and Droughts Linking California, Mesoamerica, and South America over the Past 2,000 Years. *Holocene* 13:763–778.
Schoenherr, Allan A.
1995 *A Natural History of California.* University of California Press, Berkeley.
Schoenherr, Allan A., C. Robert Feldmeth, and Michael J. Emerson
1999 *Natural History of the Islands of California.* University of California Press, Berkeley.
Scott, Eric
2004 The Late Pleistocene of the Mojave Desert, the Peopling of the Americas, and Terminal Pleistocene Extinctions. In *The Human Journey and Ancient Life in California's Deserts: Proceedings from the 2001 Millennium Conference*, edited by Mark W. Allen and Judyth Reed, pp. 25–38. Maturango Museum Publication, No. 15, Ridgecrest, California.
Shackley, M. Steven
2000 The Stone Tool Technology of Ishi and the Yana of North Central California: Inferences for Hunter-gatherer Cultural Identity in Historic California. *American Anthropologist* 102:693–712.
Silliman, Stephen W.
2004 *Lost Laborers in Colonial California : Native Americans and the Archaeology of Rancho Petaluma.* University of Arizona Press, Tucson.
Simons, Dwight D.
1992 Prehistoric Mammal Exploitation in the San Francisco Bay Area. In *Essays on the Prehistory of Maritime California,* edited by Terry L. Jones, pp. 73–103. Center for Archaeological Research at Davis, No. 10, University of California, Davis.
Smith, Courtney R., and David Lee
2004 Faces on the Rocks: A Study of Face Paint-Like Petroglyphs in the Eastern Mojave Desert of California. In *The Human Journey and Ancient Life in California's Deserts: Proceedings from the 2001 Millennium Conference*, edited by Mark W. Allen and Judyth Reed, pp. 189–197. Maturango Museum Publication, No. 15, Ridgecrest, California.

Sobel, Elizabeth A., D. Ann Trieu Gahr, and Kenneth M. Ames (editors)
2006 *Household Archaeology on the Northwest Coast.* International Monographs in Prehistory, Ann Arbor, Michigan.
Spier, Robert F. G.
1978 Foothill Yokuts. In *California,* edited by Robert F. Heizer, pp. 471–484. Handbook of North American Indians, vol. 8, William C. Sturtevant, general editor. Smithsonian Institution, Washington, D.C.
Stevens, Nathan E.
2005 Changes in Prehistoric Land Use in the Alpine Sierra Nevada: A Regional Exploration Using Temperature-Adjusted Obsidian Hydration Rates. *Journal of California and Great Basin Anthropology* 25:187–205.
Stevenson, Christopher M., Elizabeth Knaus, James J. Mazer, and John K. Bates
1993 Homogeneity of Water Content in Obsidian from the Coso Volcanic Field: Implications for Obsidian Hydration dating. *Geoarchaeology* 8:371–384.
Stevenson, Christopher M., James J. Mazer, and Barry E. Scheetz
1998 Laboratory Obsidian Hydration Rates: Theory, Method, and Application. In *Archaeological Obsidian Studies, Method and Theory,* edited by M. Steven Shackley, pp. 181–204. Plenum Press Advances in Archaeological and Museum Studies, vol. 3, New York.
Stevenson, Christopher M., Mike Gottesman, and Michael Macko
2000 Redefining the Working Assumptions of Obsidian Hydration Dating. *Journal of California and Great Basin Anthropology* 22:223–236.
Steward, Julian H.
1933 Ethnography of the Owens Valley Paiute. *University of California Publications in American Archaeology and Ethnology* 33:233–350. Berkeley.
1938 *Basin-Plateau Aboriginal Sociopolitical Groups.* Bureau of American Ethnology Bulletins 120. United States Government Printing Office, Washington, D.C.
Stine, S.
1994 Extreme and Persistent Drought in California and Patagonia during Medieval Time. *Nature* 369:546–549.
Sutton, Mark Q.
1986 Warfare and Expansion: An Ethnohistoric Perspective on the Numic Spread. *Journal of California and Great Basin Anthropology* 8:65–82.
2009 People and Language: Defining the Takic Expansion into Southern California. *Pacific Coast Archaeological Society Quarterly* 41(2&3):31-93.
Sutton, Mark Q., Mark E. Basgall, Jill K. Gardener, and Mark W. Allen
2007 Advances in Understanding Mojave Desert Prehistory. In *California Prehistory: Colonization, Culture, and Complexity,* edited by T. L. Jones and K. A. Klar, pp. 229–245. AltaMira Press, Lanham, Maryland.
Sutton, Mark Q., and David Rhode
1994 A History of the Numic Problem. In *Across the West: Human Population Movement and the Expansion of the Numa,* edited by David B. Madsen and David Rhode, pp. 6–15. University of Utah Press, Salt Lake City.

Thomas, David H.
1994 Chronology and the Numic Expansion. In *Across the West: Human Population Movement and the Expansion of the Numa,* edited by David B. Madsen and David Rhode, pp. 56–61. University of Utah Press, Salt Lake City.
Thomas, David H., Lorann S. A. Pendleton, and Stephen C. Cappannari
1986 Western Shoshone. In *Great Basin,* edited by Warren L. D'Azevedo, pp. 262–283. Handbook of North American Indians, vol. 11, William C. Sturtevant, general editor. Smithsonian Institution, Washington, D.C.
Timbrook, Jan, John R. Johnson, and David D. Earle
1982 Vegetation Burning by the Chumash. *Journal of California and Great Basin Anthropology* 4:163–186.
Tushingham, Shannon
2005 An Ancient Campground: Archaeology on the Smith River. *Redwood Currents* 21:12–15.
2009 The Development of Intensive Foraging Systems in Northwestern California. Unpublished Ph.D. dissertation, Department of Anthropology, University of California, Davis.
Uhle, Max
1907 The Emeryville Shellmound. *University of California Publications in American Archaeology and Ethnology* 1–106. Berkeley.
Underwood, Jackson
2006 Discovering the Desert Kawaiisu. In *A Festschrift Honoring the Contributions of California Archaeologist Jay von Werlhof,* edited by Russell L. Kaldenberg, pp. 179–191. Maturango Museum Publication, No. 20, Ridgecrest, California.
Vasek, Frank C., and Michael G. Barbour
1995 Mojave Desert Scrub Vegetation. In *Terrestrial Vegetation of California,* edited by Michael G. Barbour and Jack Major, pp. 835–867. California Native Plant Society Special Publication, No. 9, Sacramento.
Vellanoweth, René L.
2001 AMS Radiocarbon Dating and Shell Bead Chronologies: Middle Holocene Trade and Interaction in Western North America. *Journal of Archaeological Science* 28:941–950.
Wake, Thomas A., and Dwight D. Simons
2000 Trans-Holocene Subsistence Strategies and Topographic Change on the Northern California Coast: The Fauna from Duncans Point Cave. *Journal of California and Great Basin Anthropology* 22:295–320.
Wallace, William J.
1978 Northern Valley Yokuts. In *California,* edited by Robert F. Heizer, pp. 462–470. Handbook of North American Indians, vol. 8, William C. Sturtevant, general editor. Smithsonian Institution, Washington, D.C.
1993a A Lost Opportunity? A Brief History of Archaeological Research in the Tulare Lake Basin. In *The Quest for Tulare Lake's Archaeological Past,* edited by William J. Wallace and Francis A. Riddell, pp. 1–11. Coyote Press, Salinas, California.

1993b The Luckey Collection from Tulare Lake. In *The Quest for Tulare Lake's Archaeological Past,* edited by William J. Wallace and Francis A. Riddell, pp. 39–48. Coyote Press, Salinas, California.

Wallace, William J., and Donald W. Lathrap

1975 *West Berkeley (CA-Ala–307): A Culturally Stratified Shellmound on the East Shore of San Francisco Bay.* Contributions of the University of California Archaeological Research Facility, No. 29, Berkeley.

Wallace, William J., and Francis A. Riddell (editors)

1991 *Background to a Study of Tulare Lake's Archaeological Past.* Coyote Press, Salinas, California.

Wallace, William J., and Francis A. Riddell (editors)

1993 *The Quest for Tulare Lake's Archaeological Past.* Coyote Press, Salinas, California.

Walsh, Michael R.

2000 Beyond the Digging Stick: Women and Flaked Stone Tools in the Desert West. In *Archaeological Passages: A Volume in Honor of Claude Nelson Warren,* edited by Joan S. Schneider, Robert M. Yohe II, and Jill K. Gardner, pp. 198–212. Western Center for Archaeology and Paleontology Publications in Archaeology, No. 1, Hemet, California.

2007 Artifact Assemblage Analysis: Ground and Polished Stone. In *Archaeological Investigations at CA-SCL–674, The Rubino Site, San Jose, Santa Clara County, California, Volume 1,* edited by Allen G. Pastron and Viviana Bellifemine, pp. 139–153. Coyote Press Archives of California Prehistory, No. 54, Salinas, California.

2010 A Trout in the Milk: Circumstantial Evidence for Disputed Tenancy at Seep Spring, Northern Mojave Desert. *Pacific Coast Archaeological Society Special Publication* 43(1–2):101–112.

Walsh, Michael R., and C. William Clewlow, Jr.

2004 Assessment and Mitigation of Damage to Cultural Resources Related to Construction of the Security Perimeter Fence, Naval Air Weapons Station, China Lake, California. Submitted to Naval Air Weapons Station, China Lake, California. Copies available at Naval Air Weapons Station, China Lake, California.

2006 Whatcamacallits, Doo-Dads, and Thingamajigs: Enigmatic Rock Features in the Mojave Desert. In *A Festschrift Honoring the Contributions of California Archaeologist Jay von Werlhof,* edited by Russell L. Kaldenberg, pp. 193–198. Maturango Museum Publication, No. 20, Ridgecrest, California.

Warren, Claude N.

1994 Water and Man in the Deep Desert: A Model for Changing Settlement Patterns of the Early Holocene. In *Kelso Conference Papers 1987–1992: A Collection of Papers and Abstracts from the First Five Kelso Conferences on the Prehistory of the Mojave Desert.* Museum of Anthropology Occasional Papers, No. 4, California State University, Bakersfield.

Warren, Claude N., and Carl Phagan

1988 Fluted Points in the Mojave Desert: Their Technology and Cultural Context. In *Early Human Occupation in Far Western North America: The Clovis-Archaic Interface,* edited by Judith A. Willig, C. Melvin Aikens, and John L. Fagan, pp. 121–130. Nevada State Museum Anthropological Papers, No. 21, Carson City.

Waterman, T. T.
1920 Yurok Geography. *University of California Publications in American Archaeology and Ethnology* 16(5):177–314. Berkeley.
Waterman, T. T., and Alfred L. Kroeber
1938 The Kepel Fish Dam. *University of California Publications in American Archaeology and Ethnology* 35(6):49–80. Berkeley.
Weigel, Lawrence E.
1993 Prehistoric Burning in Northwestern California. In *There Grows a Green Tree: Papers in Honor of David A. Fredrickson,* edited by Greg White, Pat Mikkelsen, William R. Hildebrandt, and Mark E. Basgall, pp. 237–242. Center for Archaeological Research at Davis, No. 11, University of California, Davis.
West, G. James
1993 The Late Pleistocene-Holocene Pollen Record and Prehistory of California's North Coast Ranges. In *There Grows a Green Tree: Papers in Honor of David A. Fredrickson,* edited by Greg White, Pat Mikkelsen, William R. Hildebrandt, and Mark E. Basgall, pp. 237–242. Center For Archaeological Research at Davis, No. 11, University of California, Davis.
West, G. James, Wallace Woolfenden, James A. Wanket, and R. Scott Anderson
2007 Late Pleistocene and Holocene Environments. In *California Prehistory: Colonization, Culture, and Complexity,* edited by Terry L. Jones and Kathryn A. Klar, pp. 11–34. AltaMira Press, Lanham, Maryland.
Whitaker, Adrian R.
2008 Incipient Aquaculture in Prehistoric California?: Long-Term Productivity and Sustainability vs. Immediate Returns for the Harvest of Marine Invertebrates. *Journal of Archaeological Science* 35:1114–1123.
White, Gregory G.
2003 Population Ecology of the Prehistoric Colusa Reach. Unpublished Ph.D. dissertation, Department of Anthropology, University of California, Davis.
White, Gregory G., David A. Fredrickson, Lori D. Hager, Jack Meyer, Jeffrey S. Rosenthal, Michael R. Waters, G. James West, and Eric Wohlgemuth
2002 *Cultural Diversity and Culture Change in Prehistoric Clear Lake Basin: Final Report of the Anderson Flat Project.* Center for Archaeological Research at Davis, No. 13, University of California, Davis.
Whitley, David S.
1992 Shamanism and Rock Art in Far Western North America. *Cambridge Archaeological Journal* 2:89–113.
1994a By the Hunter, For the Gatherer: Art, Social Relations, and Subsistence Change in the Prehistoric Great Basin. *World Archaeology* 25:356–377.
1994b Ethnography and Rock Art in Far Western North America: Some Archaeological Implications. In *New Light on Old Art: Recent Advances In Hunter-Gatherer Rock Art Research,* edited by David S. Whitley and Lawrence L. Loendorf, pp. 81–94. Institute of Archaeology, University of California, Los Angeles.
1998a Meaning and Metaphor in the Coso Petroglyphs: Understanding Great Basin Rock Art. In *Coso Rock Art: A New Perspective,* edited by Elva Younkin, pp. 109–174. Maturango Museum, Ridgecrest, California.

1998b Cognitive Neuroscience, Shamanism, and the Rock Art of Native California. *Anthropology of Consciousness* 9:22–37.

1999 A Possible Pleistocene Camelid Petroglyph from the Mojave Desert, California. *San Bernardino County Museum Association Quarterly* 46:107–108.

2000a *The Art of the Shaman: Rock Art of California.* University of Utah Press, Salt Lake City.

2000b Response to Quinlan. *Journal of California and Great Basin Anthropology* 22:108–129.

2000c Use and Abuse of the Ethnohistory in the Far West. *International Rock Art Conference Proceedings* 1:127–154. American Rock Art Research Association, Tucson.

Whitley, David S., and Ronald I. Dorn

2010 The Coso Petroglyph Chronology. *Pacific Coast Archaeological Society Special Publication* 43(1–2):135–157.

Whitley, David S., Joseph M. Simon, and Ronald I. Dorn

1999 The Vision Quest in the Coso Range. *American Indian Rock Art* 25:1–31.

Wiberg, Randy S.

1988 *The Santa Rita Village Mortuary Complex (CA-ALA–413): Evidence and Implications of a Meganos Intrusion.* Coyote Press Archives of California Prehistory, No. 18, Salinas, California.

Wilke, Philip J.

1991 Lanceolate Projectile Points from Tulare Lake, California. In *Contributions to Tulare Lake Archaeology I: Background to a Study of Tulare Lake's Archaeological Past,* edited by William J. Wallace and Francis A. Riddell, pp. 41–52. Tulare Lake Archaeological Research Group, Coyote Press, Salinas, California.

Wilke, Philip J., and Douglas N. Fain

1974 An Archaeological Cucurbit from Coachella Valley. *Journal of California Anthropology* 1:110–113.

Wilke, Philip J., Thomas W. Whitaker, and Eugene Hattori

1977 Prehistoric Squash (*Cucurbita pepo* L.) from the Salton Basin. *Journal of California Anthropology* 4:55–59.

Wohlgemuth, Eric

2004 The Course of Plant Food Intensification in Native Central California. Unpublished Ph.D. dissertation, Department of Anthropology, University of California, Davis.

Yatsko, Andrew III

2000 Late Holocene Paleoclimatic Stress and Prehistoric Human Occupation on San Clemente Island. Unpublished Ph.D. dissertation, Department of Anthropology, University of California, Los Angeles.

Yohe, Robert M., II

2000 "Rosegate" Revisited: Rose Spring Point Temporal Range in the Southwestern Great Basin. In *Archaeological Passages: A Volume in Honor of Claude Nelson Warren,* edited by Joan S. Schneider, Robert M. Yohe II, and Jill K. Gardner, pp. 213–224. Western Center for Archaeology and Paleontology Publications in Archaeology, No. 1, Hemet, California.

Zigmond, Maurice
1986 Kawaiisu. In *Great Basin*, edited by Warren L. D'Azevedo, pp. 398–411. Handbook of North American Indians, vol. 11, William C. Sturtevant, general editor. Smithsonian Institution, Washington, D.C.

Zogg, Maureen G.
1998 Archaeological Avifauna of the San Francisco Bay Area: A Comparative Analysis. Masters Thesis, Department of Anthropology, San Francisco State University. Reprinted, Coyote Press, Salinas, California.

Index